THE NEW
COMPLETE ENGLISH SETTER

A trio of Llewellin Setters, circa 1875–80. Artist, A. Pope, Jr.

THE LOOK OF AN ENGLISH SETTER

This beautiful head study of Ch. Stacia of Scyld typifies the gentle nobility and distinctive character of the breed—truly Gentlemen and Gentlewomen by nature!

THE NEW COMPLETE

English Setter

A COMPILATION OF INTERESTING FACTS, DATA, AND OBSERVATIONS ON BREEDING, RAISING, TRAINING, SHOWING AND HUNTING ENGLISH SETTERS.

by DAVIS H. TUCK

Late President of The English Setter Association of America

revised by ELSWORTH S. HOWELL

Former President of The English Setter Association of America

THIRD EDITION—ILLUSTRATED

Sixth Printing 1978

HOWELL BOOK HOUSE

230 PARK AVENUE, NEW YORK, N.Y. 10017

DEDICATED TO

my friends who have spent practically all of their otherwise leisure hours for many years of their lives in study and hard work, to the final goal of breeding, rearing, and training better pure-bred English Setters. Their tireless efforts and honest interest have always been an inspiration to me, and after a visit with them I am fired with enthusiasm and determination to do better with my own English Setters.

Redding Ridge, Conn., 1951   DAVIS H. TUCK

Davis Tuck

REVISER'S DEDICATION

This third edition is dedicated to Virginia Tuck Nichols whose contribution, together with that of her late husband Davis Tuck, to English Setters and their devotees, will never be measured by any material means.

ELSWORTH S. HOWELL

Ch. Bogota Girl's Rowdy, first A. K. C. English Setter Field Trial Champion

Contents

Introduction

IN his Introduction to the first edition of **The Complete English Setter**, published in 1951, Davis Tuck wrote:
"There are approximately one thousand English Setters of the bench type registered with the American Kennel Club each year. The life of an English Setter is about ten years, so estimating that twenty-five percent are killed by accident before their life expectancy of ten years, then there are some seventy-five hundred registered show type (Laverack) English Setters at all times in the United States being kept for breeding, hunting, showing, and as pets. In addition, there are at least an equal number who are not registered, giving a total of about fifteen thousand."

In 1964, thirteen years later, in the second edition of this book, I revised the annual number of English Setters registered by the AKC down to six hundred and the other figures accordingly.

Now—six years later, at the end of the sixth decade of this century—the annual registrations have returned to the "approximately one thousand" number of nearly twenty years ago.

Does this mean that, despite the explosive surge of interest in most pure-bred dogs during the past twenty years, show-type English Setters have lagged in the public fancy? Not really, for certain conditions in the breed have changed radically in the two decades since Mr. Tuck's book appeared. In the 1930's and 1940's English Setter registrations were supported by large kennels—for example, the Happy Valley Kennels of Dr. A. A. Mitten, which alone entered 65 dogs at one show; the Blue Bar Kennels of C. N. Myers which carried well over one hundred English Setters at a time; and Mr. Tuck's own Silvermine Kennels. Rising costs, labor shortages, shrinking acreage, and zoning ordinances have militated against such large establishments sponsoring what the public considers a large breed requiring much space. Today, the bench-type English Setter population is spread among more owners and more, much smaller kennels. Membership of fanciers in the English Setter Association of America, the breed's parent club as recognized by the AKC, and in the regional clubs devoted to the breed, is at the highest level in history. Juvenile interest in English Setters is livelier than in many, more popular breeds; it is common to see four boys and girls with English Setters in a small Junior Showmanship class of assorted breeds.

Davis Tuck recognized that quality always transcends quantity. Since he practiced what he preached, it is unlikely that a finer classic on the English Setter will ever be written. His reward for writing it derived from the peerless contribution he made to the education of English Setter devotees—and not from monetary considerations, because it took almost 13 years to sell the small printing of the first edition. The increase in English Setter owners is confirmed by the sale of the second edition in the same quantity in only five years. The worth of Mr. Tuck's effort had also been well established. And the addition of breeding records of leading sires and dams in the second edition enhanced the value of this reference source.

Now, in this third edition, Joann Dillon, recent Secretary of the English Setter Association, has updated the compilation of outstanding producers, their pedigrees and champion progeny. Other new material is included.

It was my pleasure and privilege to extend the publication of **The New Complete English Setter** through the establishment of Howell Book House in 1961. In fact, the existence of this Tuck masterpiece was a leading factor in my acquisition of the Denlinger dog book publishing business then. And today I am happy to present to English Setter fans here and abroad the third edition of this great work on my own favorite breed.

Darien, Conn.   ELSWORTH S. HOWELL

Reproduction of a painting representing the ideal English Setter of the English Setter Club of Italy, 1949.

Reproduction of an etching by Leon Danchin showing a beautiful English Setter on point and another backing. It is interesting to note the slight dish face of these two dogs, as this dish face is still much to be desired in France and Italy. Compare these heads with the ideal of the breed shown in the yearbook for 1949 of the English Setter Club of Italy. Copyright Camilla Lucus, Art Publishers, New York.

CHAMPION STURDY MAX was considered by many to exemplify the closest approach to the standard of perfection of any modern English Setter. He was a big-boned dog with lovely dark eyes and typical English Setter expression. A good showman, with personality and gaiety. There is no doubt but that he set the style for the modern English Setter. This print can well be the breeders' ideal for which to strive—their star at which to aim. Data on Ch. Sturdy Max is shown in this book. Photograph by Tauskey

English Setter Pointing in Turnips.
By Philip Reinagle, R. A. (1749–1833)

1

Origin and History

F ROM the best authorities on the subject, it appears that the English Setter was a trained bird dog in England approximately four hundred years ago. A perusal of some of the old writings leads us to believe that the English Setter had its origin in some of the older of the land spaniels that originated from Spain. We are indebted, however, to Hans Bols, who, in **Partridge Shooting and Partridge Hawking,** written in 1582, presents quite definite pictorial evidence that the setter and the spaniel breeds were quite different in appearance, and even at that time the tails of the spaniels appeared to have been docked, as they are today, and the tails of setters left as nature intended them. There is some evidence in the earliest writings of sportsmen that the old English Setter was originally produced from crosses of the Spanish pointer, the large water spaniel, and the Springer spaniel, and by careful cultivation attained a high degree of proficiency in finding and pointing game in open country. We can see from examination of the sketches in many of the old writings that the setter-spaniel was an extremely handsome dog, many having a head much longer and with a more classical cut than that of the spaniel, while others had the short spaniel-like head, lacking the well-defined profile of the skull and foreface of the modern English Setters. Also most of these older setters had coats which were quite curly, particularly at the thighs. It can be seen from this brief review of the origin of the English Setter that even our oldest authorities were not entirely in accord as to the origin of this breed.

There is little doubt that the major credit for the development of the modern setter should go to Mr. Edward Laverack, who, about 1825, obtained from the Rev. A. Harrison "Ponto" and "Old Moll." The Rev. Harrison apparently had kept this breed pure for thirty-five years or more. From these two setters Mr. Laverack, through a remarkable process of inbreeding, produced "Prince," "Countess," "Nellie," and "Fairy," who were marvelous specimens of English Setters. Along about 1874 Mr. Laverack sold a pair of setters to Charles H. Raymond of Morris Plains, New Jersey. During the next ten years the English Setter became more and more popular, and it was about this time that many setters bred by Mr. Llewellin were imported into this country and Canada.

In considering the so-called Llewellin strain of English Setters, it is recorded in the writings of Dr. William A. Bruette that about the time the Laverack strain of English Setters was at its zenith in England, Mr. R. L. Purcell Llewellin purchased a number of Mr. Laverack's best show dogs of the pure Dash-Moll and Dash-Hill Laverack blood. These Laveracks he crossed with some entirely new blood which he obtained in the north of England, represented by Mr. Statter's and Sir Vincent Corbet's strain, since referred to as the Duke-Rhoebes, the latter being the two most prominent members of the blood. The result of these crosses was eminently successful, particularly at field trials, and swept everything before them. Their reputation spread to America and many were purchased by sportsmen in different sections of the United States and Canada, so that this line of breeding soon became firmly established in this country.

Probably the name that stands out most conspicuously in

the foundation of the field-trial setter in America is Count Noble. This dog was purchased from Mr. Llewellin by Dave Sanborn of Dowling, Michigan, who after trying him out on the prairies, was upon the point of returning him to England, but was persuaded not to do so by the late B. J. Wilson of Pittsburgh, Pennsylvania. On the death of Mr. Sanborn, Count Noble passed into the hands of Mr. Wilson, who gave him an opportunity to demonstrate his sterling qualities from coast to coast. The body of this famous dog was mounted at his death, and was in the Carnegie Museum at Pittsburgh, where it was visited by many sportsmen.

Dr. Walsh, in 1878, stated that Mr. Llewellin's dogs were Dan-Laveracks; according to him they were all either by Dan out of Laverack bitches or by a Laverack dog out of a sister of Dan. It is quite difficult to give a proper definition of a straight-bred Llewellin, but it is generally accepted that all setters may be called Llewellins which trace back in all lines to Duke-Rhoebe-Laverack. This, however, would shut out everything that had Dash II bloodlines, and this the Llewellin enthusiast does not wish to do, for under such definition it would eliminate a great number of the best known names that appear in the so-called Llewellin pedigrees. Mr. R. L. Purcell Llewellin is given credit for making the Duke-Rhoebe-Laverack cross, but, in justice to him, according to Mr. A. F. Hochwalt, one of our noted authorities on gun dogs, he is not responsible for the breed being named for him. The name was originated in America by breeders who imported dogs from Mr. Llewellin's kennels and, being great admirers of the man and the dogs he bred, they naturally gave his name to these dogs.

This somewhat orthodox or bland description of the history of the English Setter may be sufficient for most readers, but for the student or serious breeder it may be desirable to take the skeleton out of the closet and shake its bones, as thereby will be uncovered some information which has an important bearing on breeding and genetics.

The first book ever written on dogs was "Of Englishe Dogges," written by John Caius (1510–1573) and published in Latin in 1570 and translated into English in 1575. Caius

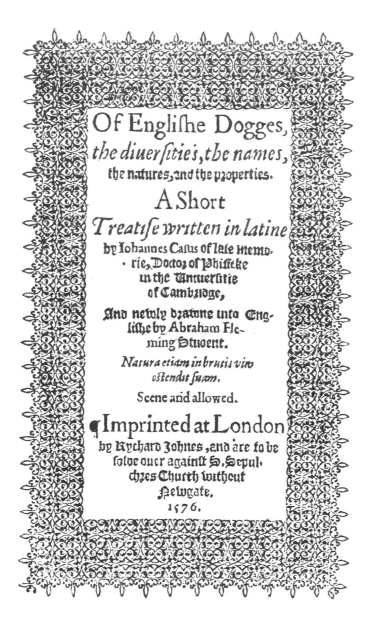

Of Englifhe Dogges,
the diuerfities, the names,
the natures, and the properties.

A Short
Treatife written in latine
by Iohannes Caius of late memo-
· rie, Doctoz of Phifieke
in the Vniuerfitie
of Cambzidge,

And newly dzawne vnto Englifhe by Abraham Fle-
ming Student.

Natura etiam in brutis viro
oftendit fuam.

Scene and allowed.

❡Imprinted at London
by Rychard Iohnes, and are to be
folde ouer againſt S. Sepul-
chzes Churth without
Newgate.
1576.

Of gentle Dogges seruing the hauke, and first
of the Spaniell, called in Latine
Hispaniolus.

 *Vch Dogges as ſerue for fowling, I*
thinke conuenient and requisite to place in this
seconde Section of this treatise. These are also
to bee reckoned and accounted in the number
of the dogges which come of a gentle kind, and
of those which serue for fowling.

There be two sortes { The first findeth game on the land.
The other findeth game on the water. }

Such as delight on the land, play their partes, eyther by swiftnesse of foote, or by often questing, to search out and to spying the byrde for further hope of aduauntage, or else by some secrete signe and priuy token bewray the place where they fall.

The first kinde of such serue { The Hauke,

The seconde, { The net, or, traine,

The first kinde haue no peculier names assigned vnto them, saue onely that they be denominated after the byrde which by naturall appointment he is alotted to take, for the which consideration.

Some be called Dogges, { For the Falcon
The Phesant
The Partridge } and such like,

The common sort of people call them by one generall word, namely Spaniells. As though these kinde of Dogges came originally and first of all out of Spaine, The most part of their skynnes are white, and if they be marcked with any spottes, they are commonly red, and somewhat great therewithall, the heares not growing in such thicknesse but that the mixture of them maye easely be perceaued. Othersome of them be reddishe and blackishe, but of that sorte there be but a very few. There is also at this day among vs a newe kinde of dogge brought out of Fraunce (for we Englishe men are maruailous greedy gaping gluttons after nouelties, and couetous coruorauntes of things that be seldom, rare, straunge, and hard to get.) And they bee speckled all ouer with white and black, which mingled colours incline to a marble blewe, which bewtifyeth their skinnes and affordeth a seemely show of comlynesse. These are called French dogges as is aboue declared already.

The Dogge called the Setter, in La-
tine *Index*.

ANother sort of Dogges be there, scruiceable for fowling, making no noise either with foote or with tounge, whiles they followe the game. These attend diligently vpon theyr Master and frame their conditions to such beckes, motions, and gestures, as it shall please him to exhibite and make, either going forward, drawing backeward, inclining to the right hand, or yealding toward the left, (In making mencion of fowles my meaning is of the Partridge and the Quaile) when he hath founde the byrde, he keepeth sure and fast silence, he stayeth his steppes and wil proceede no further, and with a close, couert, watching eye, layeth his belly to the grounde and so creepeth forward like a worme. When he approcheth neere to the place where the birde is, he layes him downe, and with a marcke of his pawes, betrayeth the place of the byrdes last abode, whereby it is supposed that this kinde of dogge is called *Index*, Setter, being in deede a name most consonant and agreable to his quality. The place being knowne by the meanes of the dogge, the fowler immediatly openeth and spreedeth his net, intending to take them, which being done the dogge at the accustomed becke or vsuall signe of his Master ryseth vp by and by, and draweth neerer to the fowle that by his presence they might be the authors of their owne insnaring, and be ready intangled in the prepared net, which conning and artificiall indeuour in a dogge (being a creature domesticall or householde seruaunt brought vp at home with offalls of the trencher and fragments of victualls) is not much to be maruailed at, seing that a Hare (being a wilde and skippishe beast) was seene in England to the astonishment of the beholders, in the yeare of our Lorde God, 1564 not onely dauncing in measure, but playing with his former feete vppon a tabbaret, and obseruing iust number of strokes (as a practicioner in that arte) besides that nipping & pinching a dogge with his teeth and clawes, & cruelly thumping him with y' force of his feete. This is no trumpery tale, nor trifling toye (as I imagine) and therefore not vnworthy to be reported, for I recken it a requitall of my trauaile, not to drowne in the seas of silence any speciall thing, wherein the prouidence and effectuall working of nature is to be pondered.

20

was physician to the ailing King Edward VI and upon his death held the same office in the household of Queen Mary and upon her death was Royal Physician to Queen Elizabeth. He was the founder of Caius (Keys') College in Cambridge and a student at Gonville Hall, Cambridge, and later became Master of this college. Caius very definitely places the setter in the spaniel class.

D. D. North, who wrote the chapter on English Setters in "The Book of the Dog" (edited by Brian Vesey-Fitzgerald, 1948), says, "At least it is certain that they were developed from spaniels." This book, 1039 pages, was published by Nicholson and Watson, London, 1948, and is an excellent one. Laverack in his book "The Setter" says, "In fact, the setter is but an improved spaniel." Stonehenge (1867) says, "There is no doubt that the setter is a spaniel brought by a variety of crosses—or rather, let us say, of careful selection—to the size and form in which we now find him." Hochwalt in his book "The Modern Setter" says, "The consensus of opinion among writers of canine literature, past and present, is that the setter is an improved spaniel."

One thing these early authorities are very explicit about is that the setting spaniel is an older breed than the pointer. They bring no proofs to substantiate these deductions, but the claim is made in order to convey the idea that no pointer blood was necessary to bring out the pointing instinct in the long haired bird dogs of the earliest days. Bernard Waters, in the "American Book of the Dog" (1891), says that the origin of the setter, like most other breeds, is obscure and all theories advanced are nothing more than guesswork and theoretical speculation. It is interesting to note that these authorities agree that the Setter was bred up from a spaniel but Setter includes all of them, the English, Irish, Gordon, and Russian, and it was not until later that the various classifications of Setters were made, and there is considerable proof that the four types were bred amongst themselves.

It is generally admitted that Laverack and Llewellin did more than any other two breeders to develop the English Setters of today, and this tendency to hero worship has possibly given more credit to them than they deserve. Edward

Edward Laverack, Esq. (1797-1877)
Broughall Cottage, Whitechurch, Shropshire, England

Laverack was a native of a Westmorland village and in his youth was a shoemaker's apprentice. Early in life he came into possession of a legacy bequeathed to him by a distant relative. This legacy gave him an income sufficient for indulging his hobby of breeding English Setters and hunting them throughout England, Scotland, Wales, and Ireland. In his book "The Setter" is shown the remarkable inbred pedigree of his Dash and he states that his Laverack setters are the result of nearly fifty years of breeding without ever resorting to an outcross from Ponto and Old Moll and that Ponto and Old Moll were the result of similar inbreeding by Rev. Harrison for thirty-five years prior to the time of his acquisition of Ponto and Old Moll. His contemporaries did not put much faith in the authenticity of his pedigrees. Laverack in "The Setter" says, "There are several secrets connected with my system of intercrossing that I do not think advisable to give to the public at present" (1872). Laverack admits that he tried several outcrosses but intimates that he promptly destroyed them and returned to his original strain, leaving the public to assume that he never used the get of these outcrosses in his breeding. In a letter to a friend about liver markings on one of his puppies he said, "He strains back to Prince's sire, viz; Pride of the Border, a liver and white. He strains back for 30 years to a change in blood I once introduced—the pure old Edward Castle breed—County Cumberland—liver and white, quite as pure and good as the blues." This letter was written in 1874, two years after the publication of his book and may be one of the "secrets" he did not think advisable to give to the public at the time. Stonehenge did not place much value on Laverack's pedigrees. Ponto was a dark blue belton and Old Moll was a light blue belton, and their breeding was supposed to be pure for thirty-five years. If Laverack did not bring in outside blood, as he claimed, where did the oranges and tri-colors come from?

The following interesting incident in Laverack's life is told by Rev. D. W. W. Horlock, who wrote the chapter on English Setters in "British Dogs," Third Edition, by W. D. Drury, Kennel Editor of "The Bazaar." "Some time ago Laverack, in the soothing atmosphere of a winter's evening fire combined with the seductive effects of some good old port, disclosed a few faint shadows of his dark secrets. One of them is related here. Once upon a time there was a tract of country on the Borders called 'the Debatable Land,' nominally belonging to the Earl of Carlisle. Now, this country swarmed with gipsies, and that strange people had from time immemorial claimed the right to shoot over this tract at their own sweet will, so on August 12th in each year, they were accustomed to form a band of thirty or more, and with a large army of setters and pointers, made a regular raid on the said moors, and it is not surprising that the keepers gave them a wide berth. Well, on one Twelfth, Laverack accompanied this mob, and he had with him one of his best dogs. Among all the Setters which were ranging far and wide, Laverack's keen eyes noted one animal, liver and white, which was outstanding, and beat the whole lot in both nose and pace, though by no means a good looking one. 'Well, sir,' the old man said, 'I hunted up those gipsies. I found the dog, I bought him, and bred from him.' "

There is some reason to suspect that in later years (1870) a judicious cross was effected with the Pointer and there seems to be very little doubt at all that the Irish Setter also was called in to refresh the blood. Although there is little doubt that Laverack introduced outside blood from time to time, his setters were more closely inbred than any other strain of the time as evidenced by the similarity of his dogs, their susceptibility to disease and their usually poor nose, although there were some exceptions, as some of his dogs were good gentlemen's shooting dogs. Contrary to Laverack's claims to outstanding hunting ability and stamina, his contemporaries claimed that many of his dogs were worthless in the field. Mr. Laverack no doubt had complete faith in the superiority of his Laveracks, but other breeders were not satisfied with their hunting ability, so Statter, Field, Armstrong and others introduced the Duke-Rhoebe-Laverack cross.

Mr. Purcell Llewellin was a son of a noted Welsh sportsman of that name and began with Gordon Setters and some of the old fashioned English Setters. These he crossed and was badly beaten at the field trials. He then purchased some

24

R. LL. Purcell Llewellin, Esq. (1840-1925)
Ashby-De-La-Zuche, Leicestershire, England.

of the best Irish Setters in the country and crossed these with his other Gordon and English Setters. Not yet satisfied he crossed his Irish Setters with Laverack Setters and secured some outstandingly beautiful specimens which at the shows were practically invincible. Among them was a bitch named "Flame," a beautifully formed red and white of outstanding quality. This bitch is most noteworthy to modern English Setter breeders because a large number of the notable show winners of today carry her blood. For instance, the well known Mallwyd English Setters (Mr. Thomas Steadman, Merionitshire, Wales) contained a great preponderance of Mr. Llewellin's "Flame" and "Carrie." The Mallwyd importations to the United States and Canada were the very backbone of our present Bench Show type English Setters (Laverack). Mr. Kruger's Mallhawk Kennels of English Setters was founded on Mallwyd dogs, and we find the Mallwyd influence strongly in Rummey Stagboro's pedigree.

These Irish Setter-Laverack English Setter crosses, although outstanding at the bench shows, were almost entirely lacking in field performance. Llewellin was still dissatisfied. These years of hit or miss haphazard crossing of Gordon, Irish and English Setters had not given him what he was looking for—field trial winners, so when Statter and others were producing good field trial English Setters from the Duke-Rhoebe-Laverack cross he attended the field trial at Shrewsbury in 1871 and bought "Dan" and "Dick," both by Field's Duke out of Statter's Rhoebe, for the purpose of crossing with his Laverack bitches. This was Llewellin's beginning of the so-called Llewellin type of English Setter, and it should be stressed that Statter, Field, Armstrong, and others had really started the strain. Rhoebe was a cross of Gordon Setter and a black, white and tan English Setter of Lord Lovat's breeding. From this it will be seen that the so-called pure Llewellin blood is in reality a mixture of Gordon Setter and English Setter and what else nobody knows.

Thus we find by shaking the skeleton in the closet that our so-called Laverack bench show setters are a mixture of Irish Setter and Laverack English Setter with probably some "spice" thrown in on the side, and that our so-called Llewellin

26

Mr. R. Ll. Purcell Llewellin with Kitty and Rosa Wind'em.

field trial type was not invented by Llewellin, and that they are a cross of Gordon Setter and Laverack English Setter with probably a little seasoning added when no one was looking. The Kennel Club in England was founded in 1873 and their stud book started 1874, so before that time pedigrees were not officially recorded and were therefore subject to considerable suspicion.

We occasionally hear reference to the Russian Setter. Laverack in his book "The Setter" (1872) refers to them as scarce in England at that time. They were white, lemon and white, liver and white, and black and white. They looked more like large spaniels than English Setters, and he did not consider them as good field dogs as his own Laverack Setters. He may have been somewhat prejudiced, because they were thought very highly of by others, as many English Breeders of the time of about 1840 used the Russian Setter for the purpose of improving high head air scenting and stamina. In 1841 Mr. Lang wrote an article in the **Sporting Review** in which he highly praised the Russian Setter as a bird dog and especially a cross breed (English and Russian Setter) belonging to Mr. Joseph Manton which he bought for a hundred guineas. These Russian Setters are interesting because they are evidently in the blood of our present day Laverack and Llewellin Setters. They were also used as an English Cross again in our early native (American) English Setters.

The "Native Setter" is referred to occasionally and without doubt these setters have had a considerable effect on our present field trial Llewellin English Setters and our bench type Laverack Setters because they stemmed from the same origin as the Llewellins and Laveracks, i.e., a mixture of English, Irish, Gordon, and Russian Setters. When our forebears settled America they brought with them or later imported various types of setters to satisfy their sporting instincts, as the entire new country was heavily populated with game birds. The owners cared little for pedigrees and usually bred the best to the best in a given locality, mixing up the various setter breeds. Most of these Native Setters were orange and white and were of medium to large size. They did their share of winning both in the field and on the bench. A native of the

A typical Russian Setter slightly crossed
with English Setter blood. From Stonehenge.

Campbell strain, "Joe Jr.," a mixture of Gordon and Irish and English defeated Gladstone on several occasions, and on December 15 and 16, 1879, he won by a very considerable margin against Gladstone, who at the time was considered the greatest exponent of the Llewellin Duke-Rhoebe-Laverack strain. Other well known strains of Native Setters were Gildersleeve of the Maryland section, Ethan Allen strain in Connecticut, and those bred by Mr. Theodore Morford of Newton, New Jersey.

Summary

Looking back at the history of the English Setter during the period between about 1819 and 1874 we find that from our modern breeding standpoint this was a most important period for English Setters. We had two outstanding breeders of some means who could indulge their fancy. Laverack was a sportsman who loved to hunt, especially in Scotland. He definitely wanted an English Setter of excellent appearance that would find birds for him. He and his keeper, Rattray, would break eight dogs in six days and a party of four would bag 3,000 grouse in a single day. In other words his ideal was a fine looking "meat dog."

Llewellin's idea was to breed a dog who could win field trials. The appearance of the animal was secondary to him. He floundered around for years trying all kinds of crosses, Gordons, Irish and English to each other but did not find what he was looking for until he copied Mr. Statter's cross of English to Gordon to Laverack's English.

Thus our English Setter accepted nomenclature of "Laverack"—the Bench Show English Setter—and "Llewellin"—the Field Trial English Setter—is not founded on fact, but was adopted from these men's **ideals** and not their accomplishments, because Llewellin crossed the English and Irish and accidentally got the show type (Mallwyd), and Laverack furnished Llewellin the missing link that produced Llewellin's field trial type.

In recent years annual registrations of English Setters have ranged between 600 to 1,275 individual dogs, ranking the breed between 44th to 54th in popularity among the 116

Photograph of Ch. Donora Prince, A.K.C. 94159. A typical Laverack type who was imported from the kennels of J. J. Holgate, Surbiton, England. He was a thoroughly broken field dog. and was at the height of his Bench Show career in 1906 and 1907. He was owned by Mr. William Rockefeller of Greenwich, Connecticut (Rock Ridge Kennels).

Donora Prince had seven Best of Show awards, including Westminster K.C. in 1907, over two thousand entries, and three Best of Show awards in England. He sired Donora Prince II, who was also a thoroughly trained field dog and was a consistent winner at the major Bench Shows in 1908–1913. Donora Prince II will be found as the great-great-grandfather of Kanandarcue Chief. The boy in the photograph is Clarence Lewis, who judged N. W. Conn. Show in 1948 and Hartford in 1949.

This photograph is interesting, too, as a comparison of top flight English Setters of 1906 with our present day winners.

Typical Bench Type (Laverack) English Setter, CH. RIP OF BLUE BAR—C. N. Myers, Hanover, Pa., owner.

Typical Field Trial Type (Llewellin) English Setter, CH. SAM L'S SKYHIGH—Sam Light, Punxsutawney, Pa., owner.

breeds recognized by the AKC. In show competition, their popularity has been somewhat higher among the breeds, their position being in the lower thirties. Between 80 and 90 new bench champions are made each year from 2,000 to 2,500 entries. Since many dogs are shown often, the number of individual dogs is much less than the number of entries. Each year the American Field registers several thousands.

During the last seventy years a difference in type has appeared and constantly widened, so that in the United States and Canada there are now two distinct types of English Setters being bred, each having its own devotees. The Llewellin type is a comparatively small animal as compared with the Laverack type, although from a size standpoint the two types will overlap. The Llewellin type is the field-trial dog, and is usually distinguished from the Laverack type by the color—white, for the most part, with large black patches and, more often, white with large black patches and tan ticking on the head, muzzle and legs. Their heads are thicker through the skull; their muzzle, in comparison to their length of skull, is shorter than similar measurements for the Laverack type. The nose is inclined toward snipiness. They excel in speed and have a keen nose.

In color the Laverack type is usually blue belton, orange belton, or tricolor. Large black patches are usually undesirable. They are, on the average, larger than the Llewellin type—higher at the shoulder and generally heavier in build. Their heads are larger and narrower through the skull; the muzzle is longer and more square than in the Llewellin type.

There is a tendency for the devotee of either type to look down his nose at the other type, though actually each has its place. The field trial enthusiast's setter would usually make a sorry showing at a bench show as compared to a Laverack-type setter, while the bench show follower would generally have an "also ran" in a field trial of Llewellin-type setters. Both setters have one characteristic in common: both will do a good job at finding, pointing, and retrieving birds.

Intolerance is a defense mechanism to hide from oneself his own shortcomings. Intolerant people usually magnify the shortcomings of others, not admitting the good characteristics,

Reproduction of an oil painting by the incomparable dog artist G. Muss-Arnolt. The painting was owned by Anton Rost of New York and was sold to Mervin Rosenbaum of California.

This picture shows the Duke-Rhoebe-Laverack cross at its best from a conformation standpoint, and any English Setter breeder would love to produce a pair like these. Note again the slightly dished foreface. Col. Corn. Schilbred in his book *Pointer og Setter*, Oslo, 1927, remarked on the desirability both from the standpoint of keen nose and beauty, of this slightly dished foreface.

34

and amplify their own points of excellence, suppressing their own faults. The intolerance exhibited between the followers of the field-trial English Setters (Llewellin) and the bench-show English Setters (Laverack) is a good example. The fair-minded will admit that the Llewellin English Setter from the field-trial standpoint is the last word in performance, but that it is not a very good looking dog, and that the Laverack English Setter is a beautiful specimen but lacks speed and bird-finding ability. The intolerant followers of the two sports, however, will not admit any good in the other type of English Setter.

The modern bench-type English Setter was developed in England from Laverack stock by Mr. Thomas Steadman of Mallwyd Kennels, his brother, Mr. D. K. Steadman of Maesydd Kennels, Dr. Price of Crombie Kennels, and by others. Many dogs from these kennels were imported from England to the United States and Canada. This English breeding will be found in many of our modern bench-type English Setters at the 12th to 14th generations.

It is interesting to trace the background of one of America's outstanding English Setter kennels whose breeding we find in the majority of our present-day show specimens—the Mallhawk Kennels of Mr. Kruger. The Mallhawk Kennels is a combination of the Mallwyd and Mohawk kennel names. The Mallwyd strain traces back to Llewellin's cross of Irish Setter to Laverack Setter, and the Mohawk Llewellins trace back through Rodingo to Count Noble who was one of Llewellin's crosses from Gordon—Old English Setter to Laverack. Thus it will be seen that our top breeding of today is not too far away from a mixture of Gordon, Old English, Irish, and Laverack Setters.

Reviser's Note: Confirmation of parts of the foregoing history, and additional information, appeared in an article by the noted author on dogs, John T. Marvin, in the December 1968 issue of **Pure-bred Dogs—American Kennel Gazette**. Several years ago Mr. Marvin found in an old Memphis, Tenn., book shop a copy of Arnold Burges' **The American Sporting and Kennel Field** published in 1876 as the first formal stud record published in the U.S.A. Mr. Marvin writes:

This particular copy was originally owned by a Dr. R. Liston of Albany, N.Y., who undoubtedly had a strong interest in the English Setter . . . . he had used the book as a filing folder for a great and important accumulation of information on the breed.

One of the most interesting items is an article from the February 1896 issue of *Outing*, written by L. H. Smith and titled 'The Llewellin Setter.' The article offers a brief but illuminating history of the development of the English Setter . . . and begins with the efforts of Edward Laverack in the 1820's. The strain, which carries his name, was begun with two animals, Ponto and Old Moll, and was brought forth through the breeding of brother and sister for some five generations whereby all of the strain traces back directly to these two progenitors. For those who decry inbreeding, this effort offers a strong counter-argument. In any event Laverack developed the strain which was absolutely tops for many decades. Circa 1870, Mr. Llewellin bought a couple of the Laverack bitches and in hopes of improving their hunting abilities decided to out-cross them with a dog named Dan, a consistent field trial winner. Great things came from these matings and a new strain was begun. Many of the Llewellin Setters came to this country, but two of the best were Druid and Queen Mab brought over by the aforementioned Burges and campaigned on the bench by him.

Another startling insert is a pedigree of the dog 'Fly' which is a massive folded vellum sheet with no less than eight generations outlined thereon. Fly was a black and white dog bred by Ed. H. Lathrop of Springfield, Mass., circa 1876. He was by Duke ex Luna. Duke was a pure Laverack with pedigree traced back a full eight generations to Ponto and Old Moll. Luna had a less disciplined background and included at least one Gordon Setter among her ancestors. In any event, the pedigree traces back to the 1820's, a phenomenal task and an amazing revelation of the breeder's skill and records.

Many other added pedigrees are included . . . Last was a tipped in 'Catalogue of Thoroughbred English Setters' owned by Mr. Goodsell, 1883. E. I. Martin was listed as the manager of the kennel which was located in Wilmington, Del. This 31 page brochure offered five dogs at stud including Ch. Plantagenet at fees of fifty dollars each and another of lessor note for forty dollars. All were listed as 'Pure Laverack' strain. In each case a pedigree was provided together with a full listing of his winnings in England with a pen and ink sketch of the dog. Many of the kennel's bitches were also listed including the 'Pure Laverack Brood Bitch,' Ch. Petrel II.

Throughout the book, Dr. Liston has jotted down thoughts and opinions and some of these, with respect to his own dogs, indicated an honest and proper approach. For example, his dog 'Pinto' was described as 'long, low-dark brown, white ticked (good).' Actually, the information added by Dr. Liston, taken with the excellent exposition and records of English Setters that form an important segment of the Burges book, offers the student a rather complete history of the breed until about 1900.

Roderigo   Paul Gladstone

Reproduction of an etching by J. M. Tracy of Roderigo on point with Paul Gladstone backing. The gun is the Artist Tracy. Roderigo, whelped 1883, was a son of Count Noble, an importation from Llewellin, and was owned by W. B. Gates, Col. Arthur Merriman and J. M. Avent. As a producer he stood at the head of English Setters of the period. He sired twenty-seven winners. Paul Gladstone was a son of Gladstone, whose dam, Petrel (Laverack), in whelp to the Duke-Rhoebe dog Dan, was purchased from Llewellin by L. H. Smith of Ontario. Paul Gladstone was a field trial winner, a bench show winner, and the sire of seven field trial winners and one bench show winner.

The English Setter bitch "Countess" was purchased from Laverack by Llewellin. She was a sister to Laverack's "Dash," who was the culmination of Laverack's long line of inbreeding from "Ponto" and "Old Moll." The pedigree is reproduced here for its historical interest.

Countess was no doubt a beautiful specimen of what a good English Setter should be, with correct shoulders, wide, deep, well-angulated hind quarters, good back line, and well-carried flag. Her neck is long and well curved, and her head shows the well-defined stop with a suggestion of dish face which has been mentioned several times in this book as being very pleasing and much sought after in Europe today.

Pedigree tree:

- **DASH 2nd** (Blue mottled)
  - **STING** (Blue mottled)
    - **ROCK 2nd** (Black and White)
      - **REGENT** (Black and White)
        - PILOT (Black and White) — DASH 1st / BELLE 1st
        - MOLL 2nd — DASH 1st / BELLE 1st
      - **JET 1st** (Black and White)
        - PILOT — DASH 1st / BELLE 1st
        - MOLL 2nd — DASH 1st / BELLE 1st
    - **CORA (BLAIR'S)** (Black and White)
      - **REGENT** (Black and White)
        - PILOT — DASH 1st / BELLE 1st
        - MOLL 2nd — DASH 1st / BELLE 1st
      - **JET 1st** (Black and White)
        - PILOT — DASH 1st / BELLE 1st
        - MOLL 2nd — DASH 1st / BELLE 1st
  - **CORA 2nd** (Black and White)
    - **FRED 1st** (Lemon and White)
      - **ROCK** (Lemon and White)
        - ROCK — PILOT / MOLL 2nd
        - PEG — DASH 1st / MOLL 2nd
      - **MOLL 2nd** (Orange and White)
        - DASH 1st — PONTO / OLD MOLL
        - BELLE 1st — PONTO / OLD MOLL
    - **CORA 1st** (Black and White)
      - DASH 1st (Black and White) — PONTO / OLD MOLL
      - BELLE 1st (Orange and White) — PONTO / OLD MOLL

- **MOLL 3rd** (Black, White and Tan)
  - **FRED 1st** (Lemon and White)
    - **ROCK 1st** (Lemon and White)
      - ROCK (Lemon and White)
        - PILOT — DASH 1st / BELLE 1st
        - MOLL 2nd — DASH 1st / BELLE 1st
      - PEG (Lemon and White)
        - DASH 1st — PONTO / OLD MOLL
        - MOLL 2nd — DASH 1st / BELLE 1st
    - **MOLL 2nd** (Orange & White)
      - DASH 1st (Black and White) — PONTO / OLD MOLL
      - BELLE 1st (Orange and White) — PONTO / OLD MOLL
  - **BELLE 2nd** (Black, White and Tan)
    - **ROCK 2nd** (Black and White)
      - REGENT (Black and White)
        - PILOT — DASH 1st / BELLE 1st
        - MOLL 2nd — DASH 1st / BELLE 1st
      - JET 1st (Black and White)
        - PILOT — DASH 1st / BELLE 1st
        - MOLL 2nd — DASH 1st / BELLE 1st
    - **CORA (BLAIR'S)** (Black and White)
      - REGENT (Black and White)
        - PILOT — DASH 1st / BELLE 1st
        - MOLL 2nd — DASH 1st / BELLE 1st
      - JET 1st (Black and White)
        - PILOT — DASH 1st / BELLE 1st
        - MOLL 2nd — DASH 1st / BELLE 1st

Pedigree of Laverack's English Setter "Countess."

Audubon and his English Setter. By Chappell.

John James Audubon (1770–1851), American naturalist. Father, French Naval Officer; mother, a Spanish Creole. Educated in Paris. Returning to America in 1798 he settled on a farm near Philadelphia where he made his bird drawings. In 1826 he went to England to secure subscribers for his book "Birds of America" (1838). In 1842 he purchased an estate on the Hudson River, now Audubon Park in New York City, where he, with John Bachman, published "The Quadrupeds of America" (1854). He died in New York City January 27, 1851.

That such a naturalist would choose an English Setter as his companion while in search of specimens, is additional proof of the unequalled disposition of the English Setter.

2

Disposition

THE English Setter has retained its popularity since its introduction into the United States primarily because of its usefulness, beauty, lovable disposition, loyalty and devotion. There is no doubt that its usefulness has been a prime factor in its popularity, and as a result of intelligent breeding it has been brought to a high state of perfection. There is always to be found a representative entry at bench shows and field trials. It is interesting to note, however, that at least half of the spectators at the ringside are not hunters or breeders of English Setters, nor even interested in showing them, but love them as pets. English Setters have a way of getting at your heart—as I write, a champion bitch of mine is under the table at my feet, content as long as she is with me.

The mild, sweet disposition characteristic of the English Setter, together with its beauty, intelligence and aristocratic appearance in the field and in the home, has endeared it both to sportsmen and to all lovers of a beautiful, active, rugged dog. Their lovable disposition makes them ideal companions for children.

Contrary to the opinion expressed by some, the hunting ability of the English Setter is not spoiled but enhanced by making it a family pet. To this dog, love and affection are as necessary as food. Indeed food often will be left in the pan for a kindly word or a friendly pat. In fact, the pleasanter the association with people, from weaning through life, the smarter the English Setter will become; and its inherent good qualities will be more fully developed when there is more frequent chance of expression. Their natural instinct for bird-hunting cannot be developed unless given the opportunity to find birds in the field, nor will their outstanding characteristics of love and devotion be fully developed without close association with people.

I used to travel a great deal by car, and always took my favorite bitch, Racket's Nell, with me as a companion. I learned that when I would leave her in my hotel room in the morning, while I went out, she would follow the maid from room to room as the day's cleaning was done. She would then ride the elevator with the operator. In the evening when I returned I would find her either with the chef in the kitchen or with the room clerk behind the desk.

I mention this experience as it describes another English Setter trait, which is, as Dale Carnegie would express it, "the ability to make and hold friends." An English Setter can get under your skin and into your heart before you know it. As additional proof of this, I quote from a letter from a man who had just bought an English Setter puppy:

"I certainly would be remiss if I did not thank you for selling me such a wonderful creature as Clarissa. She is a sweetheart! Jim [our kennelman] raised a question as to how Clarissa would stand the trip home and he certainly called it. I don't think we had gone five miles of our 150 homeward trip when she started her siege of car sickness and she was one miserable girl all the way back. To shorten her misery we kept going without lunch. Well, you wouldn't have recognized that poor pup when we got her out of the car. . . .

42

English Setters are excellent with children. This photograph was taken at a Shooting Dog stake held by the English Setter Club of New England. The three-year-old child of one of the spectators was snapped by our photographer while playing with one of the English Setters who was entered in the stake. The child and dog had never seen each other before. This photograph is a good example of the incomparable disposition of an English Setter.

"She just looked like hell. We bedded her down in her new home and gave her about an hour to settle down and then gave her some warm soup. She went for this and took about half of it. An hour later we fed her regular dinner and she wolfed that in no time flat. Her day ended with a bedding down for the night.

"Sunday morning I spent a half hour with her—calling her by name and when she came to me, fed her a cracker. We got fairly friendly and I put a check cord on her collar and took her into the field. After a few nervous minutes she got used to the cord—the crackers helping quite a bit. We spent about an hour in the field getting used to each other and the lead. Later in the day I went down to her house and she surprised me by greeting me like an old friend—jumping up on me, muzzling, etc. I put the cord on her again and off to the fields once more—and this time she really showed her class for the first time. She looked beautiful. In fact she put on such a show posing that I figured there's a little ham actress in her.

"As we went through the woods we hit a fresh deer trail and I got quite a kick out of Clarissa who insisted on showing her instinct by pushing her nose into every blessed track on the deer trail. Well, I guess I overdid the courting of Clarissa because when I put her back in her home she started to cry—which was the first sound we had out of her in thirty-six hours. I stood outside to see how long it would last and she quieted down in about five minutes. She's a great gal, and we're all deeply in love with her and indebted to you."

Well, it took Clarissa just thirty-six hours to get under this man's skin, and if I know English Setters she was living in the house within the week.

When English Setter puppies are a week or so old their mothers love to have you and your friends come to see them, and never resent their being handled; in fact they seem quite proud of the attention and the opportunity to show off their children. I know of no better way to teach your child the facts of life than to let him in on the entire procedure, from breeding to whelping. Two of my English Setter breeder friends have allowed their children to witness the entire breeding and whelping procedure since they were quite young and

This photograph was sent me by Mrs. Ramona C. Albert of Baltimore, Md. Mrs. Albert taught a troop of Girl Scouts obedience training, and it is interesting to note that seven dogs in the class of fourteen are English Setters. This kind of training is, of course, the fundamental yard-breaking for a shooting dog, and English Setters are a natural for it, having been trained in this way for generations.

45

Ch. Jiggs Mallwyd D at Camp, after a day's pheasant shooting in
Pennsylvania. Jiggs was very fond of beer and would start begging
as soon as a bottle was opened. His owner, Clint Schneck of Allentown, Pennsylvania, had steins with Jiggs' name on them in several
taverns so Jiggs could have a beer with him.

Ch. Jiggs Mallwyd D and Comet D with their owner, Clint Schneck
of Allentown, Pa., and one of his nephews, three years old. English
Setters love small children, respect their age and size, and are under
no circumstances ugly with them. The dogs were bred by the late
Dr. Daw of Vancouver, B. C., the suffix D denoting his kennel and
breeding. Dr. Daw bred many champions that were sold in the United
States, some of the better known of which were Ch. Jiggs Mallwyd D,
Sandy D, Ch. General D, Freckles D and Ch. Gore's Blue Pal.

46

they point out that it is the best and most natural way for them to learn the truth about reproduction.

Dr. Gantt, in charge of the Pavlovian Laboratory at Johns Hopkins University, shows, in his studies of the behavior of dogs, that contrary to general belief dogs have a good memory. One of the dogs in his experiment remembered for nine years the type of food given him during his unpleasant experience at the laboratory, and remembered for eight years the man who handled him there. Dogs, like humans, Dr. Gantt reasons, may resent being uprooted from their home, and resent a routine that seems like punishment, and they may be frustrated by confinement in a place from which they cannot escape.

"English Setters are gentlemen by nature; they are of the best disposition, without fear or viciousness, mild-mannered, loving and devoted every moment of their lives, and a setter's eye is one of the jewels of the entire animal kingdom." (Capt. Will Judy)

English Setters react exceptionally well to obedience training which has become so popular in the last few years. This is only to be expected because they have been bred for training in the field and therefore take up obedience work willingly and naturally. In the pedigree of Ch. Frenchtown Favorite Son, it is interesting to note that Freckles D was the second obedience trained English Setter to win his C. D.

English Setters by nature are very sensitive to punishment. They are not so much afraid of the physical pain of the punishment as of the act. A sharp reprimand or a light slap with a piece of newspaper is an entirely sufficient punishment. A command should never be given unless you are in a position to enforce it. As with children, continual nagging invites disobedience. A system of reward consisting of a scrap of food or an affectionate pat as an acknowledgment of compliance is much better than punishment for disobedience.

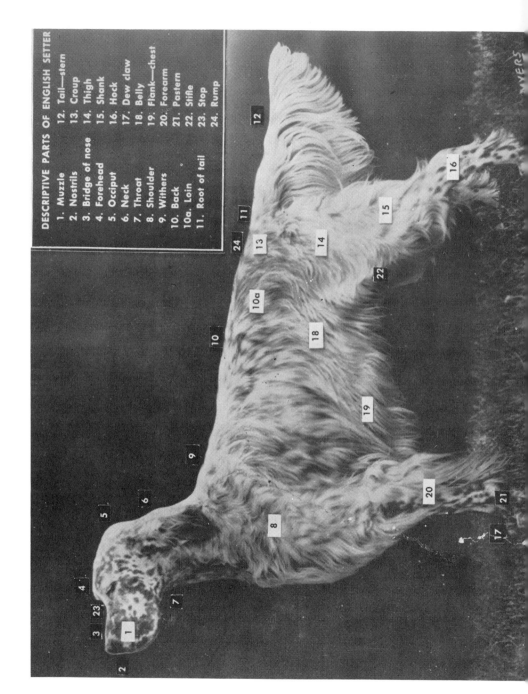

DESCRIPTIVE PARTS OF ENGLISH SETTER

1. Muzzle	12. Tail—stern
2. Nostrils	13. Croup
3. Bridge of nose	14. Thigh
4. Forehead	15. Shank
5. Occiput	16. Hock
6. Neck	17. Dew claw
7. Throat	18. Belly
8. Shoulder	19. Flank—chest
9. Withers	20. Forearm
10. Back	21. Pastern
10a. Loin	22. Stifle
11. Root of tail	23. Stop
	24. Rump

THE ANATOMY OF A SETTER

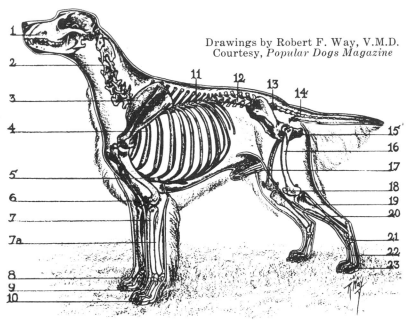

Drawings by Robert F. Way, V.M.D.
Courtesy, *Popular Dogs Magazine*

1 Skull, 2 Seven Cervical Vertebrae, 3 Scapula, 4 Ribs—thirteen pairs, 5 Sternum,
6 Humerus, 7 Radius, 7-A Ulna, 8 Carpal Bones, 9 Metacarpal Bones, 10 Phalangeal
Bones, 11 Thoracic Vertebrae—thirteen, 12 Lumbar Vertebrae—seven, 13 Sacrum, 14
Coccygeal Vertebrae, 15 Os Coxae, 16 Femur, 17 Os Penis, 18 Patella, 19 Fibula, 20 Tibia,
21 Tarsal Bones, 22 Metatarsal Bones, 23 Phalangeal Bones.

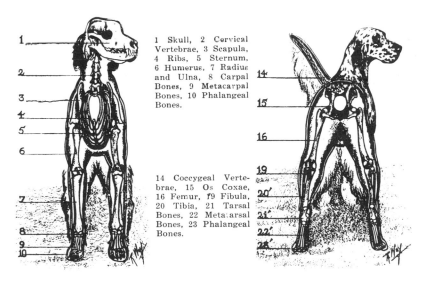

1 Skull, 2 Cervical
Vertebrae, 3 Scapula,
4 Ribs, 5 Sternum,
6 Humerus, 7 Radius
and Ulna, 8 Carpal
Bones, 9 Metacarpal
Bones, 10 Phalangeal
Bones.

14 Coccygeal Verte-
brae, 15 Os Coxae,
16 Femur, 19 Fibula,
20 Tibia, 21 Tarsal
Bones, 22 Metatarsal
Bones, 23 Phalangeal
Bones.

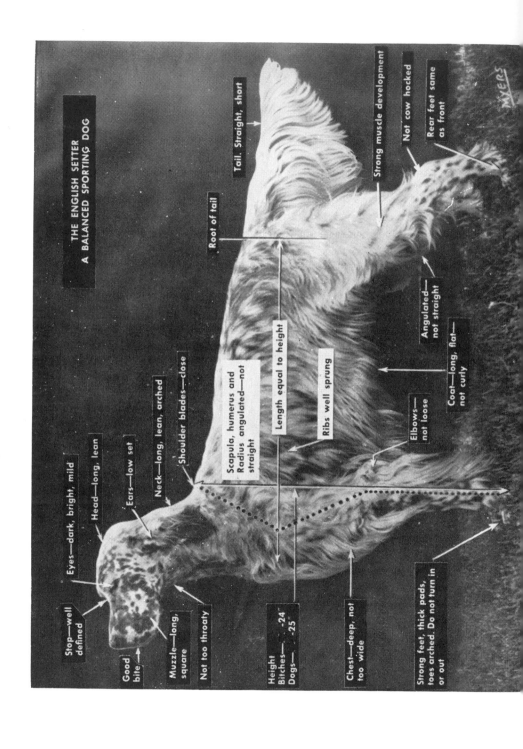

THE ENGLISH SETTER
A BALANCED SPORTING DOG

Tail. Straight, short

Strong muscle development

Not cow hocked

Rear feet same as front

Root of tail

Angulated — not straight

Coat — long, flat — not curly

Scapula, humerus and Radius angulated — not straight

Length equal to height

Ribs well sprung

Elbows — not loose

Shoulder blades — close

Neck — long, lean, arched

Ears — low set

Head — long, lean

Eyes — dark, bright, mild

Stop — well defined

Good bite

Muzzle — long, square

Not too throaty

Height
Bitches — 24"
Dogs — 25"

Chest — deep, not too wide

Strong feet, thick pads, toes arched. Do not turn in or out

MYERS

3

Description of
Standard of Points

(By courtesy of the English Setter Association of America)

Head. Long and lean, with a well-defined stop. The skull oval from ear to ear, of medium width, giving brain room but with no suggestion of coarseness, with but little difference between the width at base of skull and at brows and with a moderately defined occipital protuberance. Brows should be at a sharp angle from the muzzle. Muzzle should be long and square, of width in harmony with the skull, without any fullness under the eyes and straight from eyes to tip of the nose. A dish face or Roman nose objectionable. The lips square and fairly pendant. Nose should be black or dark liver in color, except in white, lemon and white, orange and white, or liver and white dogs, when it may be of lighter color. Nostrils should be wide apart and large in the openings. Jaws should be of equal length. Overshot or undershot jaw objectionable. Ears should be carried close to the head, well back and set low, of moderate length, slightly rounded at the ends, and covered with silky hair. Eyes should be bright, mild, intelligent and dark brown in color.

Neck. The neck should be long and lean, arched at the crest, and not too throaty.

Shoulders. Shoulders should be formed to permit perfect freedom of action to the forelegs. Shoulder blades should be long, wide, sloping moderately well back and standing fairly close together at the top.

Chest. Chest between shoulder blades should be of good depth but not of excessive width.

Ribs. Ribs, back of the shoulders, should spring gradually to the middle of the body and then taper to the back ribs, which should be of good depth.

Back. Back should be strong at its junction with the loin and should be straight or sloping upward very slightly to the top of the shoulder, the whole forming a graceful outline of medium length, without sway or drop. Loins should be strong, moderate in length, slightly arched, but not to the extent of being roached or wheel backed. Hip bones should be wide apart without too sudden drop to the root of the tail.

Forelegs. The arms should be flat and muscular, with bone fully developed and muscles hard and devoid of flabbiness; of good length from the point of the shoulder to the elbow, and set at such an angle as will bring the legs fairly under the dog. Elbows should have no tendency to turn either in or out. The pastern should be short, strong and nearly round with the slope from the pastern joint to the foot deviating very slightly forward from the perpendicular.

Hindlegs. The hindlegs should have wide, muscular thighs with well developed lower thighs. Stifles should be well bent and strong. Hocks should be wide and flat. The pastern should be short, strong and nearly round, with the slope from the pastern joint to the foot deviating very slightly forward from the perpendicular.

Feet. Feet should be closely set and strong, pads well developed and tough, toes well arched and protected with short, thick hair.

Tail. Tail should be straight and taper to a fine point, with only sufficient length to reach the hocks, or less. The feather must be straight and silky, falling loosely in a fringe and tapering to the point when the tail is raised. There must be no bushiness. The tail should not curl sideways or above the level of the back.

Coat. Coat should be flat and of good length, without curl; not soft or woolly. The feather on the legs should be moderately thin and regular.

Height. Dogs, about 25 inches; bitches, about 24 inches.

Colors. Black, white and tan; black and white; blue belton, lemon and white; lemon belton, orange and white; orange belton; liver and white; liver belton; and solid white.

Markings. Dogs without heavy patches of color on the body, but flecked all over preferred.

Symmetry. The harmony of all parts to be considered. Symmetrical dogs will have level backs or be very slightly higher at the shoulders than at the hips. Balance, harmony of proportion, and an appearance of breeding and quality to be looked for, and coarseness avoided.

Movement and Carriage. An easy, free and graceful movement, suggesting rapidity and endurance. A lively tail and a high carriage of head. Stiltiness, clumsiness or a lumbering gait are objectionable.

RELATIVE WEIGHT OF VARIOUS POINTS

Points

Head

Skull	5	
Ears	5	
Eyes	5	
Muzzle	5	20

Body

Neck	5	
Chest and Shoulders	12	
Back, Loin and Ribs	10	27

Running Gear

Forelegs	5	
Hips, Thighs and Hindlegs	12	
Feet	6	23

Coat

Length and Texture	5	
Color and Marking	3	8

Tail

Length and Carriage	5	5

General Appearance and Action

Symmetry, Style and Movement	12	
Weight and Size	5	17
Total	100	100

4

Blueprint of the English Setter

MANY English Setters are scattered about the country of whose merits their owners have no conception. Many of these dogs are of exhibition quality although, because of their owners' lack of awareness of that fact or indifference to it, they may never be entered in a dog show; while of others the owners know only that they have bought dogs with pedigrees and have them registered with the American Kennel Club. They assume that the pedigrees are an assurance of the excellence of the animals to which they are attached. It has often been said that there are more excellent show specimens tied up in someone's back yard than are at the shows. There are also a great many poor well bred dogs.

A pedigree, even a good one, does not guarantee a good dog; otherwise a poor one would be an exception. A superior dog will almost certainly have a superior pedigree, but the converse to that statement is not necessarily true. A pedigree is only a record of an animal's ancestry for some three, four, eight or ten generations. It may be good or mediocre, but while it may indicate the attributes the dog to which it is attached is likely to possess, it is no assurance of the quality of the dog. It is merely a guide to be used in the employment of the animal for breeding purposes and in the choice of mates. If the animal is sterile or is not intended to be used for breeding, its pedigree is about as useful as a second tail.

A dog may win in one show under one judge and never be heard from in the prize lists again. On the other hand, a dog may fail to be within the ribbons at three or four shows at the beginning and finally attain recognition as one of the outstanding members of its breed. Such reversals have occurred with my own dogs several times. Some judges may demand in a prize winner certain attributes that other judges may ignore. Some judges appear not to know just what they are looking for. Many judges so take a dog to pieces and analyze his parts that they fail to see the dog as a whole functioning organism. Such a judge may become so engrossed in the minutia of type, the exact placement of an eye or the ears, or the length of the tail, that he may lose sight of the more important matters of shoulder placement or running gear. The old Army axiom applies here—"Quibbling over the minutiae is indicative of failure to grasp the spirit."

People who have an eye for dogs will be broadminded, having the capacity to appreciate various viewpoints. The true sportsman is a connoisseur, and the true connoisseur would rather revel in the perception of beauty and achievement than join the unhappy hunt for imperfections. Every expanded mind is first appreciative; every mean mind is first depreciating.

Thus the awards at a single show provide no absolute criterion of the merits of a dog. However, it is more to be wondered at that the opinions of judges are so much alike than that judges differ as much as they do. Excellence cannot be denied continually, and an outstandingly all over good dog will, in the long run, win. In this connection we must not lose sight of the fact that as a dog is exhibited several times he "catches on to the ropes" and so does his handler, so that after a few shows both he and his handler put their best foot forward.

As to the alleged dishonesty of dog judges, it should be discounted heavily. This is not to say that the integrity of all judges is absolute or categorical, or that the possession of an American Kennel Club license to judge English Setters is a guarantee that a man or woman is more than human; but most judges are avid to make their awards as nearly in conformity with the merits of the respective exhibits as they possibly can. They take their judging assignments seriously, and their failures are to be charged more often to ignorance, nervousness, or inexperience than to undue influence brought to bear upon them or to outright dishonesty.

Then, possessing an English Setter, how is one to know whether it is good enough to warrant exhibiting it, even whether it is good enough to justify the owner's pride in it, whether it can be rightly claimed to be a representative specimen of the breed? The published Standard of the Breed as officially adopted by the English Setter Association and accepted by the American Kennel Club, is presumed to provide a guide to such an evaluation. However, the Standard of the Breed is compiled by men who are already familiar with canine anatomy and for other men and women who understand the more or less esoteric terms employed. Standards are of little use to the uninitiated, however valuable, even invaluable, they may be to persons familiar enough with the lore of the dog to understand or surmise their meaning and intent. Any breed of dogs requires to be officially defined, and the standard provides that official definition.

For the layman the specifications of the Standard of the Breed require to be taken apart, analyzed, interpreted and applied to the individual dog or bitch. That is what I shall try to do in this—**The Blueprint of the English Setter.** Nothing said here is intended to supersede or distort the specifications set forth in the Standard; that Standard, interpreted as best I can interpret it, must govern the breed. However, it is hoped that this **Blueprint** may enable the intelligent, serious minded amateur owner to apply the terms of the Standard to his individual dog and to reach some conclusions about the dog's merits and faults. It will help the owner to determine whether the dog is worthy of exhibition in a dog show, to be compared with other English Setters by a judge who may be depended upon to recognize its merits.

Perfection, it may be noted, is not to be sought; it can only be approximated. There are no perfect dogs of any breed. Since we are not going to look for perfection, how much shall we penalize the faults we find? A well-balanced dog, one with a multitude of minor faults, a trace short of perfection here, there, and yonder, is to be preferred over a dog with a single outstanding fault which is so glaring as to be obvious at the first casual glance. And a fault that interferes with the usefulness of an animal for the purposes for which the breed was intended may be considered to be more grievous than a violation of some merely arbitrary specification of the Standard. For instance, it is more important that an English Setter shall have good feet than that the length of muzzle be as we should like to see it; correctly angled and powerful hindquarters are more important than a coat absolutely free from wave or curl.

The scale of points which is appended to the English Setter Standard of the Breed is not to be too seriously accepted, nor did the men who wrote the Standard intend it should be. It merely designates roughly the comparative importance that is to be attributed to the respective parts of the dog, with twelve points allotted to symmetry, style, and movement.

These twelve points can be added to any gross penalty for any fault that seriously mars an otherwise good dog, and they serve as justification for any judge to place a dog he considers to be a bad one under a good one in his awards, whatever their respective score might otherwise be. Symmetry, style, and movement cover a lot of territory.

For instance, let us take an extreme but by no means an unusual example. An otherwise excellent dog with miserable hindquarters, a veritable cripple, can be penalized only twelve points for his hindlegs. A better dog all over may be cut several points in each of the various departments so that his final score is less than that of the crippled dog. However, by adding the twelve points for symmetry, style, and movement to the twelve-point penalty already assessed for bad hind legs, a judge is able to justify his decision to put the cripple down to the dog with many well distributed but minor faults. To amplify this important consideration, I once made an additional breakdown of the point system so that I had 100 separate points to cover the various parts of a dog. Armed with this breakdown I went to see a dog that was for sale and bought him for a fair price based on his rating of 92%. I showed him consistently at the same shows for a year with another dog who rated only 80%. The 92% dog never went Winners Dog, but the 80% dog quickly finished his championship and afterwards proved his superiority by siring good dogs, whereas the 92% dog never sired anything outstanding.

Actually, the judges are called upon for no such official justifications. Their awards are final, and the American Kennel Club sustains them in whatever decisions they may make. They are under no obligations to explain or justify their decisions to disgruntled persons whose dogs have met defeat, nor to anybody else. However, most judges wish to be able to rationalize their decisions to themselves, and the twelve points in the scale for symmetry, style, and movement enable them to make decisions on the merits of the exhibits without being hampered by the exact terms of the scale of points.

The judge's task at a dog show is simply to evaluate a dog's merits in comparison with the merits of other exhibits and to declare by his awards whether the dog is, in his estimation, a better or a poorer specimen of the breed than his competitors. A judge's time is limited, and he is forced to make his decisions more rapidly than he sometimes would like to do. His knowledge of what to look for and his experience in comparing dogs together enable him to make decisions quickly and with comparative sureness. We, on the other hand, are not comparing our own dog with other dogs, but rather are comparing it with absolute perfection. We are trying to ascertain how good or how bad a specimen we have, not in comparison with some other dog or dogs, but in comparison with an ideal. We are not limited as to time, and we may ponder our decision indefinitely. We must not expect to make a cursory examination of our dog and determine for all time whether he is a sure champion or whether he is an arrant mutt. Dogs change from time to time, and opinions about them alter—sometimes because of changes in the dog and sometimes because of our own changed viewpoint. So let us survey our dog, digest our conclusions, and survey him again.

We are seeking now only to assess his worth as a show dog. It is not our purpose at this time to ascertain how smart he is, nor to assay his performance in the field. It is true that among sporting dogs the ideal show specimen is presumed to be the one best fitted for field work, but the show awards take no account of the heart, mind, disposition and instinct for hunting a dog may possess except as they may have a bearing on "CLASS."

It is assumed that the dog under evaluation has been bathed and groomed, that his nails have been shortened, and that his teeth have been scaled. It is further assumed that he is free from worms, is in good general health, well-nourished, neither a bag of bones nor hog fat. His flesh should be hard from plentiful exercise; his eyes should shine from health and from the enjoyment of living. No dog can endure neglect and appear at his best. That he is just a family pet, not destined for show dog competition, is no acceptable excuse for permitting a dog to go filthy and ungroomed any more than for letting his health stagnate through faulty nutrition or for an accumulation of parasites in his interior, or for that matter, on his exterior.

CLASS

Class as applied to animals and people means that they have an extra something that it takes to lift them from the mediocre to the top. Class is a well-known slang word and like so many slang words expresses in one word a meaning that would otherwise require paragraphs to explain, e.g., "The dame has **class**," or "She is in a **class** by herself." Class is an integration between zero and infinity of all the desirable attributes plus an extra something else. It is doubtful if class can be entirely cultivated, as it would appear that the individual must be born with it or without it. An old saying that you cannot make a silk purse from a sow's ear very aptly expresses this idea. It is also doubtful that class is an inherited characteristic. Well-known examples of class in their fields are Jack Dempsey, Sonja Henie, Man O'War, Sturdy Max.

Class is something that is easily and instantly recognized by the layman as quickly as by the initiated, and it is doubtful if any animal or person can go to the top pinnacle of endeavor unless he is gifted at birth with this quality. It does not follow, of course, that an individual endowed with class can attain top honors without hard study, discipline and training. An individual having class, however, and who is fortunate in having an understanding teacher, and given the opportunity of competition, has the best opportunity of becoming famous.

Class is the one outstanding desirable quality that is so seldom seen and which can go a long way toward putting over an otherwise mediocre individual. In English Setters it is well to recognize class at an early age and lavish your time in training, feeding, exercising, grooming and housing this individual. A kennel may breed a lifetime and produce only one or two specimens who are in a class by themselves.

COLOR

Although color is not the most important consideration in the Standard and counts only three points out of one hundred in relative weight of the various component parts, it is, from a practical standpoint, of more importance than one would assume from the three-point rating. The Standard of the Breed allows a wide latitude in color, but actually the only colors that will ordinarily receive consideration in the show ring are blue belton, lemon belton, and orange belton. All the beltons are marked alike. The ground color is white, and for the blue belton the black hairs fleck through the white to give a mottled or marbled appearance. In the case of the lemon and orange beltons the lemon or orange hairs take the place of the black ones in the blue belton. Sometimes the black, lemon, or orange hairs predominate so that practically no white appears, and such marking is called roan; that is, blue roan, lemon roan, and orange roan. The roans are not as desirable as the beltons.

Another color combination that is often seen is the tri-color. This is a blue belton with some tan markings on the muzzle, over the eyes, and on the front legs. This is the usual color for Llewellin or field trial type English Setters, and while permissible under the Standard is usually undesirable in hot competition. This tri-color marking is no doubt caused by the Gordon Setter blood introduced during Laverack's and Llewellin's time (1870).

We occasionally see the color mark of the Irish Setter also in our English Setters, especially in the blue beltons where the black hairs sometimes have a red or copper tinge, just as with the Irish Setter who sometimes has a tinge of black on his red hairs, due no doubt to the Gordon influence.

The orange beltons are particularly free from color abnormalities, which is one of the reasons for their popularity from a breeding standpoint.

Very dark blue beltons are an undesirable color as they do not show to advantage in the ring and are not attractive as compared with lighter colors.

Large black, lemon, or orange patches are also undesirable except in the case of the ears, which can be solid black, lemon or orange. A color spot at the root of the tail is not too undesirable and in fact often accentuates a good tail set or a merry tail. Sturdy Max had this characteristic orange patch at the root of the tail.

The blue beltons usually carry a more profuse coat than do the lemon and orange beltons, and this characteristic is also shared by the tri-colors. This more profuse coat, however, is more subject to curl, which is a penalty. The texture of the blue belton and tri-color coat is usually harder and more difficult to control and keep in order than is the case of the lemon and orange beltons.

The winning dogs at the shows today are mostly orange beltons, and the next in number are the blue beltons, with the tri-colors last in numerical popularity. There was a strong tendency years ago to breed blue beltons, but the available breeding stock was limited due to the overwhelming popularity of the orange belton. It would seem that the breeders' desires had not changed much since 1576 when Caius stated that Englishmen were "greedy gaping gluttons after things that are seldom, rare and hard to get."

There is another advantage of the lemon and orange belton color over the blue belton as regards trimming. Usually, though not always as regards individuals, the undercoat of the blue belton is darker than the outer coat, so that when any trimming is done on a blue belton it must be months in advance of the show, else we will have a two-toned job on our hands, which is most undesirable in the show ring. Many judges who have not bred and shown blue beltons assume that the trimming job was done on the tack crate before the judging and unconsciously penalize the two-tone effect as it gives a most amateurish appearance.

There is no doubt that there is some complicated multiple gene factor between coat color, eye color, and vigor, because when orange beltons are bred together for too long a time the eye color is apt to become lighter and lighter, and vigor, vivaciousness, pep, and steam seem to lag. When the blue beltons and the orange beltons are bred together, approximately one third of the get are tri-colors. Tri-colors are more prevalent in England, though they seem to be increasing in America.

COAT

Laverack in his book **The Setter** (1872) says, "A setter cannot have too much coat for me, as it is indicative of the spaniel blood. Quality of coat is a great desideratum, and denotes high breeding. The coat should be slightly wavy, long, and silky. The forelegs nearly down to the feet should be well feathered, as well as in the breeches; you cannot have too much of it as long as it is soft, bright, and silky."

The Standard of the Breed states that the coat should be flat and of good length, without curl; not soft or woolly. The feather in the legs should be moderately thin and regular. In the relative weights for various points the Standard allows 5 points for length and texture of the coat.

There is no doubt but that good coat is an hereditary factor and when we hear exhibitors say, "Summer is a poor time for showing English Setters because they are out of coat in hot weather," then this is an admission on their part that emphasis on coat has not been of prime importance in their breeding program. An English Setter with a really good coat, that is, thick and profuse, will always be in good coat provided of course that the basic elements of English Setter management are practiced.

Coat is best grown from the inside. There is no hair tonic that can substitute for good food such as meat, eggs, starch, minerals from vegetables (not from the bottle), and vitamins (also natural instead of from the drug store). With this grade "A" food should be added plenty of fresh water, fresh air and sunshine, exercise, and daily grooming.

The importance of grooming cannot be overestimated. It must be done faithfully at least once, or better twice, every day, and the longer the time the owner devotes to it, the greater his dog's chances of winning. This conditioning of the coat is closely tied up with "Class," and the very routine of standing your dog on a grooming table every day has a definite training value for the ultimate show ring. The dogs enjoy this daily grooming and quickly learn to jump up on the bench for this special devotion.

In grooming an English Setter the following routine is recommended. First, take him out for his exercise, which should be of about one half to one hour's duration. This exercise can be walking on a hard road on a lead or allowing him to run (attended) in a field. Each method has its advantages, as the hard road on a lead helps his feet and at the same time gives him lead experience, while on the other hand, running free in a field is greatly enjoyed by an English Setter and has the advantage that several dogs can be taken out at a time, which is a great time saver where several dogs must be exercised. When the dog is brought back to the kennel, put him up on the grooming bench and brush him over to get any dirt and weeds out of his coat. A large-tooth comb may be used if necessary to loosen up any mats or to get burrs or brambles out of the coat. He should then be brushed thoroughly, using a stiff-bristle brush with bristles at least one inch long, preferably one and one half inches. (The new Nylon brushes are excellent.) This

64

operation will require about twenty or thirty minutes. Then should come the grooming with the bare hands, which is the one means of putting on a high polish. This hand grooming should include the front and hind legs, the length of the ear, head, body, and tail. Not only does this hand grooming take out the loose hair and make the coat lie properly, but it gives the owner the opportunity of looking over the dog carefully and feeling him over minutely so that any lumps, bumps, or skin trouble just starting can be caught before it becomes serious. It also gets the dog used to being man handled. It is recommended that the owner not wear rubber-soled shoes, as the static electricity developed causes disagreeable shocks to both the owner and the dog, and the dog's coat becomes so charged with static electricity that it is difficult to make it lie as desired. The next step is to sponge him off lightly with soft water. (Rain water or distilled water is preferable, especially in those cities where the tap water is heavily charged with chlorine, alum, and other chemicals.) He should then be dried off with a turkish towel, blanketed, and put in a crate for about two hours to finish drying.

When this coat conditioning routine is faithfully kept up day after day for several weeks, and proper diet and exercise are given in the meantime, and did the judge's decision rest solely on condition of coat, the dog to which this treatment has been faithfully administered would be a sure winner over all others that had been denied it.

Doubtless some English Setter owners will take the attitude that it is simply an impossibility for them to devote so much time to their dogs. Let him who takes this view be the last to complain when a good judge puts a poorer dog whose coat is in the pink of condition over his dog.

Of course a certain amount of trimming of the coat must also be done so that the entire dog will appear to best advantage. An entire chapter has been devoted to trimming an English Setter, and for the first time this important phase of putting down an English Setter in show form has been explained and illustrated in detail.

You may not have the best English Setter at the show, but you can have the cleanest and the best put down.

HEAD

A great deal of importance is placed on the head of an English Setter, as is indicated by the relative weights of the parts of the dog of 20 points out of a total of 100. Laverack describes his ideal head as one long and rather light, though not too much so. He did not like a heavy-headed or deep-flewed dog, as to him it indicated sluggishness. The Standard of the Breed subscribes to Laverack's ideal, as it also calls for a long and lean head. Some people object to a lean head on the basis that there is not enough "brain room." Actually a dog has a comparatively small brain, and only a fraction of the total is ever used. The size of a dog's brain has no bearing on the dog's intelligence. So it is with human beings. Many men with extra large heads are morons. The Standard of the Breed mentions "Brain Room," but modifies it by saying, "But with no suggestion of coarseness."

Contrary to the Standard's conception of the ideal head, there has long been the feeling among sportsmen that superior noses were somehow tied in with broad heads. T. B. Johnson in his "The Sportsman's Cyclopedia," published in 1831 and reprinted in 1848 by Henry G. Bohn, discusses the sense of smell of various breeds and relates this sense to the broadness of the head.

The reproduction on Page 14 (engraving by Scott) of an English Setter painted by Philip Reinagle, R. A., and published in the "Sportman's Cabinet" in 1803, illustrates an artist's conception of what a good English Setter was about one hundred and sixty years ago, and we immediately recognize many excellent points that they had then and that we today are trying hard to hold. Note the excellent stop. The Setter is on a close point with a black pheasant practically under his nose, yet he has a high head and is taking the scent from the air rather than from the bird's body. The expression in the dog's eyes and the overall bearing of the dog are most desirable. The excellent muzzle and wide nose compare with the very best that we have today. Note the wide head which again follows the idea that large nose, deep flews, and wide head denoted superior scenting powers.

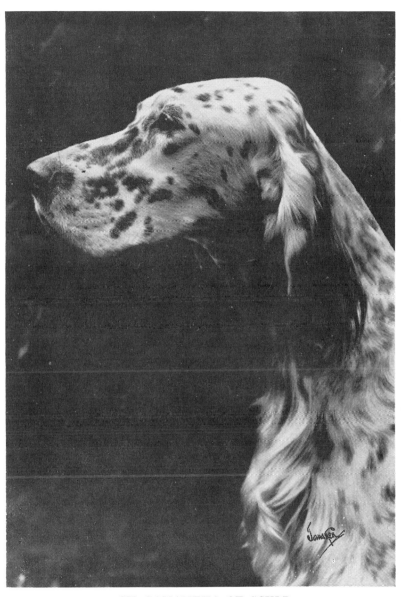

CH. SAMANTHA OF SCYLD
A Good Head

The stop or abrupt change in direction at the junction of the foreface and the skull should be well defined. An English Setter whose head is so formed that a straightedge can be placed from the tip of the nose to the skull has a most undesirable wedge-shaped head and has little or no stop. A line drawn across the top of the head and one drawn along the top of the muzzle should be parallel to one another, but at different levels, the difference in level representing the stop.

The length of the skull from the stop to the occipital protuberance should be equal to the length of muzzle from the stop to the end of the nose. The muzzle should be deep enough so that a line drawn across the nose and foreface and one drawn across the lower part of the foreface should be parallel, but with sufficient depth to make the entire head in proportion and a pleasing picture. Compare the photograph of a poor head (Page 70) with the Standard of the Breed Illustrated (Page 50). The occipital protuberance is the bump at the back of the head and gives another almost right angle (the stop being close to 90°) between the end of the head and the beginning of the neck, which again makes a most pleasing picture. The occipital can be too well defined, and when this is the case it forms a bump on the back of the head that is not pleasing. This overdefined occipital is often seen in English Setter puppies about six months old and usually blends out properly later. A bone injury during puppyhood sometimes causes this overdefined occipital.

Fullness under the eyes and cheekiness spoil the chiseling of the face and are undesirable.

The nose should be black for blue beltons and tri-colors and dark liver in color for lemon and orange beltons. Sometimes during the winter the nose of lemon and orange beltons turns a lighter color due to the dog's rooting in the snow. When prevented from this habit the nose color will resume its dark liver color.

A dish face is objectionable in the United States, although as already pointed out, a tendency in this direction is much to be desired in France and Italy. I am inclined to agree that a suggestion of dish face, as with a Pointer, is quite attractive,

CH. RUSTY OF HAON
A Good Head

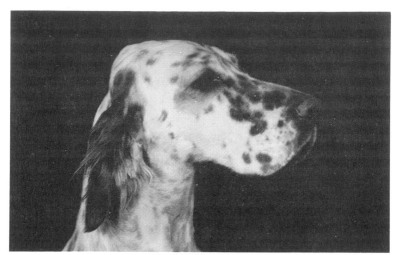

CH. MARY OF BLUE BAR
A Good Head

An example of an extremely poor head for a Laverack type English Setter. Note the snipey foreface with lack of flews and the general wedge-shaped appearance from skull to nose to neck.

70

although I also agree with the Standard that a real dish face is most undesirable. A Roman nose is the opposite from dish face. For instance, the top of the muzzle instead of being a straight line is concave for a dish face and convex for a Roman nose. The Roman nose is undoubtedly hereditary. Not as many Roman-nosed English Setters are seen today as there were about forty years ago, at which time they were quite common, stemming for the most part from two kennels.

The nostrils should be wide apart and with large, as compared with small, openings. This nostril placement and size are supposed to have some bearing on the scenting ability, but at any rate, when the openings are close together and small they are not as attractive as when correctly formed. Spots on the nose that do not pigment in uniformly are objectionable and unsightly.

Overshot and undershot jaws are most objectionable for an English Setter, not only from the standpoint of conformation, but also from a utility standpoint. When the front teeth are too far out of line a bitch cannot properly deliver her puppies, because she cannot bite off the cord. The overshot jaw is where the upper jaw is longer than the lower and gives the face a chinless appearance. The undershot jaw is where the lower jaw is longer than the upper and gives a most unattractive appearance to the muzzle, both from the front and the side. It has been believed that both over- and undershot jaws are hereditary, but there is recent evidence that it may be caused by a diet deficiency. This condition has become so bad with chinchillas that some of them cannot eat and starve to death. Studies are now being made to determine its cause. Until this work is completed, however, it is best to assume that poor mouths are hereditary, as the preponderance of evidence at present points in this direction. Puppies do not usually exhibit the tendency toward overshot or undershot mouths until they get their second teeth at about four and one half months of age, so in buying a puppy for show or breeding purposes it is wise to buy an older puppy and pay the extra price and be sure that it has a good mouth. Breeders should destroy puppies having bad mouths and under no circumstances sell or give them away, as they are potential

71

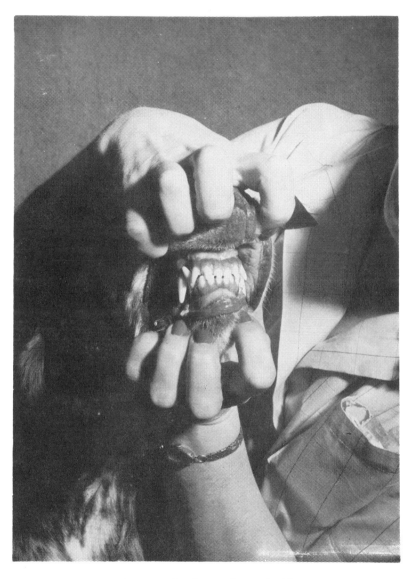

1. An example of a good mouth. Note
the scissor bite of the front teeth.

breeders of poor mouths. In the show ring a poor mouth can spoil the chances to win of an otherwise good dog.

The ears are a very important part of the head of an English Setter, as their placement and texture frame the entire head. The ears should be set low on the head, at least level with the eye, and well back on the skull. Measuring from the occipital to the stop the distance from the ear set to occipital should be about one third, and the distance from the ear set to the stop should be about two thirds. The ears should lie close to the head and not stick out, especially where they are joined on to the skull. By trimming the hair out from between the ears and the skull they will lie closer to the head. There is a tendency in some strains of English Setters to raise the ears when inquisitive, and this trait is objectionable. The leather of the ear should be moderately thin and pliable and not of a thick cartilage type. This permanent thickness of the ear is often caused by a cankerous condition which in turn causes a swelling of the leather. Trimming the top of the ear is discussed in the chapter on trimming and is also important in giving the ears their most pleasing appearance.

EYES

And last but not least by any means in making a good head are the eyes. The Standard of the Breed calls for eyes to be bright, mild, intelligent, and dark brown in color. While this is an excellent definition, it does not mention specifically their size, shape, and placement, or the pigmentation of the eyelids. Although the eyes have only five points in the relative weight classification, these five points may be called heavy points in the show ring, as the "Setter's eye is one of the jewels of the entire animal kingdom." He can ask the judge to put him up with his eyes just as well as if he could speak, and in a much more eloquent manner under the circumstances. I had this experience when I took a nine-months-old English Setter bitch to a match show for experience. She handled beautifully and when the judge went over her and then backed off to see her "all together," she slowly turned her head and looked him over also. The fineness and coyness were irresistible, and she finally ended up best of match. Her lovely dark eyes played no unimportant part in her win.

The eyes should be round rather than almond shaped (Oriental). They should be set neither too close (pig eyed) nor too far apart. They should be bright and clear and shining, suggesting health and energy. They should be dark, and the darker the better. The lame excuse, so frequently advanced, that the eyes, while not really dark, are dark enough for a lemon or orange belton is only wishful thinking. The Standard does not say that an orange belton can have light eyes.

Prominent haws are unsightly and while not a specific disqualification in the Standard are nevertheless undesirable. The haw (membrina nictitans) is often termed the third eyelid or winking mechanism. It shows itself as a red and prominent covering over the eye, usually at the inside corner. The haw is prone to chronic inflammation and is most unsightly. Sometimes this inflammation can be temporarily helped by astringent washings of boracic acid, argerol—5% solution, sulfathiazol salve, etc. The only permanent cure is its removal by surgical means.

A not uncommon fault with English Setter eyes is incomplete pigmentation of the eyelids, so that the entire lid or parts of it are pink instead of black for a blue belton or tricolor, or dark liver for a lemon or orange belton. While this condition is not a disqualification by the Standard it cannot fail to be on the minus side when the competition is hot.

NECK

The Standard of the Breed gives the neck specification in a nutshell. However, there are some helpful hints that might be of value. A long neck gives a graceful appearance in the show ring and has its advantage in the field for winding birds. Its apparent length can be accentuated by careful trimming so that by comparison it shows to its best advantage. Trimming the neck is treated with thoroughness in the chapter on trimming. In posing an English Setter the neck should be almost perpendicular to the ground so that at one end the head will make almost a right angle and at the other end the

2. Photograph of a throaty English Setter. Compare with No. 3, showing a good clean neck.

3. This is an example of several good points. Note long arched clean neck, excellent top line, correct tail placement, fairly good angulation, good feet.

shoulders will make almost another right angle. When an English Setter is set up with head and neck stretched out in front, it gives the dog an unbalanced appearance like a man with baggy-kneed trousers. The arch of the neck between the occipital and the shoulder is much admired and should be accentuated when trimming.

The Standard calls for the neck to be not too throaty. Of course a dog must have some throat, but in the show ring the less the better. We often see a handler, who thinks he is smart, gather the loose folds of skin which cause throatiness and pull them away from the judge or hide them in his hand. With all his efforts the dog is still throaty. The ringside sees it, the other exhibitors see it, and the judge sees it. A clean-throated dog will often become throaty with age, just as people get double chins with advancing years. There are some "fakes" whose only desire is to win and who care little or nothing about breeding who have the excess throat cut out of their dogs just as some people have their faces lifted. This practice is to be considered poor sportsmanship and is in the same class as a card shark cheating for money stakes. The owners get by on the theory that their competitors are too white to squeal on them.

Trimming the throat must be done carefully so that the coat will blend evenly from the throat to the chest. Otherwise the dog will have a goat-like appearance if there is an abrupt line between the throat and the chest.

SHOULDERS

From an examination of the rating of the relative weights of the various points one would gather that the shoulders are not too important, as the chest and shoulders together carry only twelve points out of the one hundred, and if we assume they are of equal importance, then the shoulders are worth only six points. However, when we consider that the shoulder takes into consideration only two bones, the scapula and the humerus, and that the remainder of the forequarters is taken into consideration under another classification, then the relative weight of six is not unreasonable. However, with some judges a good or poor shoulder may be a deciding factor in his placement, while other judges scarcely notice a poor shoulder. When it is considered that the rear legs of an English Setter are the real driving power and that the front legs are only to hold the dog up and guide him, then perhaps the shoulder is not too important. Yet an otherwise good English Setter can be spoiled by being loaded or too straight in shoulder.

It will be noted from the dotted line in the photograph illustrating the Standard of the Breed that two bones forming the shoulder, the scapula being the upper bone and the humerus being the lower bone, are placed at quite an angle and act with their connecting muscles as a shock absorber. Should this angle be too straight, the shock absorber action will be reduced in proportion. The scapulae are curved in a lateral plane so that the two when they nearly meet at the top of the shoulder should be close together so that one or two fingers only can be placed between them when the dog is standing with his head up. A trick of some handlers is to lower the head and neck when the judge feels for the closeness of the scapulae, as this movement automatically brings them together. The shoulder should lie flat against the body so that the neck and shoulder flow together.

CHEST

The chest should be deep but not so wide as to interfere with the movement of the shoulders. When a dog is viewed from the front and the chest is too wide, then also the shoulders must be separated so that the space between the two scapulae will be wide, and the legs will then not be under the dog. When the chest is too wide the elbow will point outward and the toes will be turned inward. When this fault is present, it will be more noticeable when the judge pushes down on the withers, as the elbows then swing out and are called loose or out in elbow. When, on the other hand, the chest is too flat, the toes will point outward and the elbows inward, and the dog is said to be French or fiddle-fronted. Anyone can try this for himself by turning his two hands in or out and noticing what happens to his elbows. The chest must be roomy and deep, and extend far back so that the distance from the back rib to the upper rear leg, the flank or loin, will be short. This short loin is important because it is the weakest part of a dog, having no support except the backbone and the muscles. The ribs should, be connected to the backbone at almost a right angle and then curve gracefully to the bottom of the chest. The depth of the chest should be such that the distance from the top of the shoulder to the bottom of the chest is one half the height at shoulder of the dog. (This does not include the feathering under the chest. You will notice judges pushing the chest feathers out of the way to establish this half way measurement.) The chest houses the heart and the lungs which are the dog's furnace, and without ample capacity of both, the English Setter cannot have endurance.

Some faulty chest conformations are called barrel-sided when the chest has insufficient depth, slab-sided when there is insufficient spring of rib, and razorbacked when the ribs do not spring out at the top.

BACK—LOIN—RIBS

The back line should be a gradual slope from the shoulder, being the highest point, to the root of the tail. The loin should be short. There should be no dip in the back line either just behind the shoulder or at the loin. A dip at the loin is a structural weakness, and an upward curve at the loin, although strong, is undesirable and is referred to as roached back. The loin should be supported by muscles and not fat. Some exhibitors try to make a dog appear short in loin by laying on fat, but this does not deceive an intelligent judge. A short loin is very important because the loin of a dog, like the small of our own back, is structurally weak. Bridges are arched in the center to give them strength, and if they were concave they would not carry the load for which they were intended. A slightly arched loin is therefore preferable to a dipped loin, although a well-muscled loin is preferable to either.

A not uncommon fault in English Setters is to be found where the back ends and the tail begins. The tail when stretched out should form a graceful continuation of the top

78

line, for after all, the tail is only a continuation of the vertebrae of the back. Sometimes the back has a sudden drop or shelf between the hip bones and the tail which gives the dog a constipated appearance and interferes with his movement. You will usually find this faulty tail set connected with the tendency of a dog to sit down at every opportunity.

The rib formation is very similar to that of a boat and it is for the same purpose, being a framework to protect the inner cavity which houses the vital organs—heart and lungs. The angle at which the ribs are joined to the backbone (the keel for a boat) will vary from the shoulder, being the sharpest there, to the center where the angle will be quite flat, and then gradually to a lesser angle. The spring or curve of the ribs should be minimum at the front, maximum about the center, and less again toward the loin. Just as with a boat, the lines, beauty, or symmetry of the chest will be governed by the way the ribs are formed. Round barrel-like rib formation lacks the gradual spring from front to center to rear and is not only unsightly but interferes with the shoulder action.

FORELEGS

As already stated, the forelegs' function is to hold the dog up and is similar to the front wheel of a wheelbarrow, where the driving power is the pushers' two hind legs. The front legs absorb the shock of the dog when gaiting, the dog being continually in a state of falling on his face. The front legs are similar to knee action in an automobile, and the muscles which hold the bones together are the shock absorbers. Viewed from the front the front legs should drop absolutely straight and parallel to each other to the pasterns, and still viewed from the front the pasterns and feet should still be in the same straight line. Viewed from the side the front legs should be angulated as illustrated by the dotted line in the illustration of the Standard of the Breed. It is from this side view that it will be noticed that the pasterns should be short and very slightly angulated forward to form another shock absorber. When this slight deviation from the perpendicular toward the front is too pronounced, it becomes a weakness, as the shock absorber leverage becomes so flat that it can no

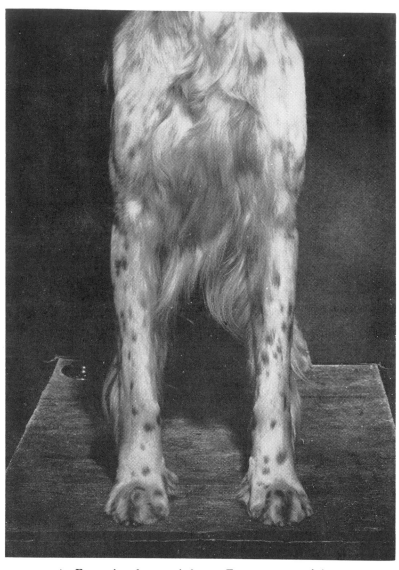

4. Example of a good front. Feet not turned in or out. Not too wide or narrow at chest. Elbows not out.

5. A poor front. Legs bowed in, and too wide at chest. Compare with No. 4 showing a good front.

longer take the shock. This condition is called being down on the pasterns. It is a common fault in English Setters and is no doubt caused by incorrect management during puppyhood. Many judges will overlook a perfectly straight pastern (no shock absorber) because of their extreme dislike for the deformity of a dog that is down on his pastern that the pastern looks like part of his feet. The pastern corresponds to a person's wrist.

Viewed from the side the forelegs should be well under the dog so that the radius (the bone in the front leg that is perpendicular to the ground) is in a vertical line with the top of the scapulae (shoulder blades). When the forelegs, shoulder, and elbow are not properly angulated the front legs are not well under the dog and are placed forward about under the neck. When viewing the dog from the front the front legs should not be too wide apart nor too close together. When the humerus and radius are in line the front will be correct. The length of the bones and the chest depth should be so proportioned that the lower part of the chest and the elbow should be in line.

HIND LEGS

The hind legs are naturally considered important in the relative weights of various points of the English Setter as they are his engine that give him the power to move. Twelve points out of one hundred are assigned to the hindquarters, being rated as of equal importance as chest and shoulders, or symmetry, style, and movement. The hindquarters or engine or propelling power must naturally be in harmony and in keeping with the remainder of the dog. A big car with a little engine or a little car with a big engine would be out of balance. The hind legs should be rugged with big bones and powerful muscles and should tie in generally with the overall animal. The hind legs are a series of levers and shock absorbers with muscles to coordinate these levers and shock absorbers. The bones which make up the leverage are the ilium, which is the hip bone and joins with the back bone or vertebrae. This hip junction is really the main bearing, as the entire effort of the hindquarters is transmitted through

82

6. Example of a fairly good rear. The hocks could be more nearly perpendicular to the floor, but this can be considered a good rear.

7. A poor rear. Note the cow hocks and the toe out which is a weak structure.

this joint to the vertebrae (the reason for a short muscular loin). The next bone is the femur or top thigh bone and sockets into the ilium. The next is the tibia or lower thigh bone and sockets into the femur so that the angle made by the two is about 120 degrees. This angle is called the stifle and is what is referred to as a well-angulated stifle when it is about 120 degrees, or a straight stifle when it is considerably more than 120 degrees, and overangulated when it is considerably less than 120 degrees. The reason for the 120-degree desideratum is that this particular angle gives the maximum driving power. The last bone of the rear leg is the metacarpus which is really an assembly of five bones and corresponds to the human instep. This is also called the rear pastern, and the junction of the metacarpus and the tibia with its protuberance, the oscalcis, is called the hock. The pastern should be short and round, and angulated very slightly forward. Looking from the rear the femur, tibia, and metacarpus form an angle so that if they are not in line the dog is called cow hocked. Associated with cow hocks, naturally, the back feet are turned out. In looking for cow hocks, especially in a puppy, the animal should be at ease, as when frightened a hocked stance is often displayed, even when the bone formation is correct. When posing a dog at the show the pastern should be just about perpendicular to the floor when viewing the dog from the side and the rear, and when viewing from the rear the stifle should be in a vertical line dropped from the rear of the buttocks. For instance, looking at the illustration of the Standard of the Breed, the dog illustrated is pulled out too far so that the pastern is not perpendicular to the floor and this poor unbalanced position also reacts unfavorably on the desirable sixty degree angulation at the stifle. The muscles around the femur and the tibia should be thick and hard as against thin and flabby.

FEET

As with man, the feet are a most important part of the body, although a dog is more fortunate in having four to support its weight. Man's hands correspond to a dog's forefeet and it is interesting to note that when a man falls, he in-

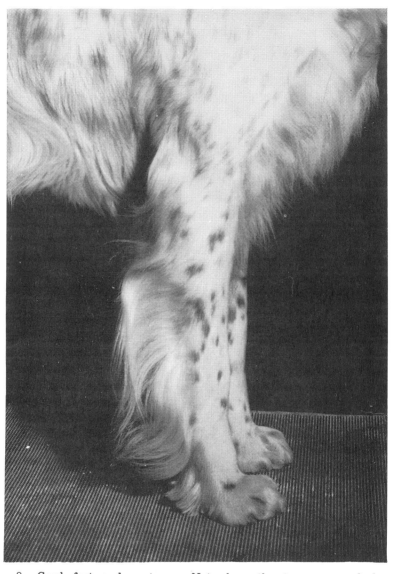

8. Good feet and pasterns. Note how the toes are arched.

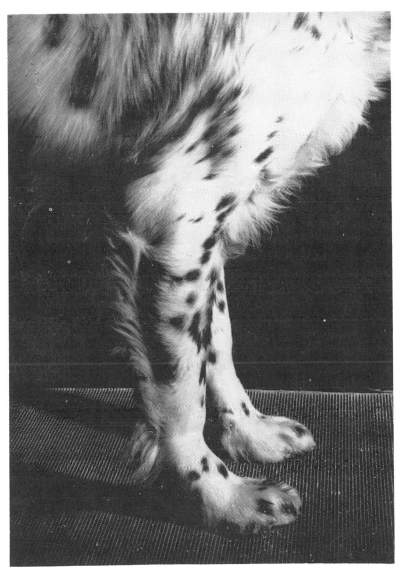

9. Example of poor pasterns, sometimes mistaken for poor feet. The feet are not good but the main fault is in the pasterns.

stinctively makes an effort to break the fall by using his hands and arms as they were probably intended in the dim era of the past.

The feet on an English Setter should be strong with toes close together and arched, with the pads thick as against thin. A dog literally walks on his toes, although in some extreme cases of malformation they are inclined to use their pastern (our foot arch) and their hock (our heel). Poor feet are a serious fault in an English Setter and a common one. Poor feet are the result of a combination of inheritance, overfeeding when a puppy, and lack of exercise. The combination of flat toes (not arched), splayed toes (not closely fit together), and thin pads is often coupled with poor pasterns (sloping too far forward). Attention should be called to the effect of long toenails as a contributing factor to poor feet, as when the nails become too long they interfere with the proper action of the toes and pads. Of course long toenails and lack of exercise, another contributing factor to poor feet, go hand in hand. It is doubtful that the toenails will ever be too long if a dog gets sufficient exercise, as he will keep them worn down to the point where the toes and pads function properly. While on the subject of toenails it is well to mention dew claws. English Setters have dew claws on the front legs only. They serve no useful purpose that we know of and mar the beauty of the front. They often become torn in the field and should be removed when the puppies are three or four days old.

TAIL

Next to the eyes, the English Setter's tail or flag is the most expressive part of his makeup and even when you cannot see the eyes, the tail tells you without doubt just how he feels about it—whatever it is. A tail carried down or between the legs indicates a disposition that is not characteristic of an English Setter. Although the Standard places considerable emphasis on the tail, it specifies its static requirements and does not mention specifically its dynamic action. The tail should be carried approximately level with the back so that a line from the base of the neck to the end of

10. Photograph of an excellent tail set. Note how it continues the top line without a dip to tail set. This is also shown in No. 3 of the same dog.

the tail should be a continuous pleasing slope. The Standard states that the tail should not curve sideways or above the level of the back. In fact, in the field trial (Llewellin) setters this is most desirable, as this high flag helps the handler locate the dog in heavy cover. English Setters are inclined to carry a high tail when they are in fine fettle or are looking for a fight. At any rate, a high tail carriage will usually not be penalized as much as a tail carried too low or between the legs. The tail should be animated and wag continually and in time with the dog's movement.

The tail is not merely an ornament and a means of expression, but has the useful purpose of serving as a rudder and a brake. The length of the tail should be not greater than to reach the hock. A shorter tail than this maximum is desirable. The tail should be covered with a silky fringe below, which should taper to a point at the end. A heavy bushy or fox tail is not desirable and much can be accomplished in this direction as well as length by careful trimming as explained in the chapter on trimming. In taking the superfluous hair off the tip of the tail, care should be exercised so that in our zeal to make the tail appear as short as possible it is not trimmed so closely as to cause a bleeding tail end when the dog is worked in the field. This word of caution is especially apt in the case of a dog with an exceptionally merry tail.

HEIGHT AND WEIGHT

The latest revision of the Standard of the Breed (1950) by the English Setter Association omits any reference to weight and defines the Standard for Dogs as height at shoulder about twenty-five inches and for Bitches about twenty-four inches. The intention of the committee on standard revision was twofold: (1) To raise the height standard of English Setters and (2) By the use of the word "about" to permit some variation in height above and below the suggested twenty-five inches for Dogs and twenty-four inches for Bitches. An examination of sixty-three English Setter Champion Dogs of earlier years showed that the average height at shoulder was 25.4 inches, so the change in the standard to 25 inches has a

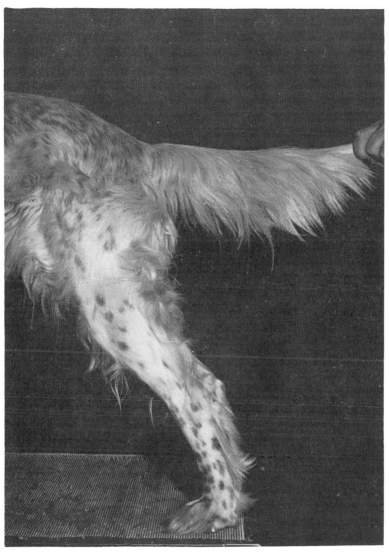

11. An illustration of low tail placement which gives a poor top line. Compare with the correct tail placement of No. 3.

definite background. A similar study of twenty-two Champion Bitches showed an average height of 23.8 inches. While the word "about" is somewhat indefinite, as was the intention of the committee, its practical definition may be considered 24-26 inches for Dogs and 23-25 inches for Bitches with a preference for the 25 inches for Dogs and 24 inches for Bitches.

There is a marked tendency toward breeding English Setters higher than 25 inches for Dogs and 24 inches for Bitches (height being measured from top of shoulder). This is allowed under the standard by the word "about." It should be pointed out, however, that it is extremely difficult to produce a really good dog or bitch larger than the height suggested. Extreme care must therefore be exercised when breeding in this direction. In general, if the breeder will try to stay at about the height suggested, his chances of breeding acceptable specimens will be greater. Quality, not quantity, is desirable. In spite of the arguments against breeding for extra large size, it cannot be disputed that a larger dog has a better opportunity of receiving attention from the judge in the Sporting Group, assuming that it is otherwise good.

SYMMETRY

Some years ago a cartoon appeared in one of the dog magazines showing a store where they stocked and sold dog parts for all the various breeds. Heads, tails, feet, ears, fronts, and all other parts for each breed were orderly arranged in bins. If such a store really existed, it is extremely doubtful if anyone could go there and buy all excellent parts and from them assemble a dog that would have symmetry.

Symmetry is an integration of all the parts to form a whole which will be pleasing to the artistic eye or to the trained eye of the experienced dog judge. Amateur breed judges often become so engrossed in the "parts store" that they do not see the entire picture, good or bad. It is for this reason that a good experienced judge will usually pick out the symmetrical dog who is fairly good all over, while the breed judge may put up a specimen who excels in several parts but lacks symmetry. All too often a breed judge will forget to back away sufficiently to lose the details of the fine points and look for a picture of proportion or symmetry. Included in symmetry is "Class" which has already been discussed in detail.

We often hear the gallery and the ringside express disapproval of the judge's selection. They were too far away from the dogs to see the fine points but at their distance they recognize symmetry and express themselves accordingly. I well remember the judge of English Setters at the Morris and Essex show in 1938. He had a quick and trained eye for symmetry. He had very large classes and stood at about the center of the ring and watched the dogs as they came in the ring. He would motion the handlers as they came in to the right or left, and when the entire entry was in the ring he had the symmetrical dogs lined up on the right and those lacking in this quality on the left. To me it was a remarkable exhibition of an eye trained for and appreciating the beauty of symmetry.

From the foregoing one may assume that an artist, sculptor, or industrial designer, whose eye is trained in form and function, would make a good dog judge. This, unfortunately, is seldom the case, as to most of them a dog is just a dog, and they do not know enough about the different breeds to appreciate the fact that what may be symmetry for one breed may not be the same for another breed. Quite often our Best of Show judges are people in the public eye, "name bands," and do not know much about the fine points of many, if any, of the breeds. They rely upon the breed and group judges to send them a representative specimen of the breed and therefore judge practically entirely on conformation, which is another word for symmetry.

MOVEMENT AND CARRIAGE

We have all seen dogs who when they move seem to get in their own way or who slink along like they were afraid of the unknown. This is the very antithesis of what is correct in movement and carriage. We want an English Setter who functions and coordinates perfectly and who is bold and gay with it all.

The gait should be free and without apparent effort. We have often seen dogs who make a great show of moving by picking up their front legs high and making a big effort, but not going anywhere. This action reminds me of a Mississippi River steamboat. The paddle wheel goes around and around furiously, but the boat moves very slowly. This is sometimes caused by the handler using a tight lead so that the handler is holding up the front of the dog, and the front legs, whose function is to do this, are practically useless.

A smooth clipped lawn or a carpeted strip on the floor, if indoors, should be used for moving your dog and in teaching him to move on a loose lead. It is best to use all types—grass, carpet, rubber mat strip, and grass mat strip—as your dog will later find all types for moving at shows, and may balk if he is not used to them. When attending a show with an unseasoned dog it is a good idea to get there early and move your dog on the floor of the ring to get him accustomed to the particular kind of floor. You will want the proper kind of slip show lead and not a collar and chain or too heavy a lead. A slip show lead measuring ⅜" or ½" wide will be correct for an English Setter. And by the way, never leave a collar on a show dog as it makes a ridge in the neck coat. The best position for observing a dog's action is to kneel or squat so that your eyes are about level with the dog's back. Perfect or very bad action can be easily seen from a standing position, but when comparing dogs of almost equal gait qualities it is best to be practically on a level with them.

The first thing to look for is parallel hocks. A good handler can stand a cow-hocked dog so that it is fairly good, but when they are moved the truth will out. Also once in a while we will find hocks turned out, called "bandy legs," which is also a fault. Dogs with cow hocks will move with their rear feet turned out.

A narrow base with the rear feet moving so close together as to threaten interference, the one with the other, is poor movement and is a common fault with English Setters. There should be five or six inches between the hocks as they pass one another. However, a spraddling action of the rear legs

94

is just as bad a fault as when the hocks are carried too close together.

As the dog returns toward him the examiner should look for the much desired perfect parallelism of the front legs, the elbows held close to the sides, but not bound or held too tightly. There should be no crossing of one foot over the other, known as weaving or trussing or paddling of the front.

While the dog in the walk or the trot (in fact in all gaits except the gallop) supports himself upon alternate front legs of necessity, the transition should not be apparent in the shoulders, which should be joined to the body so they do not slide up and down loosely as the dog changes from one foot to the other in the course of his locomotion. This is a common fault in English Setter movement. This movement is similar to the "tough strut" used to portray a bully in the movies, where the opposite shoulder goes up when the leg goes down.

The excessive lifting of the front feet and pasterns when moving on a level surface, called hackney action or steamboat action, is often applauded by the gallery and at best forgiven by some judges. It is a waste of energy and a definite faulty movement. This gait, although spectacular to the gallery, is a fault and should be penalized. It is frequently seen in the Pointer ring. This is not to say that an English Setter should drag his feet; he should lift them smartly so that from behind you can see his pads at every step, but he should not indulge in any goose-stepping calisthenics. Sometimes a similar high action of the rear legs is seen, especially on dogs with too wide a rear stance, and they are inclined to throw their feet outward as in a "Charleston" dance. Such dogs have, to the gallery, a spectacular but deceptive style, lots of action but little progress, like sawing wood with a dull saw.

Having watched the dog move away and toward the observer, we should next watch him move from the side or profile. His top line should be good without rolling and without dips behind the shoulder or loin. His joints should move with rhythm, and his leg action should be long and free, simulating a glide forward with no ups or downs, as you would want in a good saddle horse. His head should be in the air, and his tail active. He should show liberty in his gait as well as sound-ness and power.

A smooth moving Setter with plenty of action forward and covering the space with minimum effort, head up and tail wagging in time to his movement with restrained enjoyment never fails to make an impression on the Group or Best in Show judge as well as the gallery. He is always a Best in Show contender.

FAULTS

The faults for English Setters are given in the following tabulation. Those preceded by an asterisk are not common faults for English Setters as a breed; these points usually come good. Knowing which faults are not common is a help in breeding, as the drag of the breed will help to eradicate these faults; e.g., a short foreface is not a common fault for a Laverack type English Setter, so I would not hesitate to breed to an otherwise excellent dog who was slightly short in foreface, as I would not expect this fault to carry through to the puppies.

There are naturally various degrees of faults, such as a long tail. The maximum length of the tail should be such that it just reaches the hock; of course if it were one-quarter of an inch longer it would not be too bad, but if it were two inches longer it would be classed as too long. It is well, therefore, to qualify the fault by an adjective—eyes on the light side; slightly hocked, coat slightly curly, etc. Many of these faults are the result of the operation of the law of variation and are to be expected in your breeding operation. In the chapters on breeding, possible ways of minimizing them are suggested.

Several usual faults are illustrated in the group of photographs (pages 72-91), and a companion photograph of a good part is shown for comparison.

The head studies (pages 67-70) of several dogs and bitches will give the reader a good general idea of what is desirable in English Setter heads. Mr. Earl C. Kruger of "Mallhawk" fame and who judged the 1949 Morris and Essex Kennel Club Show, placing Ch. Mary of Blue Bar Best of Breed, described the ideal English Setter head for a dog weighing 60 pounds and 25 inches at the shoulder as measuring 10 inches overall, $4\frac{1}{2}$ inches wide at ears, and $4\frac{1}{4}$ inches deep through the muzzle. A great deal of importance is attached to a pleasing head of an English Setter as evidenced by the relative weight assigned by the Standard of the Breed. One fifth of the total points going to make up a good English Setter are for a good head.

Admitting that a poor head may spoil the integrated picture of an otherwise good dog, the other eighty per cent of the dog is also important, so a word of caution is not remiss lest we unconsciously sacrifice the eighty per cent in favor of the twenty per cent.

I know English Setters who are admittedly weak in head but whose other eighty per cent is so superior that they have easily gone on to their championships over dogs that were much superior in head but weak by comparison in the other eighty per cent.

LIST OF ENGLISH SETTER FAULTS

Light eyes
*Eyes too small
*Eyes not correctly placed
Eyelids not pigmented
*Curly coat
Not enough coat
Poor spring of rib—slab-sided
Straight stifle—structural
    fault
*Poor expression
Tail set too low
Tail carriage too high
Sickle tail
Slight bone
Lack of substance
Long loin
Snipey foreface
Short foreface
*High ear set
Cow hocked
Front toe in or out
Rear toe in or out
Angulation of front and rear
    not balanced
Too much throat
Too large
Too small

*Splayed feet
*Thin footpads
*Flat-footed
Short neck
Poor stop
Thick skull
*Undershot mouth
*Overshot mouth
*Deaf
*Roman nose
*Shy
Roach back—structural fault
Sway back—structural fault
Out in elbow—structural
    fault
Front paddles when moved
Rear too close when moved
Front and rear not in line
    when moved
High rump
*Undescended testicle
Straight in shoulder—struc-
    tural fault
Lack of brisket depth
Lack of back rib develop-
    ment
Body rolls when moved
Tail too long

---

* Faults which are not common with the breed.

5

Care and Management

THERE are several excellent books covering the feeding, housing, basic training and diseases of the dog in much greater detail than could possibly be included in this work. Certain information on these subjects is particularly applicable to English Setters, however, and is included below.

In raising puppies, it is interesting to know what an English Setter puppy should weigh for any age. Such information is not only valuable for evaluating a puppy or grown dog for purchase, but it is well to watch the weight of developing puppies to see if they are gaining as they should. Available data of known accuracy on weight versus age of good English Setter puppies is somewhat meager. The following curves for dogs and bitches have been taken from two main sources* and adjusted to fit the standard of the breed, and further adjusted between birth and maturity by several series of measurements

---

* *American Kennel Gazette*, November and December, 1937, Horswell. Kellogg Company, 1938, Battle Creek, Michigan.

These two-month-old puppies exhibit good bone development. Notice the tight feet from feeding little and often, and unlimited exercise. They all weighed approximately fourteen pounds.

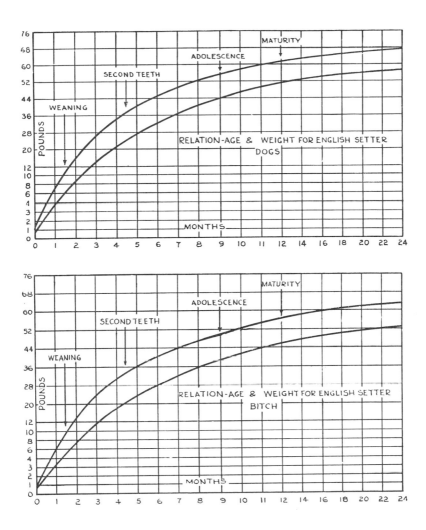

RELATION-AGE & WEIGHT FOR ENGLISH SETTER DOGS

RELATION-AGE & WEIGHT FOR ENGLISH SETTER BITCH

made independently by the author and Mr. Ward C. Green of South Norwalk, Connecticut.

It is obvious that age-weight records for dogs and bitches who at maturity did not weigh the minimum required by the standard of the breed should not be included in the age-weight chart, so such animals have been omitted as we do not care

101

to know the age-weight curve for substandard English Setters, but rather those who come within the limits of the Standard of the breed. Age-weight records are not complete, and the curve for dogs or bitches may have to be slightly revised when additional accurate data is available. It is believed by the author that sufficient data is available to establish within practical limits the age-weight curve up to six months of age. Additional data is needed for six to twenty-four months.

Such age-weight curves are very valuable to the breeder because they enable him to know at a relatively early age if a puppy is going to make the grade or not when mature.

These English Setter puppies are six weeks old which is the age for weaning, worming, distemper protection, training to ride in a car, crate breaking, lead breaking, house breaking, first trimming, teaching to stand, and generous feeding of the best food. They should weigh six to eleven pounds for dogs and five to ten pounds for bitches, and should gain weight according to the age-weight chart shown in this book.

From the charts showing the relation of weight and age for English Setter **Dog** and **Bitch** puppies who at maturity will meet the weight corresponding to the height requirement of the Standard of the Breed (revised 1950) it is obvious that a dog puppy at the age of five months weighing thirty-six pounds will, if kept increasing normally without severe setback from sickness, mature within reasonable limits of the Standard of twenty-four to twenty-six inches at the shoulder. On the other hand, should this five-months-old dog puppy weigh only twenty pounds, it is unlikely that he will reach the standard height at maturity. In using these curves some display of good judgment must be made, as evidently these curves do not apply to puppies who are hog fat or thin.

In compiling the data for the age and weight of English Setters similar data has been kept of age and height at shoulder, but such data is not sufficient for drawing any accurate conclusions. It was found, however, that there is a definite relation between the height at shoulder and the weight of good adult dogs and bitches. Using the data for the seventy-three good dogs and bitches it was found that the square of the height at shoulder in inches divided by the weight in pounds is 10.

$$\left(\frac{ht^2}{wt} = 10 \right)$$

This formula is substantiated by many careful measurements of height and weight made by the author, and it has been found that when the height at shoulder of a good dog or bitch in show condition is carefully determined by using a scale and spirit level, the ratio of height squared divided by the weight is very nearly ten. This ratio is valuable in getting a dog in show condition, as show condition weight can be accurately forecast by measuring the height at shoulder.

Training

English Setter puppies are fairly easy to house-train, given sufficient and frequent opportunity to perform outdoors when nature calls. A puppy from two to eight months of age should be taken outdoors the first thing in the morning, about every two hours during the day, after every meal, and the latest possible hour before its owner retires at night. Fresh water should be available all day until 5 or 6 p.m. so that the puppy will not drink too much at any one time during the day.

Training to paper in the house is **not** desirable, since sooner or later the paper habit itself must be broken. If the puppy wets in the house, wipe up its urine with a rag or cloth which can be placed outdoors in the location best suited for the puppy's toilet habits. Always take the puppy to this location and it will soon get to know the place where it may perform without disciplinary action.

A normal, healthy dog will not foul its own nest or bed. For this reason, confining a puppy in a wire or wooden crate at night helps in the house-training process.

Crate-Breaking

Crate-breaking comes in very handy later for confining him and keeping him out of mischief when you are away for an afternoon or evening, or taking him to a match show, or along on your summer vacation. In later years many occasions will arise when you will bless the day that you crate-broke your dog. If you intend to show him at the dog shows or enter him in gun dog trials, crate-breaking is a great help, and the sooner he learns it the better.

It is also a very good idea to teach your dog to relieve himself while on a lead. This is very easy to do, especially if you catch him just at the time he really wants to go (first thing in the morning and immediately after eating). You will have to lead-break him anyway, so you will be killing two birds with one stone. In the city, on vacation, at the dog show or gun dog trial, you will be glad you trained your dog to relieve himself while on lead.

104

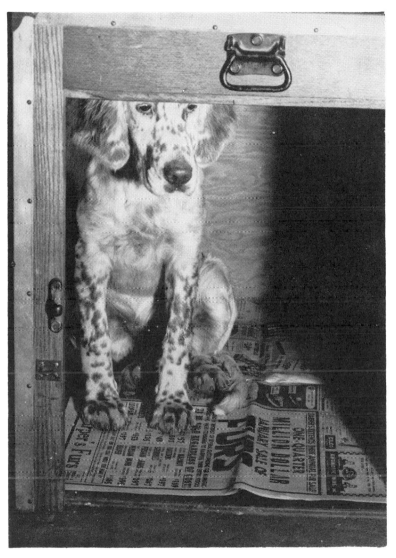

Photograph of a five-months-old puppy who has been thoroughly crate-broken. He is outside all day but sleeps in his crate at night. At bedtime he runs most willingly into his crate. Recently, wire crates have become available and they can be folded for carrying.

Allowed to roam at will, most dogs sooner or later connect with an automobile. Since they are hunting dogs, English Setters will roam. Assuming you love your dog, want to save him from injury and hope to avoid big veterinary bills, please fence him in! This need not be large nor expensive—a run 20 feet long, five or six feet wide and six feet high is sufficient. It can be made of wire called farm or turkey fencing, or of chain link if one can afford it.

Chaining any dog to a post or pulley wire is to be avoided at all costs. Chained dogs bark a lot and often become vicious.

English Setter puppies up to four months of age will normally get enough exercise running about their yard and playing in the house. Older puppies and adult dogs (and their owners as well) will benefit from a brisk daily hike of one or two miles, or a run free from restraint in a field or woods far removed from traffic or other perils.

Manoah Kennels' (Heathmont, Vic. Australia) Dual Ch. Manoah Moonlight, himself the sire of Dual Ch. Manoah New Moon, here baby-sitting his owner's daughter.

Puppies are easily lead-broken by coaxing them along with frequent petting and patience. They may balk a little for the first few days, but they will quickly learn to go along nicely. Do not be too severe with them; they do not know what you want them to do.

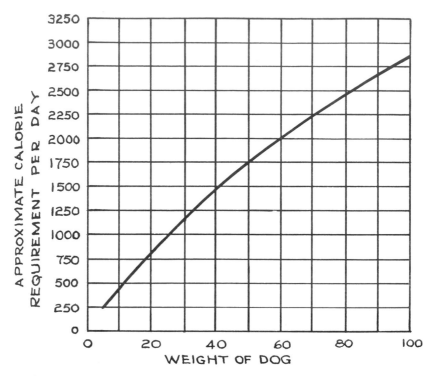

Relation of English Setter's weight and daily caloric requirements.

Except in illness, English Setters require no specialized, esoteric or exotic diets. A healthy, parasite-free puppy or adult will thrive on a balanced diet containing the proper amounts and ratios of protein, carbohydrate and fat without fancy or expensive foods. Those interested in calories will want to know how many calories are required by a dog of given weight. A graph is reproduced in this chapter showing the relation of weight and caloric requirements.* Though interesting, such charts should serve only as a general guide and not as an exact ideal. More useful to English Setter owners are the charts herein that show the age and weight relationships for dogs and bitches from birth to two years. Such age-weight curves are valuable to the breeder because they enable him to know at a puppy's early age if it will make the grade or not when mature.

Until recent years, breeders believed in stuffing young puppies until they become roly-poly butterballs. Today veterinarians are recommending that breeders keep puppies of the larger breeds somewhat on the lean side to avoid taxing muscular and bone development. The ideal at any age is neither thin nor obese.

It will be noted that considerable importance has been given to vegetables as a part of the dog's food, and it is believed that they deserve even greater considerations. Modern meat and grains have lost much of their vitamin and mineral content, not only due to processing but also because they are more or less artificially grown. The so much publicized trace elements are also deficient. These necessary vitamins and minerals are better utilized when fed in a biological form than in chemical or synthesized form, so that vegetables, although largely water, do have a food value in their vitamin and mineral content. It has been suggested that raw vegetables such as ground carrots, alfalfa leaf meal, etc., may actually allow the dog to synthesize, to a more or less extent, his own vitamin requirement.

Diseases of dogs are treated thoroughly by a number of authors, and space does not permit sufficient coverage herein to be of material value to the reader. The prevention and treatment of illness and the removal of internal and external parasites are best left to the experts—the veterinarians. Consult a veterinarian if your dog displays any of the following symptoms: loss of appetite for more than a day, fever, listlessness, diarrhea, lameness, cough, runny nose, watery eyes, evidence of pain, incontinent urination, vomiting, unusual thirst, skin eruptions, bad breath, persistent scratching of any area—or any other uncommon or unusual behavior.

Hip Dysplasia, or Subluxation

This disease, once unrecognized or considered uncommon, is far too common in many breeds, including English Setters. Until recent years, little information was available on hip dysplasia. Either an increase in its incidence or greater awareness of it among breeders and veterinarians has elicited much study of the disease lately.

Even today the cause and cure are not known. In later puppyhood the head of the femur (thigh bone) slips out of the acetabulum (hip socket) and the socket fills with calcium deposit. The outward symptoms may be stiffness in hindquarter action, a desire to sit down most of the time, a straightening of stifle or lack of angulation, lack of muscle in the lower thigh, and evidence of pain. However, only one or two—or none—of these symptoms may be present in certain afflicted dogs. Cases of "HD" vary from slight displacement on only one side to radical separation of femur heads from the sockets on both sides. Veterinarians have assigned grade numbers, from I (slight) to IV (severe), to the degrees of HD. In many cases, X-ray of both hips by an experienced veterinarian is the only sure method of detection.

Since so many puppies are sold as pets before HD manifests itself, the quantitative incidence among English Setters is unknown. The inexperienced owners of pets only slightly affected are often unaware of HD's presence.

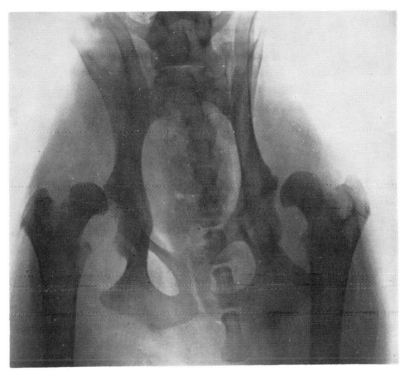

X-ray photograph showing how the femur bones are out of their
sockets and how the sockets have filled up with calcium deposits.

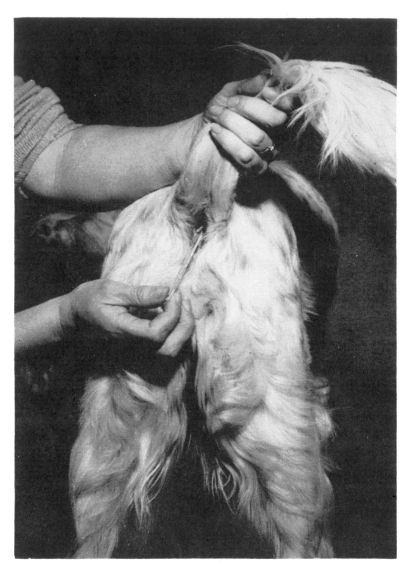

Taking the temperature of an English Setter with a rectal fever thermometer. Shake the thermometer down, grease with vaseline, insert in the rectum about two inches for about three minutes. Wipe off with a piece of cotton and read the temperature. A fever thermometer is a "must" when raising dogs.

112

The eradication of HD requires constant vigilance by breeders in X-raying their stock and refusing to breed or sell for breeding those specimens which X-ray positive. Even showing such dogs should be discouraged, since shows are held for "the improvement of the breed" and what improvement derives from the exhibition of unsound animals?

Afflicted puppies may be sold as pets, if HD is not causing pain, without papers to avoid breeding and showing them. Fortunately, in time most cases of HD compensate by themselves, and though the dogs cannot now be cured they may live happy, useful lives as companions.

The Orthopedic Foundation for Animals, affiliated with the School of Veterinary Medicine, University of Missouri, Columbia, Missouri, renders the following useful service to breeders for determining the absence or presence of hip dysplasia in individual dogs:

The OFA provides a kit for the taking of a pelvic radiograph, or X-ray, with a 14″ x 17″ film and instructions for the veterinarian in properly placing the dog to obtain a satisfactory X-ray. The dog's name, owner, American Kennel Club registration number, and other data must be imposed on the film for identification. The veterinarian or owner sends the developed film to the OFA which in turn sends it to three certified veterinary radiologists. The diagnosis sent to the owner is a consensus opinion of these three qualified experts. If this evaluation indicates the dog is clear of hip dysplasia, the OFA mails the owner a certificate so stating and bearing an OFA #. At present, the minimum age accepted by the OFA for X-ray evaluation is one year.

Dr. Fletcher Vinson, late President of the English Setter Association, playing with two of his English Setter puppies who were sired by Ch. Rip of Blue Bar. These are typical of the show prospect type puppies. Note the heavy pigmentation of nose and eyelids, the heavy bone development and the large feet.

6

Buying a Puppy

YOU want to buy an English Setter puppy for
a pet, a show dog, a shooting dog, or a combination of any two
or all three uses. Where to go to look for a puppy, how much
you should pay, what you should look for in the puppy, and at
what age to buy it, are important questions to you.

The best place to look for a puppy is at your local dog show.
You should attend the show and watch the English Setter
judging, paying particular attention to the dogs that the judge
places first and second in the various classes. Also watch the
animals who are placed winners and reserve winners dogs and
bitches, best of breed, and best of opposite sex. You can
meet and talk to the owners at the benches where the English Setters are kept when not in the show ring, and you can
find out if they have any puppies for sale. If you do not find
the owner of a particular dog at the benches, you can easily
locate him by inquiring from some of the other exhibitors.

Should your local dog show date be too long away for you to wait, your next best bet would be to write the American Kennel Club, 51 Madison Avenue, New York, N. Y., asking them to recommend several reliable breeders in your vicinity, and then write or phone to visit these breeders.

English Setter fanciers are among the most helpful sportsmen and sportswomen in dogs. Even when they have puppies of their own for sale which might not suit your requirements, they will often recommend other kennels. So do not hesitate to approach them, and professional handlers who show English Setters, for their good and usually reliable advice.

You should let the breeder know what kind of a puppy you want, pet, show, or hunting prospect, as the kind of dog you want will not only have a bearing on the price but also the breeder can recommend the proper puppy for your needs. If you want a pet, a loving affectionate disposition is of first importance to you. If you want a hunting dog, then the nose and interest in birds will be the deciding factor. If you want a show prospect, the conformation, gait, and marking will be important.

The price will probably range from $75 up for a pet, $100 and up for a hunting prospect, and $150 and up for a show prospect. A pet should be bought at from six weeks to any age; a hunting prospect from four months to a year old, and a show prospect from four months to any age.

While the price will be about the same for a pet or hunting prospect, regardless of age, the price of a show prospect will advance steadily with age. Buying a show prospect is a gamble, both for the breeder and the buyer. If you buy a good show prospect for $150 at an age of four months, the breeder is taking a chance of selling you for $150 a puppy that may be worth $1,000 when it is two years old. On the other hand, you may be buying a puppy for $150 that may be worth only $75 to $100 when it is two years old. There is no positive way of telling at four months of age just how a show prospect will finish up when grown.

When picking out your puppy, place a considerable amount of confidence in the recommendation of the breeder, but also make some examinations of your own. If you are picking out a pet, look for a friendly happy disposition, and under no circumstances pick out a shy puppy. If you are looking for a hunting dog, pick one that is alert and watches anything that moves—a falling leaf, a butterfly, a sparrow, a grasshopper—and one that moves fast with a high head and tail carriage. A show prospect should have a good mouth, not under- or overshot, and a dark eye. Second teeth and permanent eye color come at four and a half to six months of age. Examine the belly for a possible navel hernia. Look for a dog that is bold and a good mover, with a long neck and high head carriage. The tail should not be set too low at its root. The muzzle should be square and not snipey. The length of the body should be about equal to the height at the shoulder. The puppy should not be cowhocked. It is best to watch for movement and hocks when the puppy is using his natural gait. Before going to look for a show prospect, review the chapter on the Standard of the Breed.

When going to a breeder to buy a puppy, make up your mind in advance the purpose for which you want the puppy and the maximum price you can afford to pay. Do not overlook the "priceless ingredient," the honor and integrity of the breeder. Inquire about this before you visit him. On the other hand, tell him the truth and do not ask for a pet because you think you can buy it cheaper and then select his best show prospect. Most breeders will give the buyer a good break in price on a show prospect if the breeder can be assured that the puppy will be shown consistently, but he does not want to sell one of his best show prospects only to have him lost in some back yard. On the other hand, a sincere breeder does not want to sell a poor show prospect as it will ultimately reflect unfavorably on his kennel.

The trait of bargain hunting with its attendant misstatement of facts and haggling over price is very apt to take possession of a buyer who has a dream of finding a "dumb" breeder who will sell him a top show prospect at a pet price. Such a buyer is usually not as smart as he may think and in almost every case gets at least no better than he pays for. My advice to a buyer wanting a puppy that has a good chance of turning out to be a show winner is for him to be perfectly honest with the breeder. Tell him the very top price that you can (and I do not mean afford to) pay and just what your intentions are from a show standpoint. Do you want a blue ribbon winner or one that can win the Sporting Group? Are you going in for breeding or do you just want to have some fun at the shows? If you will take this honest attitude, you will get what you are after. If, on the other hand, you insist on bargain hunting, you will end up about third or fourth in your class with "just another fifty-dollar dog."

When buying a puppy the purchaser has a responsibility as well as the seller. It is unfair for the purchaser to go from one kennel to another on the same day and handle puppies at each one as virus diseases can easily be carried on the hands, clothing and shoes and so by not thinking or being selfish one may easily be the cause of many litters of puppies becoming seriously ill or dying.

A woman bought a four-months-old English Setter puppy for her husband's Christmas. On December 23rd she went for the puppy explaining that she would take the puppy to a near-by boarding kennel for one night and a day. She was warned that although the puppy had been permanently immunized against distemper, a boarding kennel was a risky place for a puppy at the time. She felt, however, that the boarding kennel in question was clean and safe. Five days later I accidentally happened to find out from a veterinarian that the puppy was being treated by him for a virus infection whereas the litter brothers and sisters remaining at the breeder's kennel were well and healthy, proving that the puppy picked up the infection after he left his original home. The woman, however, had had dogs before and knew where her puppy contracted the virus infection and did not even report her trouble to the kennel where she had purchased the puppy.

Many people who are not animal-wise would, under similar circumstances, immediately assume that they had been sold a sick puppy and I am sorry to say their belief is often abetted by their veterinarian who, for some reason, associates ten days with the incubation period for virus infection.

When examining a litter of puppies with the idea of buying one, look for uniformity of size, alertness, boldness, and general health and well being. This litter of eight puppies were eight weeks old when the photograph was taken.

Best of Breed English Setters being judged by Dr. Thomas D. Buck of Rochester, N. Y., at the 1933 Morris and Essex Kennel Club Show. The Best of Breed dog on the right, was Ch. Gilroy's Chief Topic, owned and shown by Mr. W. F. Gilroy. The Best of Winners was Maesydd Modesty of Bromiley, owned by the late Mr. Irving Bromiley, being handled by Harry Hill. Modesty was an imported bitch from the Maesydd Kennels of Mr. D. K. Steadman of Merionitshire, Wales. Modesty was the most beautiful English Setter bitch that I have ever seen. The dog on the left is Ch. Hearthstone's Orkney Chief owned and handled by Mr. Richard Jennings of N. J.

7

Training for Shows

THERE is not much difference in training an English Setter for the show, training for a pet, or training for a shooting dog stake or for hunting birds. In all cases he must be trained to be obedient, to go on a lead at his owner's will, to ride in a car without getting sick, to be crate-broken, to stand as his owner wishes, and above all to be happy about the whole thing. We have already discussed training for car riding, training to go on a lead, and crate-breaking, all in the process of house-breaking and general training. It is advisable to start grooming your dog from an early age as well, for this will help the coat, making it lie well, and to teach him to stand still in the position you want him to stand, when and where you want him to stand. It also prevents him from becoming hand-shy, through the frequent handling of various parts of his body.

An English Setter should be groomed at least as well as his owners. His hair should be washed, combed, brushed, and trimmed with the same care as you give yourself. His nails should be cut and filed. The hair on his head, ears, neck, shoulders, tail, hocks, and feet should be kept neatly trimmed to accent his beauty of form and to show off to the best advantage his good points. It is difficult for a veteran English Setter breeder to see the good points of a dog or bitch through a mass of unruly hair, let alone the dog show judge who has only a short time to look your dog over.

In grooming, trimming, lead-breaking, and other training you give your English Setter, do not forget the reward of a small piece of kibble or liver and some loving. Do this during the training process so he will associate this training with a good time and be merry about it. Remember you have more to learn than your dog, but the difference is that there is no one to reprimand you when you make a mistake, so take it easy and develop your patience. It is often said that the professional dog handler has an "in" with the judge and usually wins with his dog over an amateur handler. There are two reasons for his many wins:

1. A top professional dog handler usually shows top dogs.

2. He knows how to handle a dog to get the most out of him.

The professional dog handler has been doing for years what you are just starting to learn, so instead of finding fault, watch him closely, and you will learn to win over him when you have a better dog and should win. Just remember that the top jockey usually wins the race, and you will find the lowest odds on the top jockey's horse.

Your dress and deportment in the show ring are very important. A man handler should have on a clean shirt, pressed suit, polished shoes, but should **not** wear a hat. He should have a recent hair trim and a shave. He should not be overdressed.

A woman handler should **not** wear slacks. Her shoes should have low rubber heels. Her skirt should be slightly full and not so tight as to restrict easy movement, and should have a pocket for a small comb, a bit of liver, etc. Her blouse should not be extreme in cut—remember, you want the judge to keep his eye on your dog.

Applying both to women and men dog handlers, the color of your clothes is important. The color should silhouette your dog, not blend with him. For example, a white blouse and a light orange belton English Setter will blend together so that it will be difficult for the judge to see the dog's top line. Most all English Setters are orange and white (orange belton) or white with black ticks (blue belton), and your clothes should therefore be darker or lighter than the dog. Bright colors are acceptable, but very loud, vivid, or screaming colors are not suitable. A good rule to keep in mind is that you are showing your dog to the judge and the ringside, not yourself.

You must train yourself to gait with your dog, and this will require practice. Move with decision and precision and do not assume a pussyfoot, coaxing, or slinking movement.

The best training for you and your dog is to show at all the sanctioned matches that are near enough to you. You can usually find one or two a month. These matches are dress rehearsals preparatory to the point shows, and are well worth the trouble. Both you and your dog will gain confidence and ring manners. Ask for and profit by constructive criticism of both your dog and yourself.

Join your local English Setter Club and attend the sanctioned matches as well as their point shows. Also join your local all-breed dog clubs and take an active interest in them. If you really love English Setters, and you must if you ever hope to do anything with them, you will find that you will enjoy your new associations with dogs and doggy people much more than the movies, stage shows, night clubs, and other forms of paid-on-the-barrel-head entertainment where you do not participate in the fun.

To summarize, it is easy to train an English Setter for the shows if you will start with them young and have the time and determination to work on them.

Posing for Shows

Some dogs are much easier to teach to pose for dog shows than others. In this connection I have often noticed that the ones who are well-balanced are the easiest to teach to pose in the desired show position, as when they are well-balanced, the pose position is a natural position which is easy to maintain for a considerable period of time without shifting. For example, when a dog naturally toes in or out in the front, it is an unnatural pose for them to stand with their feet placed as they should be, and you will find them taking their natural position at every opportunity.

Posing for the shows is best taught at an early age, four weeks being not too early for starting their training. Make it fun for the puppy by a reward of playing afterward so that it will associate fun and not punishment with the posing lesson.

Dirt in Coat

Dirt and sand often get in the long coat and should be thoroughly combed and brushed out before trimming, as it dulls the tools very quickly. No English Setter should ever be taken into the show ring without a bath. If you do not have time to bathe the dog, then do not show it. Unkempt, dirty animals are a discredit to the breed and disgusting to the judge. B. O. applies to dogs as well as to people.

Chalk

It is customary to chalk the feet, tail, and feathers before an English Setter goes into the Show ring, as a final touch to give a well-groomed appearance. The chalk should be rubbed in and then thoroughly brushed out. Excess chalk should never be left on a dog in the Show ring, as it gives a most undesirable artificial appearance and is against the rules of the American Kennel Club.

Harness

A harness should not be used for leading an English Setter. A round collar with a ring for snapping on a lead or a show-type lead is the proper equipment. A well-trained English Setter can be led by a piece of thread, and one who is continually tugging and pulling simply indicates lack of control. A harness on an English Setter is as much out of place as a pair of handcuffs on a man.

When bathing an English Setter you will find that a built-up bathtub
will keep you from getting an aching back, especially when several
dogs must be bathed in one evening before a show.

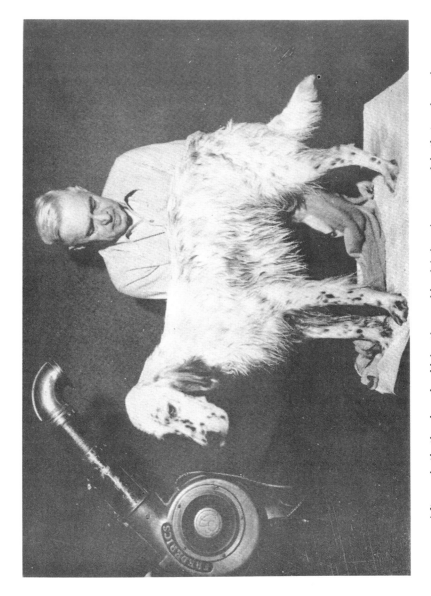

After a bath the dog should be thoroughly dried, using several bath towels and a hair drier. While the drier is not essential, it cuts the drying time almost in half.

126

The same dog as below after drying before blanketing.

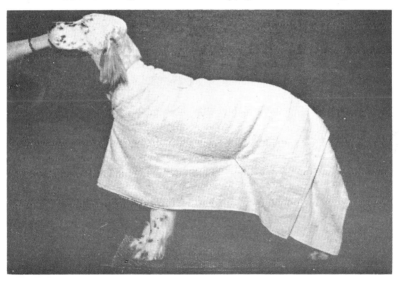

After drying, the dog should be blanketed tightly and put to bed in a crate. Pin the blanket with large safety pins. Special blankets are available that tie on with tape. Light-colored dogs should sleep on another blanket instead of newspaper as the ink will rub off the paper and get them dirty again.

As already pointed out, an English Setter should be kept looking his best. He needs about the same care and grooming at about the same frequency as his owner. His hair should be combed and brushed every day—it takes only about five minutes. Once a month he should have a hair trim, a bath, ears cleaned, toenails cut and filed, and the excess hair cut off his feet. If he is being shown he will require this attention before each show.

For bathing you will find Ivory soap as good as any. Soap all around his neck first to keep fleas, if any—and there is no excuse for your dog ever having fleas—from moving up from his body to his ears. Then soap to a good lather all over. After thorough rinsing, give him an additional rinse with Hilo Dip* which will kill any fleas, ticks, or lice, and leave him with a pleasant smell. This rinse should include his entire head and ears. Don't worry about getting a little in his eyes, as Hilo Dip will not hurt them; you will soon find this out when he shakes Hilo into **your** eyes. Dry him thoroughly with turkish towels and a hair dryer, if you have one. Then blanket him with a large turkish towel pinned with large safety pins under his neck and under his loin, then put him in a crate to sleep and give his coat time to set flat. The entire bath routine will require about one and a half hours.

There is very little data and detailed instructions on trimming an English Setter and, judging by many that I have seen in the show ring, I believe more or less complete illustrated instructions on trimming an English Setter will add considerably to the practical value of this book.

---

* Registered U.S. Patent Office by The Hilo Company, Norwalk, Connecticut.

8

Trimming and Grooming

SOME may ask, why is it necessary to trim an English Setter: Why not leave it as nature intended? The answer, of course, is plainly indicated by the illustrations of an English Setter, shown before and after trimming in Plate numbers one and two on page 133. At the present time, style dictates that an English Setter be trimmed approximately as indicated in the following series of photographs.

There are other methods of trimming an English Setter, such as plucking, without the use of mechanical time savers, and the use of a stripping knife only, or a combination of plucking and stripping. The method outlined in the following photographs, however, is the usual practice and will give a finished job equal to that of any other method if carefully and expertly done.

An English Setter for show purposes cannot be trimmed properly in a day. He should be roughed out as shown by the

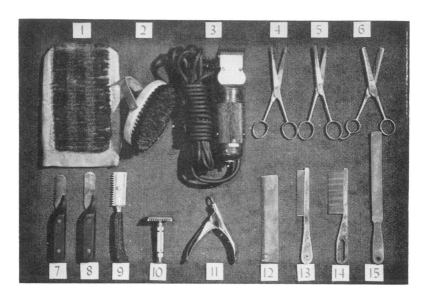

Tools used for trimming an English Setter: 1. Hound glove. 2. Brush. 3. Oster Clipper with No. 7 head. 4. Barber's scissors. 5. Curved blade scissors. 6. Thinning shears. 7. Coarse stripping knife. 8. Fine stripping knife. 9. Durham Duplex stripping tool. 10. Safety razor. 11. Resco nail clipper. 12. Furrier's comb. 13. Fine comb. 14. Medium comb. 15. Nail file.

illustrations and then worked over a small amount at a time every day. By taking off a little hair here and there as needed, a finished job can be done in about two weeks. While trimming it is a good plan to stand off from the dog at about ten feet now and then and look him over so as to get the over-all balanced picture.

The following group of photographs was made to illustrate the various steps to be followed in the first rough trim, after which daily touching up, a little at a time, is necessary for a finished show trim. The dog used as a subject was in show trim February 15, 1949, and had purposely not been trimmed since until April 28, 1949, when these photographs were made.

The photographs in this trimming section were made by William Joli, one of our top dog photographers, and I want to acknowledge his skill due, in no small measure, to his patience and understanding of dog psychology.

Photograph No. 1 shows the dog before any trimming was done and for convenience in comparison of what can be accomplished in accentuating the dog's good points. No. 2 shows the same dog after the various roughing out operations had been completed. The time for roughing out was two hours, using two people, one to hold the dog in the desired position so that he would not interfere with the person trimming, and the other to do the trimming.

Before starting to trim, the one doing the trimming should stand off at as great a distance as the room will allow and look the dog over, just as a judge would look at the dog to get an idea of his over-all picture. This first survey should be made from one side and then the other, and then from the front and the rear.

This general survey will disclose that the dog illustrated has several good points, such as a short loin, good feet, good tail set, good shoulders, good depth of brisket, good pasterns. Moreover, the dog has several other things good about him that are not so apparent from the survey. For instance, he has dark eyes, a good expression, good teeth, and good bone, and when moved is gay and full of life, and carries a merry stern.

However, the dog has some minor faults. He is inclined

to have a short neck, and a slight dip in the middle of the back, and is consequently high behind. The tail is on the long side, and the heavy coat in the wrong place makes it look unkempt. The extra heavy coat in front of the chest makes him appear straight in front, which is accentuated by the heavy neck coat. The rear quarters look particularly bad due to a straight stifle, which in turn is made to look even poorer than it is by the excess of coat behind.

All in all, the dog has a pinched, constipated appearance, and his faults show up even worse than they are. His good points are largely hidden by his general unkempt appearance.

I recently saw an excellent bitch at the shows who had been consistently turned down because of her poor trimming, who after some effort has been going Winners Bitch and rightly so, too. We must remember that with hot competition it is the little things that count. Some may say that a good judge should not be fooled by the handler's faking a dog by trimming, but we all know that a beautiful diamond does not look its best when the owner wears it while washing dishes, lifting ashes and digging in the flower and kitchen garden without subsequent care to the diamond. There are very few judges who can or who want to see beneath a poorly set down English Setter. After all, some credit must be given to the owner who spends hours keeping his dog in show condition, as compared to the indolent owner.

The same dog illustrated in No. 1 is shown in No. 2 after the roughing-out job has been completed. The dog is obviously not in final show trim, but when comparing the two photographs it is quite evident that considerable headway has been made. The constipated appearance has disappeared by taking some of the excess hair off the head, neck, shoulders, chest, rump, thighs, and tail.

Just as a well-groomed man carrying a good head of hair must visit the barber shop every two weeks to bolster his well being, so it is with the English Setter. The expression that a man has had his "ears lifted" when he gets a hair cut also applies to the English Setter, only in the Setter's case the ears have been lowered. We find many strains of English Setters who grow a typical spaniel topknot (additional proof of the

132

No. 1

No. 2

setter's forebears) which gives them a most undesirable wedge-shaped head appearance. This topknot is not easy to remove to show form because the hair is so long in comparison to that on the rest of the head that when it is stripped off in the roughing operation, it is plainly visible that something has been done, and the trimmed topknot hair sticks straight up in contrast to the hair on the remainder of the head which lies smoothly. This is a good example of why an English Setter cannot be trimmed properly on the crate before the judging, or the day before the show, or even the week before the show.

When comparing No. 2 with No. 1 it is interesting to note how the over-all color of the blue belton dog has been lightened by removing the excess hair. The darker area over the rump and at neck and shoulders will lighten more when the final show trim is completed.

This roughing-out operation is all that is given the majority of English Setters exhibited at the shows, the reason being either lack of knowledge of how it should be done, or laziness on the part of the owner or handler. At this moment I know of two excellent English Setters who are being continually kicked around because of the poor trimming job done on them.

Do not get the idea for a moment that trimming can make a poor specimen a good one, or that trimming alone means show condition. Long hours of grooming after trimming are necessary for show condition.

The first operation in the trimming process is to remove the excess hair from the throat, using an Oster Clipper with No. 7 head. English Setters vary greatly in temperament, and some make be frightened at the buzzing sound of the clipper and resent its use to the extent that it is almost impossible to hold them still enough to use the clipper properly. When a dog is jerking about, trying to get away from the clipper, there is danger of cutting him or yourself.

This resentment of the clipper noise (which sounds like a bee buzzing) can be entirely eliminated by getting the dog used to it when still a puppy. We start trimming puppies as soon as they are weaned, not that they need it, but to get

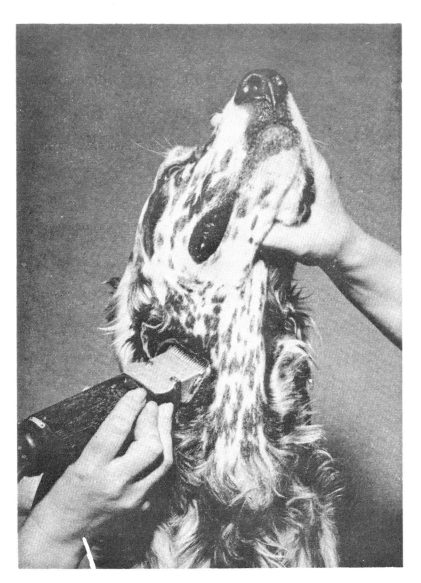

No. 3

them used to the clipper. Another advantage of getting puppies accustomed to the clipper at an early age is the attention and handling that are associated with trimming, as otherwise many puppies get so unruly that it is difficult to quiet them down without harsh measures that may spoil their disposition from a show standpoint. When a dog is acquired at older than puppy age, I have found it a good idea to get them accustomed to the clipper noise by laying the running clipper near them while combing them, brushing them, and petting them. In this way they get used to the clipper noise at some little distance and are not so frightened when it is brought nearer to them.

We have also found that if you will place your face close to their ear and talk to them in a soothing voice, telling them what nice dogs they are and other such nonsense, they will stand for the clipper much better than otherwise. In no case should they be too tightly held and forced to submit to the clipper, as they only become more frightened, and you start trouble for the next time by making them associate the clipper noise with a rough time.

In this neck trimming operation, although not done here for photographic reasons, it is advisable for the person doing the trimming to hold the dog's head with the left hand so that any sudden movement of the head can be anticipated, thereby preventing gouging by the clipper blade. The assistant can hold the rear end of the dog and pet him. Having the assistant rub the dog's belly while the clipper is being used also helps to quiet an unruly dog.

While we all dislike the use of the electric clipper, it saves hours of hard work and gives a smoother appearance than most people can get without it. However, its use should be confined to the first roughing-out work. On the under part of the neck always work upwards with the clipper, using steady continuous strokes.

The throat is now trimmed and the next step with the Oster Clipper with No. 7 head is to trim off the superfluous hair from the sides of the neck, as shown in No. 4. While doing this be sure to hold the ear up so that it is out of the

No. 4

way of the electric trimmer, and then in slow continuous strokes trim right up to the base of the ear. This is the hair that keeps the ear from lying flat against the neck.

Do not use the clipper above the line which is definitely formed by hair originating under the neck and that originating on top of the neck, as the hair on top of the neck is left longer and is taken down by hand with a stripping knife or the Duplex Dresser, as shown in No. 10. This line of demarcation is clearly defined, as the hair lies at a different angle on each side of the dividing line.

Some people prefer to remove this side-of-the-neck hair with a stripping knife or scissors and blend in the top of the neck and side of the neck by singeing with a lighted wax taper and using a comb. Dogs object to the singeing even more than they do to the clipper noise, not because it hurts them, but because of the flame and the smell of the burning hair. Singeing also discolors the hair, especially on a light-colored blue or orange belton, and a week or more is required before the discoloration disappears. We have tried all the various methods and prefer the Oster Clipper No. 7 blade. Some final touch up of the ridge between the side of the neck and the top of the neck can be made later with the scissors and comb or with the Duplex Dresser.

We will find more and more use of the Duplex Dresser as the trimming operation progresses. The Durham Duplex blades are rather expensive and a blade will retain its edge for only about five minutes. This quick dulling of the edge of the Durham Duplex blades is due to minute quantities of dirt and grit in the coat, and you will find that a thorough brushing before trimming will lengthen the life of the blade before it becomes dull.

The Durham-Enders Razor Corporation of Mystic, Connecticut, have a blade holder and strop known as the Ingersoll Stropper made especially for honing and stropping blades to a barber's edge. The complete outfit costs $1.50. Be sure to order the Ingersoll Stropper for **Durham Duplex blades,** as they also make other Ingersoll Stroppers for other blades.

When clipping the side of the neck, carry on through the cheeks to under the eyes and to the nose. When making the

138

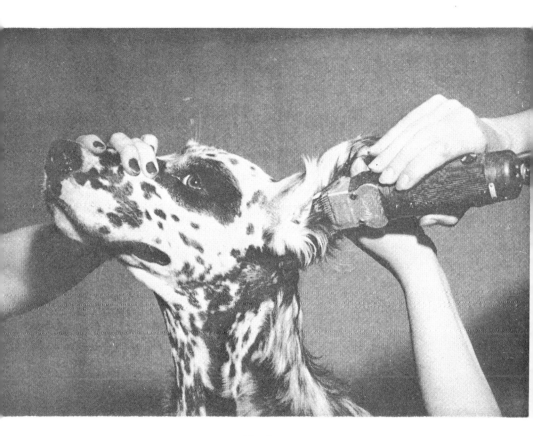

No. 5

first cut get right down as closely as you can at once and do not try to taper off, as this blending into the adjoining coat is done later.

No. 5 illustrates how to take the unwanted hair from the underside of the ears. This is the hair which with that on the sides of the neck keeps the ears from resting nicely against the neck. Use the Oster Clipper with No. 7 head, and by the way, the clipper should be oiled frequently with special Oster Oil and the blades should be kept clean of felted hair with a whisk broom. If this attention is not given to the clipper it will not run smoothly and will give a ragged result. With good care the Oster blades will need resharpening, by the Oster Service Station, about twice a year with ordinary use on five English Setters. After using the Oster Clipper wipe off the teeth with an oiled rag. (We use a small piece of blanket sample for this purpose.)

When trimming the underside of the ear watch very carefully for the small split part of the underear and do not cut it. Even with care this split is sometimes nicked, and you would do well to have a small bottle of Thymol Iodide handy, as ear cuts bleed profusely and a very light touch of Thymol Iodide powder will stop the bleeding almost instantly. It is best, of course, not to cut the ear as it often causes the dog to resent your working on his ears.

The clipper should be run against the grain of the hair, and you will find that the grain or lay of the hair changes as you approach the base of the ear, so that whereas you will start, from the photograph, west, at the end of the ear, you will be going north when you reach the base of the ear. Some of the hair in the inner ear can be removed with the clipper while you are working on the ear, but the final touches to the center ear will have to be done with a pair of sharp curved-blade scissors.

When working around a dog's ear remember that the ears, the eyes, the mouth, the nose, and the feet are the most sensitive parts of his body. It is a good idea to go slowly when trimming the ears and give him frequent rest periods with some petting and a piece of dog biscuit, just to stay friends with him.

140

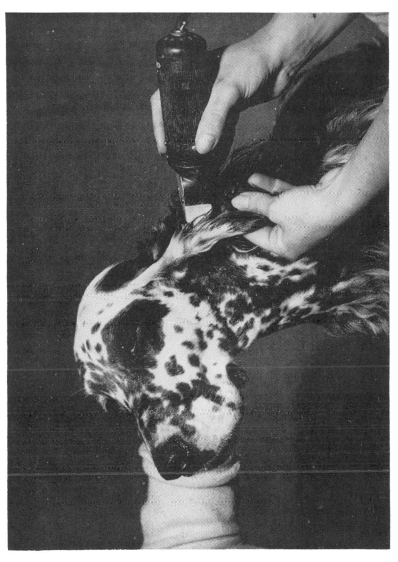

After the trimming of the under and center parts of the ear has been completed it is a good time to look after the inner ear. "A stitch in time saves nine," and if the ears are cleaned out with a piece of cotton dipped in alcohol, then dried with another piece of cotton and dusted with Bismuth Formic Iodide, canker ears will never develop. Anyone who has ever had a dog with a canker ear to contend with will appreciate this precaution.

Taking the extra hair off the top of the ear, as illustrated in No. 6, gives the English Setter's ears the utmost possible in a low-set ear. Of course the ears must be low set to start with, but this careful trimming operation will show them off to their best advantage. Trimming the top of the ears must be done most carefully for a pleasing result and is a careful blend of three operations. Start with the Oster Clipper and No. 7 head down about one quarter of its total length as shown by the position of the clipper in photograph No. 6. Go up against the grain or lay of the hair, and as you approach the junction of ear and head, gradually pull the clipper out of its depth of cut so as not to leave a stopping-off place.

Do not take the hair off the front edge of the ear, as this hair softens the ear and is most attractive in cooperation with the eyes in giving the much-desired typical mild expression that is an English Setter characteristic. The Gordon Setter looks fierce, the Irish Setter looks wild, but the English Setter must look mild and, without fear or viciousness, inspire love and confidence. The ears play an important role in this most sought-after expression as a frame or background for the eyes. This most desirable expression is why a high ear set or a high ear carriage when alert is not to be desired as it tends to convey the idea of aggression rather than of peace.

As I write this I would not wish the reader to get the idea that an English Setter is a sissy any more than a properly trimmed Standard Poodle is a rabbit. Either one can take care of himself very nicely in case of a fight. They will not start a fight, but I have witnessed a fight between a blue belton English Setter who had the most friendly disposition imaginable and a neighbor's Doberman Pinscher who had the reputation of being a killer. When I was finally able to break it up, the English Setter was unharmed, and I had to take the Doberman, who deliberately started the fight, to the Veterinary Hospital for stitches in both front legs. The old saying "Beware of the wrath of a patient man" certainly applies well to the English Setter.

In the photograph note that two people are keeping the dog steady, one the person doing the trimming and the other the helper. Dogs often resent the buzz of the clipper at their ears, and a sudden jerk of the head would cause the clipper to bite in too deeply and leave an unsightly step in this important part of the dog. A hacked-up English Setter in the show ring is a sorry sight and unfortunately we see too many of them.

Photograph No. 7 shows the finished roughing-out trimming of the ear and the top of the head. The start is made with the Duplex Dresser or a stripping knife. To make the hair cut more quickly some people chalk the hair before trimming. There is no doubt that chalking make the hair more brittle so that a quicker job can be done. I prefer, however, not to use chalk and to take more time, as with the chalk there is a tendency to strip so fast as to leave steps in the coat. Even without chalk great care must be exercised to prevent steps.

Start at the stop over the eyes and strip backward with the lay of the hair. Go all the way back past the occipital in a swath. Then start again, overlapping the first swath and carry on until the entire head is done. Then repeat the second time, taking care to make the overlapping of swaths from front to back occur at different places than the first one. If time permits, take less off on the first and second swaths and repeat four or five times. The less taken off at each bite and the more often you go over the head, the smoother the finished job.

As you work backwards from the eye you will run into the place at the ears where you left off with the clipper in No. 6. Here is your opportunity to carefully blend the head into the ear and again a much better graduation can be made by taking several shallow cuts than a few deeper ones.

In this careful head and head-to-ear blending a fairly dull blade in the Duplex Dresser is better than a new blade or a sharpened one, as the temptation is to hurry the job along with a sharp blade because it is almost lunch time or you are having friends in for dinner. The only out is to take it easy, and if you don't finish, come back after dinner and your friends will enjoy kibitzing more than they would playing Canasta or watching television.

It is interesting that the dog used as a model for this trimming chapter was not one of our own and was not easily worked on, which, coupled with the activity of the photographer and the distraction of numerous flash bulbs, made this exhibition trimming operation not an easy one. Withal the entire roughing-out operation was completed, and for purposes of illustration better than usually, with photographs and time out now and then for rest, in two hours.

Photograph No. 8 illustrates the dense shaggy coat that an English Setter (particularly a blue belton) will grow in a little over two months (February 15 to April 28). When you look at it you get the feeling of despair. How can it ever be made to look right—like the other dogs in the ring? And the longer you wait before show time to get at it the deeper the despair. I believe many dogs are not entered at the shows or are scratched because the owners just don't see how they can possibly get them trimmed in the allotted time before the show.

It is amazing how quickly things get done after you once start. Compare No. 8 with No. 9. Not only was the unruly mass of hair on the back of the neck put into shape, but all the rest was done in just two hours. Start just back of the occipital where you left off in No. 7 and with the Duplex Dresser (sharp blade) start stripping down to the shoulders in swaths, overlapping each time, as indicated in No. 10. By the time you have gone over the back of the neck once the blade will be dull, but don't change it. With the dull blade go over the same area two or three more times. A stripping knife can be used instead of the Duplex Dresser if preferred, or the two tools can be alternated with excellent results. The

144

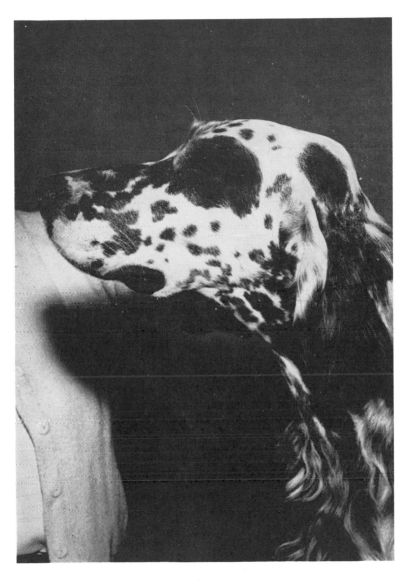

No. 7

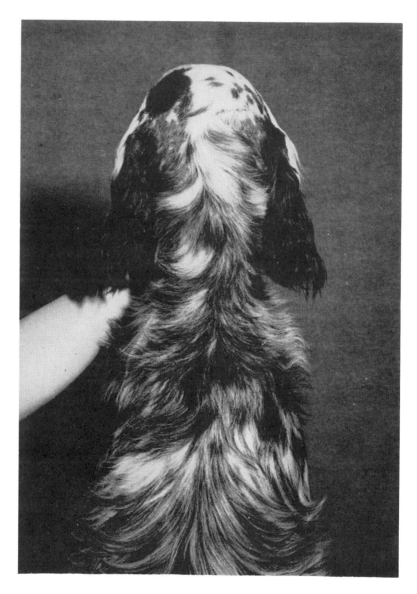

No. 8

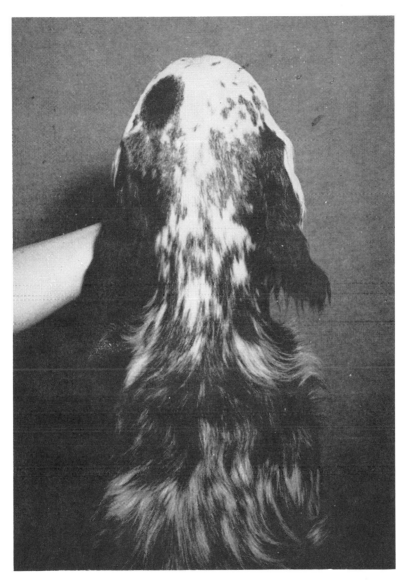

No. 9

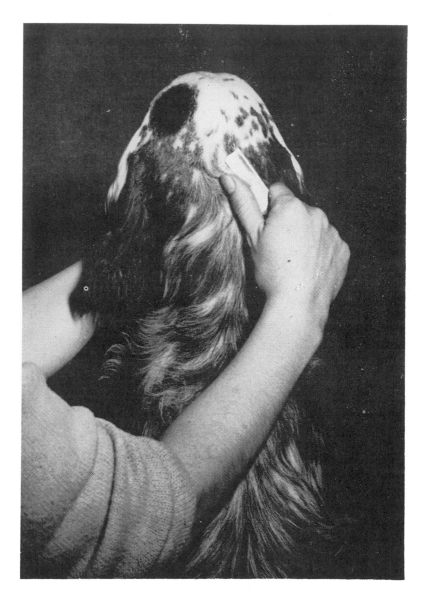

No. 10

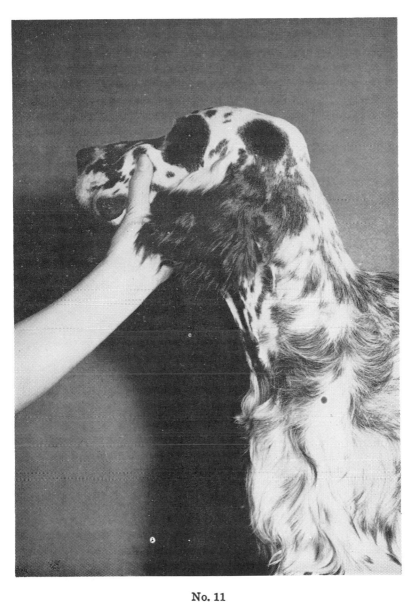

No. 11

dog can sit down during this operation and you will find that you will get more tired than he does.

Time out for a smoke and back at it again. By the way, you will find that some doggy friends and a shaker of cocktails will make the trimming job a pleasant one instead of drudgery. Throw a trimming party next time and see how the time flies and the work gets done. Do it early though, or you will find your doggy friends have the same idea at their kennel.

This work on the neck accounts for the accenting of the length of the neck which is so noticeable when comparing Nos. 1 and 2. As already cautioned, do not try to do a finished job at one operation, but rather rough it out and leave the finishing touches for a later day. This admonition is made not with the idea of getting you out of some work, but for the purpose of finishing up with a balanced dog, because you can always take a little more off but you can't put it back on. Upon looking the dog over after the roughing-out job you get an over-all picture and you immediately see that a little more off here and there will give a better and more pleasing balance.

Photograph No. 11 is a check up of what has been accomplished so far. The front of the neck, the ears, the head, and the back of the neck have been done. This photograph and the lower portion of No. 9, and No. 1 show the unruly hair between the base of the neck and the shoulder. This hair has a tendency to curl forward, which gives an unkempt appearance and contributes to the bunched-forward, constipated look in No. 1.

The careful trimming of this blend from the neck to the shoulder is very important. The chest and shoulders together count twelve points and a great deal of emphasis is placed on good clean, light, and not loaded shoulders. There have been so many poor-shouldered English Setters shown recently that the relative importance of the shoulders is being overemphasized and will, no doubt, continue to be until this fault is no longer a common and outstanding one. There was a time when some exhibitors thought a lot of extra hair would cover up or hide a poor shoulder, but now they realize that anything extra only accentuates a heavy loaded shoulder.

150

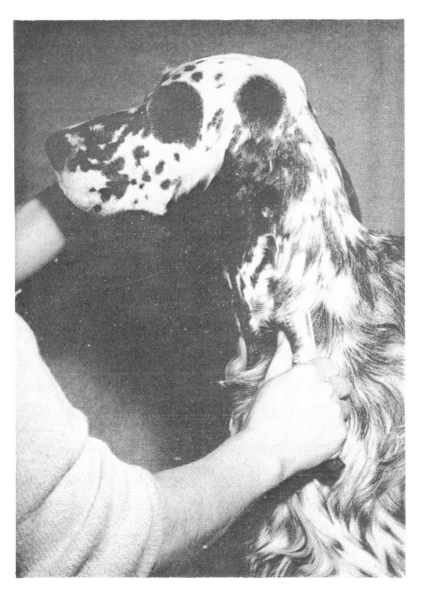

No. 12

The tendency now is to emphasize a clean shoulder. This particular part, the blending of neck to shoulder, of an English Setter can be one of beauty and grace or it can stick out like a sore thumb.

Photograph No. 12 shows how this extra hair is taken off by using the Durham Duplex trimming knife. Some practice is necessary to master the knack, but once you catch on, it becomes easy. Always strip the hair with the direction of its growth, that is, with the grain or lay and not against it. Take only a few hairs at a time. In practicing, notice the different effect when you let the hairs slide through the grip between your thumb and the blade and when you snap it or cut it off.

Even with care this unruly hair has a tendency to stick out after it is trimmed, and it will require some time and a great deal of brushing and hand grooming to make it lie correctly. The trouble is that this particular place is really a ridge or dividing line between the body and the chest where the hair lies backward toward the ribs and forward toward the chest. It is really a continuation of the similar ridge between the throat and the back of the neck. These lines of discontinuity of direction of hair lay always present trouble in trimming, but they are all important because they are the two tangent curves that go to make the beauty of form.

Photograph No. 13 shows the neck and shoulder trimmed but the front or chest not finished. It will be remembered that in No. 3 the clipper left a sharp dividing line between the bottom of the neck and the chest. This beardlike tuft of hair on the chest should be stripped down until you get a gradual blending from where the clipper started to where the chest feathering starts. This "shirt front" can be one of the most difficult places to trim, so go slowly with the Duplex Dresser or stripping knife. If too much is taken off, the dog will look unbalanced, and if too little is taken off he looks like a goat. There is a wide difference of opinion as to how much should be taken off. I feel that there is no set rule to go by except that the over-all finished picture should be balanced and pleasing.

Photograph No. 14 shows the ruff that English Setters

152

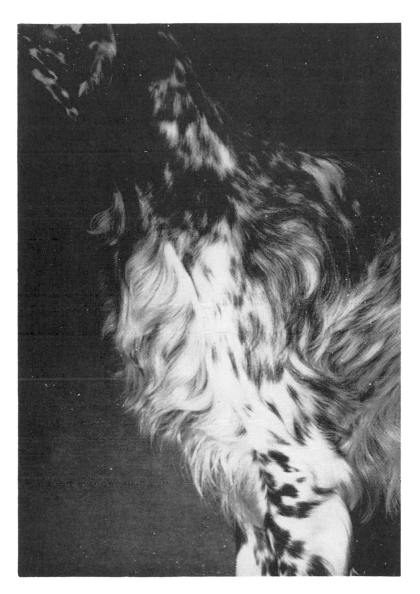

No. 13

of good coat usually grow between the withers and the shoulder. This is another of the dividing lines between the lay of the hair on the shoulder and the body, and if left untrimmed gives the shoulders a loaded appearance. This ruff is more apparent in dogs than in bitches. This excess of hair should first be stripped with the Duplex Dresser or stripping knife, taking the cuts in the direction of the grain of the hair, then thinned out with the thinning shears and comb as illustrated in No. 14, and finished up with the Duplex Dresser. Thinning shears must be used sparingly. They cannot be used too often on the undercoat or they will leave a hole in the finished job.

Thinning shears are mainly useful for the roughing-out work. I have seen handlers practically trim a dog with the trimming shears only, but it should be remembered that when they do this the roughing-out operation was done months before; they are not using the thinning shears for taking out pads of undercoat as is done in the roughing-out job, but they are using them on the surface coat to take a little off without showing the marks that ordinary scissors would make. Of course a stripping knife would do just as good and a more lasting job. It is my belief that handlers who use thinning shears habitually for trimming English Setters do so because they do not know how to use the accepted and more useful tools.

Great care must be exercised in taking out this ruff between the shoulder and the ribs or else you can make the dog look out in elbow. Better go slowly and stand back to see what you have done. Then stop and groom for a few days and see if you can't train the remainder of the ruff to lie in the proper direction. If not, some additional judicial trimming will be in order.

Photograph No. 15 is an intermediate one in the trimming process. Time out for a survey of what we have done so far. The head, neck, chest, and shoulders have been roughed out. Compare No. 15 with No. 13 and notice the smoother, improved appearance; also take note of how little total hair has actually been taken off. The hair that was removed, although small in quantity, was taken off at the right places to give the desired

154

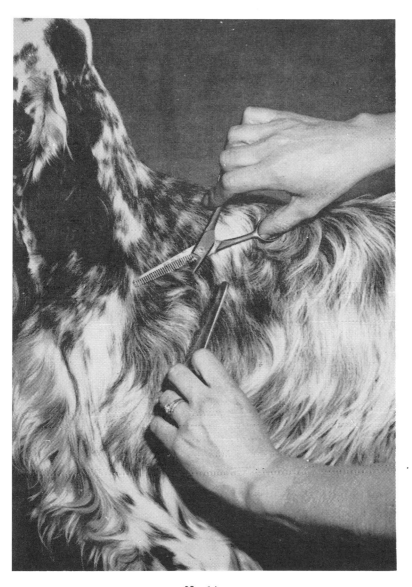

No. 14

smooth look. At this time-out period step back as far as you can and get a complete picture of what you have done, as a close-up or part view can often be misleading. Remember you are striving for integrated parts in a complete over-all picture of a well-groomed dog, not a picture of a scalped dog.

My wife numbers among her many other accomplishments that of being a sculptress, and knowing the immense value of seeing symmetry as a whole instead of innumerable details, she erected a six-foot mirror in her studio. She worked at a distance of about eight feet from the mirror so that by looking into the mirror once in a while she was able to get a sixteen-foot distance view of her work. The idea would not work as well for trimming dogs unless four mirrors were used, as her modeling platform turned on ball bearings so she could view the model from any angle in the mirror.

Trimming is tiresome work for dog and trimmer alike and these rest periods are welcomed by both and can do double duty for rest and looking over your progress.

We are never too old to learn and although we may think we know it all, it is very likely that some owner or handler can teach us some new tricks. With this in mind while at the shows waiting to be judged or waiting for closing time, it is a good idea to watch the professional handlers getting their dogs ready for the show ring. These boys have been in the game for years. They make their living showing dogs to win because unless they do their share of winning week after week they will soon see their income—their string of dogs— dwindling. It stands to reason, therefore, that the smart ones know more about putting a dog down in top show form than you do. These lessons are free and are yours for the looking. Do not confine your observations to the English Setter handlers, but watch handlers of all breeds, and I feel sure that you will be well repaid for your time.

No. 16 shows the rear and tail as we found it. The tail is bushy and where it joins the rump is not defined. The rump and rear legs are a mass of curls and lack definition. No. 17 shows the rear and tail after the roughing-out operation has been completed. When comparing No. 17 with No. 16 the im-

156

No. 15

No. 16

No. 17

mense improvement in finish is easily recognized. When one realizes that this improvement has been brought about only by the roughing-out operation, it is not difficult to imagine the finish that can be accomplished by an additional three weeks' touching up, grooming, a final bath and blanketing.

No. 18 shows how the curls and superfluous hair are removed from the rump and upper thigh with the Duplex Dresser, always making the cutting strokes along with the lay of the hair. Take it easy, a little at a bite, and do not be in too much of a hurry to finish the job. Keep in mind that trimming is creative work, not a production job, and that your feeling towards it plays an important part in the finished dog.

No. 19 shows how the unwanted hair from the rear end and under the tail is taken off with the Duplex Dresser. This hair must be graduated out to the fringe on the upper rear thigh. This is an important operation, one that is often overlooked, and if too much coat is left here it gives the effect that the dog has on a pair of pants.

Photograph No. 20 shows the operation of trimming the extra hair from around the anus, here using curved shears. This not only promotes cleanliness, but also gives the tail an attractive carriage as will be seen in No. 17. Note the break between the tail fringe and the rump, just under the tail in No. 17. This break will be slightly increased during subsequent touch up.

Referring to No. 21 it will be seen that on a well-coated dog the hair is usually too thick along the top of the tail, especially about the location shown by the position of the knife in the photograph. Using the Duplex Dresser, the hair should be thinned out to give the tail a graceful taper from root to tip. Referring to the Standard you will note that bushiness of tail is undesirable, so shape it to conform to the Standard. Some of the fringe should be stripped from the location of maximum length of fringe to the anus (about under the knife in the photograph) so that the finished tail has roughly the shape of a triangle. Note this effect in No. 17.

No. 22 shows the use of barber's shears for trimming off the extra hair from the end of the tail, leaving about one half to three quarters of an inch of hair remaining to protect the

160

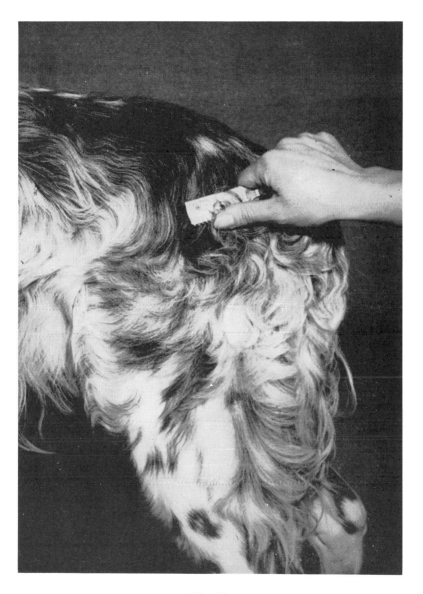

No. 18

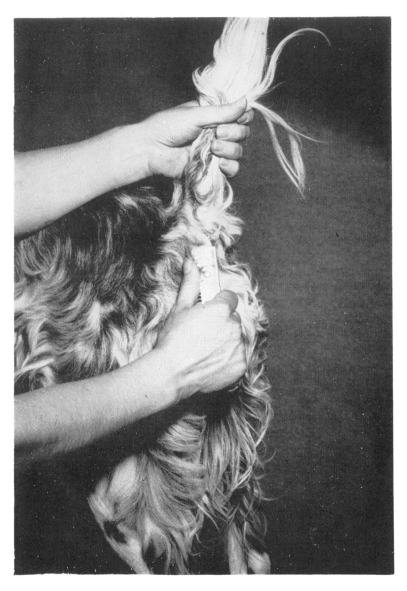

No. 19

No. 20

No. 21

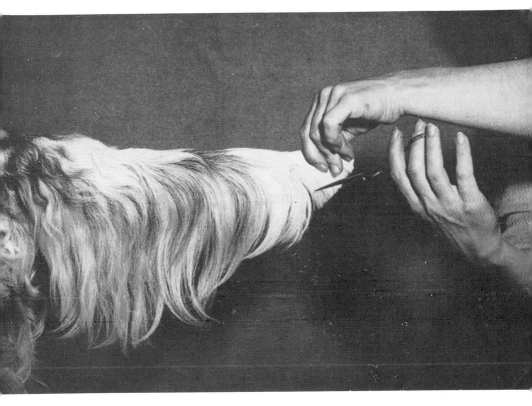

No. 22

end of the tail from injury. The underfringe should be trimmed with the shears to the triangular shape already referred to. Any subsequent shaping of the tail should be done with a stripping knife.

No. 23 shows the front feet before trimming. Compare with the trimmed feet in No. 2. The final touches to the feet are yet to be made, but, as already mentioned several times, it is wise to undertrim rather than overtrim during the first roughing-out operations. You can always take some more hair off, but you cannot put it back in time for a show.

No. 24 shows how the extra hair is trimmed from the bottom of the pads, using a pair of curved shears. This allows the pads instead of wads of hair to touch the ground and tends to make the dog use his toes in walking as he should. It also prevents the dog from bringing extra dirt into the house and is a hygienic measure for the dog, keeping his feet cleaner and minimizing the chances of infection. Be careful not to cut his pads or toes.

Referring to No. 25, the toenails should be kept cut as short as possible without cutting down into the quick or sensitive part of the nail. With light-colored nails the quick is easily seen, but with black nails it is not so easy to determine just where to stop. Care must be taken not to cut so deeply as to make the nail bleed, since this is not only painful to the dog but can easily make him foot shy. A "Resco" nail trimmer is, in my opinion, by far the best of all the available toenail clippers. A file should be used afterwards to shape up the cut nails. Keeping the toenails short helps the dog to stand up on his toes as he should and therefore should not be neglected.

No. 26 shows the use of a stripping knife in trimming off the hair sticking out from between the toes. Do not remove all hair from between the toes, only that hair which does not lie flat. The very long hair is shortened but not removed. A large percentage of English Setters have a permanent fungus infection between the toes (similar to athlete's foot) brought on by matted hair between the toes which is more or less continually damp. This hair should be kept combed and under control to prevent mats; it not only gives the foot a

166

No. 23

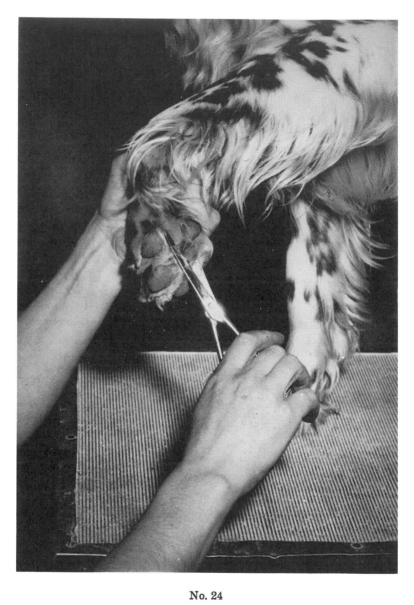

No. 24

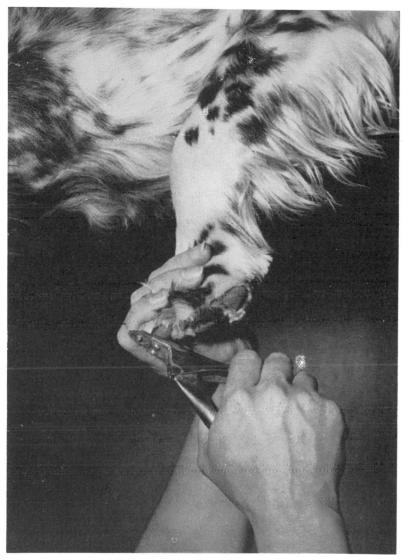

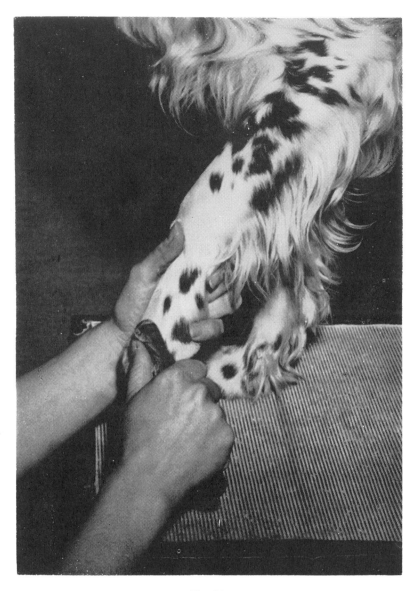

No. 26

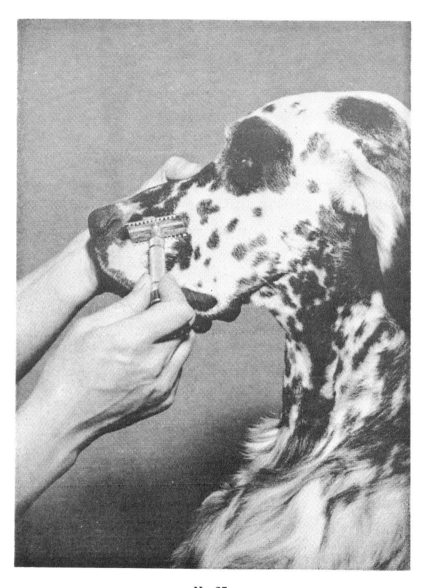

No. 27

neat, well-kept appearance, but it aids in eliminating the fungus infection. This hair is best removed with a regular stripping knife, not the Duplex type. Such a stripping knife is shown on page 130 among the necessary trimming tools.

No. 27 shows the final part of the roughing-out. Here the whiskers and eyebrows are shaved off with a regular safety razor using a new sharp blade. Blunt-nosed sharp shears may also be used. Of course it is not necessary to take the whiskers off at this time as it will have to be done again the day before the show, but is gives you the opportunity to survey your work without having to make allowances.

After the rough trimming the dog should be bathed and rinsed in Hilo-dip, dried thoroughly, blanketed and put in his crate for the night. This blanketing is important as it helps to make the hair lie flat. The next day you can start on the final touching-up here and there as required, with a vigorous brushing afterwards.

The dog should always be bathed the night before a show and blanketed. You may not have the best English Setter at the show, but you will have the cleanest.

When trimming the neck the first roughing out will show a difference in color of the trimmed part, but it will come back to its natural color in two or three weeks. This is one of the reasons for making the trimming job an extended operation. The dog also gets tired of standing on the bench for too long a time and, as mentioned before, we should try to keep the dog happy as much as possible. So for the first roughing-out operation give him frequent rest periods on the floor and play with him during such rest periods. Some handlers train their dogs to rest on the trimming bench—an excellent idea as you will learn when attending the shows.

Do not get the idea that a trimming job is as tedious an operation as it may sound from this outline. Once the dog has been trimmed, a few minutes a week will keep him in show form. Trimming should be started when the dog is a small puppy (two to three months), as it will be a part of his later training, and getting him used to the sound of the clipper when he is young is much easier than later on.

172

The dog used in these photographs illustrating the rough-ing-out operation was later worked on by his owner for about five minutes every day for a period of six weeks and then entered in some of the shows. Although the owner had little or no previous experience in trimming, her continual work a little at a time with the stripping knife resulted in as well set down an English Setter as the author has ever seen. This is a good illustration of how anyone with a little careful work every day can keep an English Setter in top show form after the first roughing-out operation, even with practically no previous experience.

SPIRON JAGERSBO pointing quail.

This great blue belton dog was the father of Rummey Stagboro and was owned by Erik Bergishagen of Birmingham, Michigan.

My Setter ranges in the new-shorn field,
His nose in air erect; from ridge to ridge,
Panting, he bounds, his quartered ground divides
In equal intervals, nor careless leaves
One inch untried. At length the tainted gale
His nostrils wide inhale; quick joy elates
His beating heart, which, awed by discipline
Severe, he dares not own, but cautious creeps,
Low-cowering, step by step; at last attains
His proper distance; there he stops at once,
And points with his instructive nose upon
The trembling prey.

—Somerville

9

Training for the Field

THIS book has been written about the show type (Laverack) English Setter. They make excellent shooting dogs for a day's sport on grouse, woodcock, quail and pheasant, but it is doubtful if one will ever be able to compete successfully with a field trial type (Llewellin) English Setter in the big time field trials when race-horse speed over long heats is required. Edward Laverack in his book **"The Setter"** (1872) has a chapter on breaking, and it is so interesting, meaty and to the point that I am sure you too will enjoy the parts that I quote.

"Young dogs vary much in their tempers, and their early predisposition to hunt and find game. I have frequently shot over my setters at nine and eleven months old, as steady as need be, and continued to shoot over them daily the whole season; some come sooner into work than others, get their strength, and furnish quicker.

"Like children, many are more precocious than others. My

breed (strain*) hunt, range, point, and back intuitively at six months, and require comparatively little or no breaking.

"The system of tuition I adopt is to take the dogs to my shootings in Scotland, uncouple, and let them chase everything (game) until they are tired, having previously accustomed them to lie down at the word 'Drop.'

"After having run themselves down, they naturally point and back. When pointing, walk quietly up, slip a thin cord through the collar, and stand behind, making no noise, holding the cord rather slack in your hand. After the dog has stood some little time, he naturally, to ascertain by his nose where the game is secreted, will prick up his ears prior to making a spring at feather or fur, whichever it may happen to be. In attempting to do so, jerk him sharply back with the cord, calling 'Drop!' Keep him down until the birds are out of sight, to teach him patience; then withdraw the cord, and let him range.

"By repeating this, the dog will very soon be broken. When I rented the shootings of Cabrach, in Banffshire, belonging to the Duke of Richmond, I and my keeper, Alexander Rattray (now keeper to the Duke of Richmond Glentiddich), by this system once broke eight dogs in six days; and all at the week's end were as steady as could be—pointing, backing, footing and free from 'chase.'

"When you get the dog to drop well to the word, it is easy to teach him to do so at 'wing' or 'fur'; to 'down charge,' to come close to heel, and to ware fence is nothing to teach.

"My dogs are invariably broken on the open moors, and not in small enclosures, which always cramps their range and checks their spirits; it is distressing to hear a breaker crying out every instant 'ware fence,' whistling and shouting: you cannot be too quiet on all occasions.

"I seldom use whip or whistle, but allow my dogs to use their own natural sagacity in making their casts and finding game.

---

* Strain has been inserted by the author as in the past the word breed was used to designate that which we now call strain. For instance, we would now say the Laverack and Llewellin strain, whereas at that time they were referred to as the Laverack or Llewellin breed.

"I have ever found those dogs who range wide turn out the best. It does not follow because a dog ranges wide he will not range close. Where game is plentiful a wide ranging dog must necessarily become a close ranger because the game stops him; he cannot get far without finding, his natural sagacity tells him to hunt close; it is his high courage and anxiety to find game that causes him to range wide.

"A wide-ranging dog too saves you a great deal of walking. Every shooting man knows that he may occasionally tramp over two or three miles without coming across anything; here it is a wide-ranging dog is of greater ability than a close ranger.

"I will give an instance of the advantage of selecting good and lasting dogs. I was one of a party of four that on September 11th had bagged 3,066 head of grouse—one gentleman killed within seven head, to his own gun, as much as the whole party, solely by having superior dogs, and in addition he lent a brace of dogs several times to his friends. I was one of another party of four on a Scotch moor. In four days the four guns had killed 1,654 head, and one of them bagged 127 brace in one day, over a brace of setters. None of us ever used relays of dogs, or did any of us possess more than two brace each.

"Many years have passed over my head, bleached my locks, and withered the sap of youthful vigour since I took my gun and dogs and made bonnie Scotland my home. I loved it then, I love it still, and ever shall. I yet go there annually, and feel ten years younger when I catch sight of those wild, glorious, healthy, purple clad mountains, far away from the busy hum of the world, and ever-crowded and ill-drained cities. It is in Scotland I find repose, contentment, amusement, and health.

"I cannot understand **Pater Familias** taking his wife and family away to the Continent, or to some expensive watering place for the autumnal months, when we have such lovely and magnificent scenery within twelve hours of us. I may be an enthusiast on this point. The used-up **blase**, worn out with dissipation and late hours, broken in health, constitution, and spirits, is often now recommended by his doctor to take a High-

177

land shooting. What for? Not with the idea that he may kill much game. He is too prostrated, too feeble for a long tramp over the hills. It is not for the sake of shooting, but to wean him in some measure from dissolute habits, which if persisted in, must eventually carry him to a premature grave. It is in the hope of saving him, invigorating him, and restoring his shattered constitution.

"I remember the remark of an old Highlander to a cockney sportsman who was grumbling at the country and asking 'What was to be found in it?' Sandy replied, 'Hoot mon, there's health behind every rock and stane.'

"Burns' beautiful lines are now recalled to my memory:

> 'Now westlin winds, and slaught'ring guns,
> Bring autumn's pleasant weather;
> The moorcock springs, on whirring wings,
> Among the blooming heather.'

"These lines again bring to mind many stories I heard; scenes I have seen, in years long gone by, never to return. Relentless old Father Time serves us all alike; shows no favour to rich or poor, and with that terrible scythe of his cuts all down in turn."

I think Edward Laverack probably had the correct psychology of hunting in the field with his English Setters. He did not care to have his dogs trained to all the niceties and etiquette of the field trial. He wanted a dog that could find and point birds day after day. He loved the sport and the comradeship of his good friends in the unspoiled open country. I suspect, however, that his keeper, Alexander Rattray, spent many hours on his dogs before he and Mr. Laverack trained eight dogs in six days. Nevertheless, his basic methods were sound. Eight years ago I followed his methods with a bitch named "Brenda" (a daughter of Ch. Sturdy Max). Five hours at a game farm made her a shooting bitch, and I have enjoyed her ever since. She placed in several field trials and never lost a wounded bird. Of course, as Laverack pointed out, "Brenda" was a precocious child.

Stonehenge, in Dogs of the British Isles—4th Edition (1882), points out that in his opinion a quiet tail is usually

Ch. Jiggs Mallwyd D maneuvered the pheasant so that it was between him and the gun, and then pointed. No chance of this bird running out on him.

accompanied by a nose of equal dullness. I am fully in accord with Stonehenge's observation as it has been my own experience also that merry English Setters make the best hunters and there is no doubt but that they show to great advantage in the show ring.

Mr. Ralph E. Yeatter is the author of a booklet, **Bird Dogs in Sport and Conservation.** This booklet, published by authority of the State of Illinois Natural History Survey Division as Circular 42, contains a section on amateur training for hunting that is so practical and simply expressed that I have secured permission to use parts of Mr. Yeatter's material here. The parts that do not apply to English Setters have been omitted. The methods outlined by Mr. Yeatter are proven, practical methods used for many years by trainers, and can be relied upon to produce results.

There are two "musts" that should be stated here at the very beginning of this chapter on training, for lack of them will result in failure in whole or in part:

1. You must have patience.
2. Your dog must be birdy and normal, both physically and mentally.

The Amateur Trainer

Sportsmen who buy trained dogs or have young dogs fully trained by professionals are relatively few compared with those who buy young dogs and train them during spare time. That numerous capable hunting dogs have been trained by their owners speaks well, on the whole, for amateur trainers. Nevertheless, many dogs develop bad hunting habits that might have been avoided or minimized if the owners had been better informed on training.

There are several books on the subject of training hunting dogs. Unfortunately for the average reader, authors sometimes fail to bridge the wide gap between the professional trainer and the amateur and they outline rough training methods which, in the hands of the beginner, may ruin the dog as a hunter.

Most dogs are by nature anxious to please their masters, but they cannot do things they do not understand. Lessons need to be repeated until they are thoroughly mastered. Patience on the part of the trainer, whether natural or acquired, is the first requisite in successful training.

Obedience training is an essential part of the education of any dog. In hunting dogs, this is especially important, since the disobedient dog hunts mostly for himself and takes most of the owner's time in trying to keep up with him or to find him. The obedient dog, which responds to directions and hunts for his owner, stands a good chance to find as many birds within gun range as the wild, disobedient dog will find for himself a mile away.

The successful amateur trainer develops a knack of teaching obedience without cowing or alienating his hunting companion. The following quotation from a widely known English authority (Carlton 1945) can well serve as a guide when the puppy's obedience training is begun:

"You should no doubt teach the puppy his name, which may be done by calling his name and patting him or giving him a piece of biscuit. You should also, no doubt, make the puppy gallop up to you on his name being called—which may be done in much the same way. And you should make him go to his kennel when desired. This presents more difficulty. Personally, if a puppy is recalcitrant in this respect, I generally get him to me, and either pick him up and carry him in or put on him a collar with a short, light cord attached and make him comply by an admixture of cajolery and gentle force, and end up with a reward.

"In these early lessons, as with all other lessons during early puppyhood, the four cardinal principles are:

"(1) Never give an order without seeing that the puppy complies with it; he has got to learn to obey you always, not sometimes.

"(2) Always be absolutely gentle, both in voice and action —when you come to work in the field, you want a bold, keen dog, not a cowed and listless wreck.

"(3) Never give an order with which you cannot secure compliance without a display of harshness.

"(4) Never persist in any lesson which is becoming a bore to the puppy.

"The nearer these early lessons can be approximated to a game, in the puppy's eyes, the better."

As the puppy develops and learns to take directions, you should become accustomed to giving them in a firm, distinct voice, making sure that each command is understood and carried out. The commands should be short, and the same words should always be used for each response expected. Be sure each command is audible, but do not get into the habit of raising your voice, or the pupil will probably think he does not need to mind unless you shout.

Teach a few basic things well rather than attempt a large number, which may be only half learned.

At each step of training, make every effort to see that the dog understands what you want, and, whenever possible, why you want it. When the lesson is learned, it should be practiced until response becomes habitual. This is the background of obedience training. Such training calls for ingenuity, common sense, and much patience in getting the lessons over to the dog. Harsh treatment and punishment not understood have permanently intimidated many promising hunting dogs. The dog's span of attention is short. Lessons should be only four or five minutes long for the young dog. They should not be prolonged until the dog becomes bored or sour, and the trainer loses patience.

Dogs vary in intelligence and temperament just as do humans. This variation calls for study of the individual characteristics of the pupil and adaptation as far as possible of the training program to his needs. Some dogs need more rehearsals of each step than others. Some must be praised and encouraged more than others.

Although considerable emphasis has been laid on the preparation of the trainer, there is no need to overrate the difficulties of training a hunting dog. Most boys can teach their dogs any number of tricks by the simple method of showing the pupil what is wanted, practicing it until well learned, and rewarding the dog's progress with praise. The amateur trainer who stresses the development of companionship with his dog, and encourages his inborn desire to do things to please his master, paves the way for progress in training.

182

Int. Ch. Tula II Jagersbo pointing woodcock. This beautiful orange belton bitch was the mother of Rackets Rummey Jagersbo. Owned by Mr. Erik Bergishagen of Birmingham, Michigan.

The man who likes hunting dogs and dog work and who is willing to acquaint himself with the fundamentals of training can usually do at least a fairly good job of training his own dog. The development of a good hunting companion will amply reward him for his work. Moreover, the skill in handling acquired during the training period will serve the hunter well in the field. Obviously, good dog work is in large measure dependent on good handling.

Training Systems

Various systems are used in training bird dogs. Some owners do little yard training and confine their programs largely to a few field trips before the hunting season, and then take the dog along on hunting trips. If the owner works frequently with his dog, the animal can eventually become a useful hunting companion, but he will make mistakes, some of which might have been avoided with more yard work and other preliminary training.

A program that combines yard training and field training over an extended period of time seems to give best results.

Training Classes

A program that combined yard training and field training over an extended period was used successfully by a group of spaniel owners in northern Illinois. They began a training class in April and continued until October. Yard (obedience) training was given first. When this was thoroughly mastered, the dogs were taken to the field and put through an intensive course of quartering, finding and flushing game, remaining steady to flush and shot, and retrieving. In the autumn a field trial was held.

Observation of the methods of a successful trainer was particularly helpful to the beginners, who had a good man to act as instructor and coach. A class met for instruction every other Sunday. At each meeting progress was checked, mistakes were straightened out, and questions were answered. Then each amateur trainer was given a mimeographed sheet of the next lesson and told to work at home.

Photograph showing how to dizz a bird. The pheasant is held with both hands and swung around fast in a circular motion five or six times.

Sound instruction of this kind is helpful in all phases of dog training, particularly in the more difficult tasks, such as training to retrieve.

Planted Game

The use of planted birds is of great assistance in training dogs for hunting and retrieving. Barn-loft or pen-reared pigeons, game-farm pheasants, and guineas are used for this purpose.

Planting or hiding a dizzied bird in cover, where its exact location is known, enables the trainer to control his dog on the approach or on point.

Flushing and shooting planted birds in flight provides the means of training a dog to retrieve under conditions that approximate actual hunting.

The Young Dog

The dog makes most of his physical and mental growth during the first year of life. At six months most dogs have developed only to the stage of simple yard training, finding and chasing game, and other relatively easy tasks. To adapt training to the mental development of the young dog, most trainers delay the start of intensive yard training until the puppy is at least eight months old or even a year or more. Some trainers, however, believe it does no harm, and may be beneficial, to do a limited amount of hunting with a puppy five or six months old before he has had advanced yard training. However, Martin Hogan warns that a young dog, even one that has been trained to the firing of a gun, can easily be made gun-shy if several hunters shoot at once when the dog is in the immediate vicinity. A young dog that seems fully trained to field hunting can be ruined by being taken into cover where there is heavy shooting.

English Setters are trained to remain steady to wing and shot in standing position, and also to "Whoa" in the same position.

The following brief training outline, based on steps followed and methods recommended by well-known professional trainers and authorities on hunting dogs, may be helpful to

The pheasant's head is then tucked under one wing.

the amateur trainer in planning his program. Numerous variations in the sequence of steps of training are employed successfully by different trainers.

PUPPY TRAINING

First Lessons. The puppy from the age of about three to eight months can be taught a few simple lessons. In addition to being housebroken, he can be taught to know his name well and the meaning of "No," and he can be given simple yard training, for example, to lead, to stand, to "Fetch," and a few other easy lessons such as those outlined below. During this period, like a child, he learns how to learn, and how to mind. He learns the meaning of a number of words (sounds to him). This preliminary training, based largely on the desire of the puppy to do things with his master, paves the way for future progress.

During this time, the young dog is usually given a period of freedom in the field, which is continued until he learns to recognize game and to handle himself well afield.

Name. Whenever you call the puppy or speak to him, make a point of using his name. He should learn always to associate the sound of his name with himself. Later, when you teach him to stand, you should be able to call him by a dozen different names, without having him move from position. He should not move until you use his own name.

Lead. The puppy should be taught to lead early and the owner should exercise care in this training. Any good dog of any breed can be cowed by an owner who handles it too roughly on a leash. You can make pups leash shy by being too rough with them at first. At the age of four months or so, a pup should have a short leash snapped on his collar so he can trail it around. Then you gradually exert pressure on the leash and guide him. He can then be taught to follow readily at the pull of the leash.

"No." When the puppy does something wrong, give the command "No" in a firm tone, and make every effort to show him what he has done wrong. His knowledge of the meaning of "No" will be very useful throughout his training.

The bird is then gently placed in some thick grass cover, lying on the side so that the body, head, and wing are toward the ground. The planter should carefully but quickly walk away. The bird should stay where planted from fifteen to thirty minutes.

Pointing Game. As a means of introducing the English Setter to game, one professional trainer uses the following device. A pheasant wing is tied to a piece of twine about ten feet long attached to a long stick. The wing is placed on the lawn close to the puppy's nose, where he will get the scent. As the puppy tries to pick up the wing, it is pulled along, just out of his reach. When he learns that he cannot quite catch the quarry he will usually begin to point instead of chase. This pastime develops pointing at an early age, but it should not be continued more than a month or it may form the habit of "false pointing" of moving objects.

Natural Retrieving. Most English Setter puppies possess a natural tendency to retrieve that can be developed by practice. Carlton points out that the puppy's inclination to pick up and carry things is present much earlier than his desire to hunt. Similar stages of development are evident in young foxes; for example, around the entrance of a fox den will usually be found dead ground squirrels or other prey animals, which serve as playthings for the young. Vixens have been observed to give to their young parts of prey animals to carry during their first hunting trips.

Early training of puppies in retrieving is partially summarized below:

1. Do not begin until you have gained the puppy's confidence so that he is eager to race up to you whenever he sees you.

2. When you begin his retrieving lessons, take him to a place where he will not be distracted by dogs, other animals, traffic or people. This may be on the lawn, if it is not his regular playground, or it may be in some area where the grass is not close cut, but where he will have no difficulty seeing a thrown object.

3. Get him interested in a knotted handkerchief or a similar easily seen, soft object that is to be used as a dummy. When he is watching the movement of your hand and moving in the same direction, throw the dummy underhand a yard or two away, at the same time telling him to "Fetch."

4. If he has seen the dummy leave your hand, the chances are he will race out to it, pick it up, and run back to you. If

Ch. Jiggs Mallwyd D was a smart pheasant dog. He knew their tricks and usually pointed them so that the pheasant was in between. He was an all-day, tireless hunter and a natural retriever. He was the most satisfactory shooting dog that I ever had the pleasure of hunting over. Owned by Mr. C. S. Schneck, Allentown, Pa. Bred by Dr. Daw of Vancouver, B. C.

he does not go to it, he probably has not seen it leave your hand, in which case pick it up and throw it again.

5. If the puppy does not come directly back to you, try to get him to do so by sitting down, or by turning your back, or by walking away from him. When he comes to you with the dummy, your object is to get it directly back in your hand. However, do not snatch it or engage in a tug-of-war with the puppy. To do so tends to develop a "hard mouth," that is, a habit of biting down hard on what is being retrieved. Place your hand under the puppy's lower jaw, so that he will not duck his head or drop the dummy, and press the dummy up and toward the back of his mouth as you remove it. If necessary, place your fingers in his mouth and open it gently.

6. When the dummy is back in your hand, reward the puppy with a bit of food or by making much of him. Probably food is the best reward for the first two or three lessons. Following these lessons, rely on praise, reserving additional food until he shows a disinclination to return to you after he picks up the dummy.

While the puppy is very young, limit the practice periods to four or five minutes at a time, and once or twice a day. He should always consider these lessons play; whenever his interest wanes, take away the dummy and discontinue the lesson.

After a week or two of practice, begin to substitute larger dummies, such as a stuffed canvas glove, a short piece of garden hose, or some other soft object that the puppy likes to pick up. For later lessons, a good practice dummy is one made of a piece of soft wood, eight or ten inches long, rounded off to a diameter of about two inches, with a number of pigeon, pheasant, or other bird feathers attached to it.

As your puppy grows and becomes proficient at picking up and returning the dummy, you must vary lessons gradually in the direction of retrieving in the field. As early in his schooling as possible, begin to throw the dummy where he will have to use his nose to find it, but not at first, in thick cover. He should return it to you in the same way as in the earlier lessons.

192

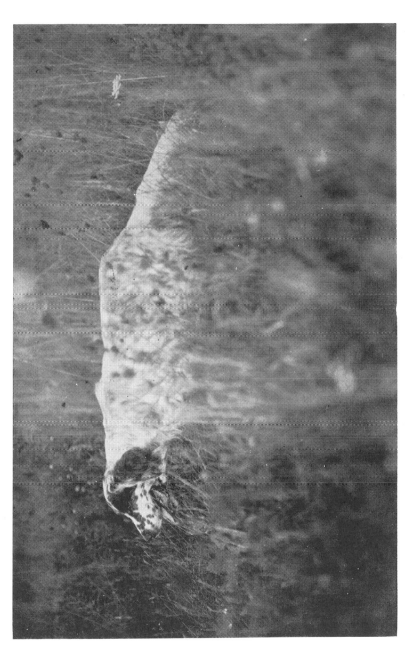

A fine bench type English Setter on quail. A large dog, but an all-day worker.

Another variation is to get the puppy to find the dummy without having seen you throw it. When you are walking downwind with him, drop the dummy when he is not looking. After you have gone fifty feet or so, turn and walk back into the wind toward the dummy, encouraging him to hunt for it. If he is familiar enough with it to recognize the scent, he should be able to draw up to it from a distance of several yards. He will thus learn to look for and retrieve something he has not seen fall.

Later, under hunting conditions, the training of natural retrievers must be extended to include retrieving of shot birds. Methods of field training vary among trainers. One of the most useful methods of teaching the dog to retrieve birds is by releasing pigeons to be shot in flight and retrieved by the dog.

If the puppy will not retrieve in play, the practice should be discontinued, and he can be force broken to retrieve after he has had some hunting experience.

Force Breaking to Retrieve. There is some difference of opinion as to the merits of natural and force-broken retrievers. It is generally agreed, however, that if the dog has been thoroughly force broken he can be depended on to retrieve, while a natural retriever may refuse to retrieve and the owner will be unable to enforce the command. Nevertheless, force breaking is one of the most difficult and time-consuming tasks of training, especially for the amateur. Unless the job is done thoroughly, it is better not attempted. If the dog shows indications of being at least a fair natural retriever, it may be questioned whether it is worth while for the nonprofessional to attempt force breaking. The amateur trainer who plans to force break his hunting dog to retrieve can find descriptions of methods in the books on the subject.

Freedom in the Field. Getting your young dog into the field and allowing him to learn to hunt by himself is an important part of his training. By the time the puppy is five or six months old you will probably find it profitable to get him into the field to gain experience in finding wild things as often as possible. Although some trainers favor delaying this period of freedom in the field until advanced yard training

An excellent action photograph taken at a recent Shooting Dog Trial sponsored by the English Setter Club of New England. The pheasant has just been flushed by the handler. Photograph by William Joli.

is begun (eight months to a year), it seems better in most cases for amateur trainers to begin to take their dogs to the field at an earlier age. Generally, the more preliminary field training and experience on game your puppy receives, the better hunter he will become.

On these trips allow him to find and chase rabbits, squirrels, birds, anything he finds, to his heart's content. Four or five field trips a week where he will have a chance to find game provide excellent training. This is his time to get acquainted with the field and to develop independence in finding likely spots for game.

The dog should be allowed plenty of freedom to learn things for himself. His early attempts at hunting may be supervised, but not too obviously. Frequent directions may take away his initiative, or give him the idea he is doing something wrong, which is likely to lead to disobedience later.

Usually a good shooting dog can be made from one that likes to hunt. The period of freedom in the field is his time to learn thoroughly to enjoy hunting. He can be got under control with obedience training after his hunting instinct is developed.

Since he needs to gain self-confidence, it is well for him to be without other dogs on at least most trips; many successful trainers believe a young dog will learn to hunt faster if taken out a few times with an older, experienced dog. If he shows a tendency to point, he should be encouraged, but no attempt should be made to enforce pointing at this time. Sooner or later he will start making points.

Accustoming to Firing of Gun. Field trips offer you good opportunities to accustom the young dog to the report of a gun. Previously you may have introduced him to a report by firing a cap pistol (not close at first) as you approach him with his food. He will thus come to associate a report pleasurably with food. In the field, begin by occasionally firing .22 blanks, at first when the dog is some distance away and **only when he is intent on chasing something he has flushed.** He will probably pay no attention to the report. Gradually you may fire the gun nearer to him, **always when he is chasing.** If he shows no nervousness, you may use a .410 or larger

Let the young dogs find and chase birds to their hearts' content. They will soon learn that they cannot catch them, and it offers you the best possible opportunity of firing light loads in the air to accustom them to the noise. An English setter will never be gun-shy if introduced to the gun while chasing a bird. Photograph by William Joli.

CHIEF MASTERMAN, a typical Llewellin type English
Setter on point. Owner, Lee White, Norwalk, Connecticut.

gauge, firing it **only when he is chasing,** and at first when he is some distance away. Do not try to kill the game during this early training. The strict observance of this lesson may easily mean the difference between a gun-shy dog and a dog steady to shot.

Fourth of July. Under no circumstances allow fireworks to be shot near your kennel, as it is the cause of many gun-shy dogs. Young stock as well as untrained grown dogs can be made permanently gun-shy by the slightest infringement of this iron-bound rule. No English Setter was ever born gun-shy, as acquired characteristics are not hereditary. It is no fault of a dog that he is gun-shy, and this condition can always be blamed on man's inconsideration, stupidity, or selfishness.

Teaching "Whoa." Another lesson that you can give the dog during field trips is the meaning of "Whoa." When the dog is ready to start his romp in the fields, but before you have unsnapped the leash, grasp him by the collar and tail, putting him in pointing position, at the same time giving the command "Whoa." Since he will be anxious to be off, he will probably stiffen to a point. Repeat this procedure at the start of each trip until he has learned to remain quiet in this position; then try stepping back a few paces, restraining him with the leash. Whenever he moves, go back and straighten him to a point. Soon he will stop on point at "Whoa" with only occasional restraint by the leash.

"Heel." In teaching a dog to heel, carry a very light, willowy switch. When you start to walk with the dog on leash give the command "Heel" and a hand signal to indicate he is to stay behind. He will not know what is wanted and will probably try to go ahead. Call him back, giving the command and hand signal, and repeat these until he understands he is to walk behind. If he is still hard to keep back, flick (not whip) him lightly with the switch, repeating the command. This will cause him to get back in position quickly. Practice with this method will teach him to walk in position at command.

Coming Promptly to Call. One of the most important lessons involves teaching the young dog to come to you when

Typical Laverack type English Setter pointing on pheasant.

you call him. If you are having difficulty in this respect, you may use a twenty-five foot clothesline rope as a lead. If the dog does not come at once when you call, use the lead to start him to you. When he comes promptly, praise him. After he learns to come promptly when called, mistakes in other phases of his training can be corrected at once. It may be questioned seriously, however, whether it is ever good handling, or fair to a dog, to call him to you to punish him. If punishment is necessary for willful infraction of rules (when your dog is old enough and well enough trained to know the rules and to know that he must obey them), you should go to him. He should not have the idea he is likely to be punished when he comes to you.

Hand Signals. Dogs learn the meaning of hand signals more readily than they learn words. During yard training, use hand signals along with commands as often as possible. For example, when you give the command to "Whoa" or "Heel," also give an appropriate hand signal. The dog should learn to respond to hand signals in the field whether he hears the command or not.

Advanced Yard Training. By the time your dog is eight to twelve months old he will probably have developed mentally to the point where he is ready for advanced yard training. We will assume that he has had preliminary lessons in most phases of yard work, and that the series of lessons has progressed gradually from the easier to the most difficult tasks.

The advanced yard training program should perfect by degrees his performance of the earlier yard lessons, or any new ones given him. Later when further freedom in the field will do no good and teaching control will do no harm, these lessons may be applied to initiate control of your dog in the field.

I have successfully practiced the yard training lesson in the living room, using an easy chair for the "kennel." At the command "kennel," the dog jumps in the chair, and upon being called by name comes to me. The advantage of house training over yard training is that it can be done at night and during bad weather, thereby saving time.

Field Training

Teaching Dog to Quarter. Eventually, in the field, you will bring your hunting dog's yard lessons into play in teaching him to remain steady to flush and shot, and in bringing him under control while working ahead of you. Do not be in a hurry to enforce control, however, until he has gained field experience. You should teach him to quarter the ground ahead of you, but he will have to learn for himself to work the birdy spots and to skirt the unlikely places. Proper working of the cover requires experience on his part.

A dog that finds and flushes game fifty yards ahead gives little chance for a killing shot. A pheasant will be at least sixty and perhaps seventy yards away before it is safe to shoot (because of the dog). From twenty-five years' hunting experience, I know that most game is shot under thirty yards. It is my opinion that most hunters and even top wing shots can't even cripple a bird at seventy yards, much less kill one. Also, a dog fifty yards in front of the gun will flush a moving bird far out of range if it is necessary to follow the line any distance before flushing. A dog ranging or quartering over a seventy- to eighty-yard front with the gun in the middle of that front is covering enough ground, even though he is crossing in front of the gun at a distance of five yards.

In training the dog to quarter, you may use hand signals to advantage to indicate that he is to turn and quarter in the opposite direction. Some trainers use their dog whistles for no other purpose than to turn the dogs. Perhaps the most useful device you can use in training your young dog to quarter properly is to follow a zigzag course over the field, always working into the wind in early lessons. When the puppy sees you change your course he will usually swing back to keep ahead. Occasionally you may find it necessary to start to run to arouse his interest in what lies ahead of you. After the dog has learned to quarter properly, you may reserve whistle signals or voice signals for special occasions when it is necessary to get his attention.

Steadiness on Point and to Wing and Shot. The well-trained dog should hold in pointing position until the hunter flushes the game and shoots; then remain steady in this position until sent to retrieve or to resume hunting.

Achieving steadiness in the young dog requires patience on the part of the trainer as well as frequent rehearsals of the lesson. It is probably better not to strive for complete steadiness early in the dog's hunting experience. The first impulse of the dog when game is flushed seems to be to leap after the quarry. The strong tendency found in all breeds of dogs to chase moving objects is undoubtedly inherited from their wild hunting ancestors.

Some dogs learn with experience that it is useless to chase birds, but most dogs, if not given careful training, repeated when necessary, are likely to develop persistent habits of breaking and chasing.

When the setter begins to point game, make a special effort to get to him when he is on point. Hold him there for five minutes or more, stroking him and straightening him to a good pointing position; let him know you are well pleased with him. Repeat "Whoa" several times to associate this command with pointing game. Pushing the dog gently toward the pointed game tends to make him lean back. This is a good way to make some dogs more staunch.

Methods of teaching steadiness to wing and shot vary among trainers. Many trainers rely on a check cord (twenty-five to fifty feet of clothesline attached to collar) to steady the dog on point or to wing or shot. Stopping the dog with enough force to cause him to turn end-for-end after he has broken point and started to chase is frequently recommended to cure these faults. Nevertheless, in most cases it seems better for the amateur to teach steadiness without the use of a check cord if possible. The check cord ruins more dogs than any other thing; it makes blinkers out of them. Many bird-shy dogs are caused by a check cord, even in the hands of a good trainer.

The following method of teaching steadiness without a check cord is recommended by a nationally known professional trainer. When the dog has been taught to "Whoa," is accustomed to the firing of a gun, and is undergoing advanced training in the field, the trainer begins the steadiness train-

Steadying a young English Setter bitch on point by the use of a check-cord. She is on a stiff point and was lifted up several times by the tail and stroked to keep her steady.

ing by firing a gun at an opportune time. The dog is probably accustomed to associate the report with the fun of chasing, and his impulse will be to be off, but in this lesson the command "Whoa" is given immediately after the report. If the dog has been sufficiently trained, and all goes well, he will stop and hold the pointing position.

If the dog does not obey the command, the trainer usually (under some circumstances it may be preferable to let the dog get his chase out) goes to him and carries him back to the exact spot where he should have stopped. The dog is put in correct position, kept there a few minutes, and allowed to think over his mistake. This procedure is repeated until the dog learns to stop at the shot and command, and finally to the shot alone.

The author believes that training a shooting dog to be steady to wing and shot is an unnecessary detail, as it serves no practical purpose. Such training is a left-over from field trials, where it may serve a definite purpose to keep these wide-ranging dogs under control at the important moment. It is against a dog's nature not to chase, which is the reason it is so difficult to break them of it. Moreover, in real hunting it is a decided advantage to have the dog under the bird when it comes down in case it is wounded. Not so many wounded birds would be left in the field if the dog were allowed to retrieve them at once. In case of a missed shot the dog can have the bird located and be on point again when you come up with him. I can see no good reason for keeping the rule of steady to wing and shot in our shooting dog trials (not field trials), and would attach more importance to the dog's being under control at all times than his being steady to wing and shot. I have discussed this subject with several trainers and have yet to be offered a sensible reason for training to be steady to wing and shot. One well-known trainer said, "Without the dog's being steady to wing and shot he lacks a finished performance," which of course is an unsatisfactory explanation.

Training the Pheasant Dog. Training an English Setter to hunt pheasants presents special problems because of the cock pheasant's habit of running ahead of the hunter and dog.

Dogs must learn by experience to follow the pheasant, rather than to keep on pointing while the bird runs away. Occasionally, one of these dogs learns by himself to circle the pheasant, thus probably causing it to lie to a point between the dog and hunter.

Instead of pursuing the cock from the rear (trailing) it is best for the dog to move out and around the bird, thereby either changing its course or causing it to lie to a point or to flush within shot of the gun. There are several methods for training the dog to handle the wily cock in this manner.

1. Keep the dog's head off the ground; never let him develop into a trailer. The best method found by the author has been to take the dog out of short cover at the first indication of ground trailing and put him down in a dense vegetation that he can best traverse with his head held high.

2. Never permit the young dog to trail the bird from behind. Train him to move around the bird. This may be done by teaching him to respond to a command. I personally like to locate a pheasant in a narrow draw with but two normal escapes, one at either end; then when it is known that the bird is there the dog is put down so that he has the advantage of the wind. When he has his bird well located, force him to leave it completely and circle around, approaching the bird from the opposite side. After he has learned to do this efficiently from command, he may be encouraged to make the same move without command. Time and much patience will eventually result in an automatic response which seems to increase with age.

3. By tethering a cock bird in dense cover, or by attaching to it a light stick, one has almost a complete control over the training. By repeatedly controlling the dog's movements when the exact location of the bird is known, the approach and the point can be steadied. This is probably the best method of training the pheasant dog.

4. Once the idea takes hold, it is advisable to give the dog plenty of opportunity to develop all of the fine technique which the particular dog is capable of developing through plenty of self-hunting, or better still through loose control when the trainer is present.

CORKING CHLOE pointing woodcock. She was sired by Ch. Sir Orkney Racket out of Red Rose Susanne. Owned by Mr. Luther Otto III, of Armsworth Kennels, Westminster, Massachusetts.

This seems to be about the only way the dog has of learning the characteristic behavior of pheasants under varying conditions.

Overhandling Undesirable. It should be the objective of the hunter to train his dog thoroughly in the essential points of working to the gun; then to allow him to work with a minimum of direction. Frequent directions will distract the dog and retard the development of initiative in finding and skill in handling game, both marks of the good hunting dog.

207

Photograph taken at a Shooting Dog Stake held in New Milford, Connecticut, by The English Setter Club of New England. The dogs are all bench type and are the winners of the various classes. The winner of the open class is a bench show champion. Another placing second in the novice class finished his bench show championship a few weeks later and many of the others had several points toward their championships. Photograph by William Joli.

F.T. Ch. Johnny Crockett, winner of the annual Purina Award for the Top Field Trial Bird Dog in the United States during the 1969-1970 season. Owned by H.P. Sheely, Dallas, Texas, and trained by W.C. Kirk.

A BREEDER'S DREAM—ALL CHAMPIONS BUT ONE!

The most remarkable litter in all English Setter history. Sired by Ch. Rip of Blue Bar out of Frenchtown Blue Feather, eleven of these twelve puppies became champions. Left to right; all carrying the Frenchtown prefix: Carrousel, Rosette, Festival, Judy, Blue Yonder, Mardi Gras, Holly, Topic, Reveler, Vanity Fair, Ripple and Blue Punch. Vanity Fair died with 10 points toward her championship.

10

Breeding

In creative work, that which is first must survive the spotlight of criticism and so becomes a target for the malicious tongues of the envious. The charlatan, the mountebank, the phony, unable to equal or better the best, tries to depreciate and destroy, thereby confirming the superiority of that which he degrades. The best is advertised by the clamor of envy by the jackals.

WHILE there is some variation, of course, in the breeding cycle of individual bitches, it is believed that this variation from the norm is not as great nor as frequently encountered as some may believe. Aside from some exceptional cases, the apparent variation is due to keeping inaccurate checks and records on the time when the cycle first starts. Also failure of the bitch to conceive is all too often blamed on the time of the mating, when in reality the blame should be placed on other factors, such as the condition of the bitch or stud at the time of service.

The following chart* shows the average mating cycle, and it will be found advisable to use it for breeding unless it is **definitely** known from accurate records of past experience that a particular bitch's mating cycle always shows a different sequence than the chart indicates. The most usual variation from the chart is the elapsed time between seasons, and irregularity in this period does not predispose irregularity in the more important interval of show of color to ovulation. I once bought an English Setter bitch who had been bred several times in the past, and her former owner reported several failures in her coming in whelp and advised me to breed her very early in her season for satisfactory results. I had known her former owner for several years and knew that he had farmed the bitch out with a more or less irresponsible party, so did not place very much store by his advice. I bred the bitch at the time I have always used, and found that she was normal in her cycle and that she produced normal litters. The trouble was that her former owner did not keep careful watch over her and did not know actually when she came in season, and after finally discovering it he became hysterical in his search for a convenient stud for immediate service for fear she was already on her last day.

Referring to the chart, it will be noticed that the bitch's vulva begins to swell about five days before color shows. The breeder's record of the bitch should show about when she is due to come in season, and she should be carefully watched every day at this time for the preliminary signs, which will be evidenced by the swelling of the vulva. This sign gives us ample warning of the coming season even if it is missed for a day or two. From the day color begins to show, count eleven days and then determine when she is willing to stand for the stud dog. It will be noted that ovulation usually begins at the sixteenth day after color shows, and the ideal time for breeding is at the time of ovulation. Keeping in mind that the bitch cannot conceive unless the live sperm comes in contact with the ovum, and that the life of sperm is not over three days (two days being safer), it is readily seen that the most opportune time for breeding is the fourteenth day after color

* Adapted from data by Leon Whitney

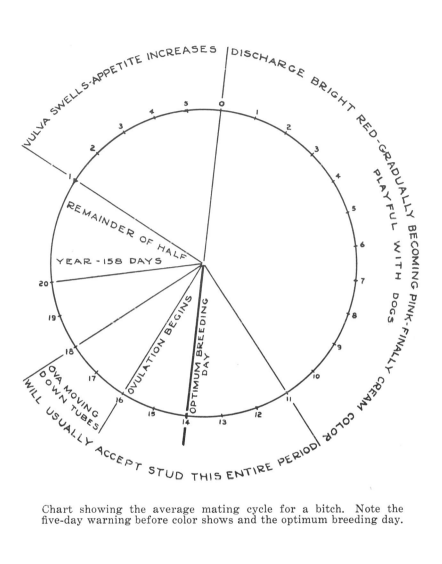

Chart showing the average mating cycle for a bitch. Note the five-day warning before color shows and the optimum breeding day.

shows, or more exactly the third day after the bitch will stand for the dog. Of course the safest procedure would be to breed the bitch on the second day and again on the fourth day after she will stand for the dog (thirteenth and fifteenth days after color shows). When only one service to the stud is available, the best selection would be the third day after the bitch will accept the stud, or the fourteenth day after color first shows. This fourteenth day is especially desirable when using an old stud whose sperm may be comparatively weak and who cannot be used for two services only two days apart.

When mating takes place on the first day that the bitch will stand for the dog, it is an exception when the bitch conceives. Another sign of the proper day for breeding is when the congestion or firmness of the vulva begins to lessen, which will be about the third day after the bitch will stand for the dog. This is a comparative condition and must be carefully watched for by feeling from day to day. Experience shows that bringing a bitch into season by artificial methods, using drugs, is not indicated, as such a season is not natural and is associated with unnatural sequence. There are, however, natural methods of hastening the coming of the season. These methods are not as quick as the use of drugs, but often produce an earlier season having a natural sequence. It is well known that additional hours of light will hasten to some extent the time of a bitch's period, and such an acceleration of the normal time of period may be practiced without apparent unnatural sequence. The practice is extensively used for stimulating winter egg production of chickens where the eggs are not only for food but also for incubation.

The whelping chart shown is based on a chart from "Gaines Dog Research Progress" (Winter 1948–1949). Various forms of whelping charts have been published, but the calendar month method shown is easier to read as it is more open. The Gaines Calendar shows a 1949 calendar with the days of the week indicated, and although it is correct for any one year, the days of the month will of course fall on different days of the week for years other than 1949. The chart given here has omitted the days of the week, and is therefore correct for any year.

214

WHELPING CHART

JANUARY

1	2	3	4	5	6	7
Mar.5	Mar.6	Mar.7	Mar.8	Mar.9	Mar.10	Mar.11
8	9	10	11	12	13	14
Mar.12	Mar.13	Mar.14	Mar.15	Mar.16	Mar.17	Mar.18
15	16	17	18	19	20	21
Mar.19	Mar.20	Mar.21	Mar.22	Mar.23	Mar.24	Mar.25.
22	23	24	25	26	27	28
Mar.26	Mar.27	Mar.28	Mar.29	Mar.30	Mar.31	Apr.1
29	30	31				
Apr.2	Apr.3	Apr.4				

FEBRUARY

1	2	3	4	5	6	7
Apr.5	Apr.6	Apr.7	Apr.8	Apr.9	Apr.10	Apr.11
8	9	10	11	12	13	14
Apr.12	Apr.13	Apr.14	Apr.15	Apr.16	Apr.17	Apr.18
15	16	17	18	19	20	21
Apr.19	Apr.20	Apr.21	Apr.22	Apr.23	Apr.24	Apr.25
22	23	24	25	26	27	28
Apr.26	Apr.27	Apr.28	Apr.29	Apr.30	May1	May2
29						
May3						

MARCH

1	2	3	4	5	6	7
May3	May4	May5	may6	May7	May8	May9
8	9	10	11	12	13	14
May10	May11	May12	May13	May14	May15	May16
15	16	17	18	19	20	21
May17	May18	May19	May20	May21	May22	Ma23
22	23	24	25	26	27	28
May24	May25	May26	May27	May28	May29	May30
29	30	31				
May31	June1	June2				

APRIL

1	2	3	4	5	6	7
June3	June4	June5	June6	June7	June8	June9
8	9	10	11	12	13	14
June10	June11	June12	June13	June14	June15	June16
15	16	17	18	19	20	21
June17	June18	June19	June20	June21	June22	June23
22	23	24	25	26	27	28
June24	June25	June26	June27	June28	June29	June30
29	30					
July1	July2					

MAY

1	2	3	4	5	6	7
July3	July4	July5	July6	July7	July8	July9
8	9	10	11	12	13	14
July10	July11	July12	July13	July14	July15	July16
15	16	17	18	19	20	21
July17	July18	July19	July20	July21	July22	July23
22	23	24	25	26	27	28
July24	July25	July26	July27	July28	July29	July30
29	30	31				
July31	Aug.1	Aug.2				

JUNE

1	2	3	4	5	6	7
Aug.3	Aug.4	Aug.5	Aug.6	Aug.7	Aug.8	Aug.9
8	9	10	11	12	13	14
Aug.10	Aug.11	Aug.12	Aug.13	Aug.14	Aug.15	Aug.16
15	16	17	18	19	20	21
Aug.17	Aug.18	Aug.19	Aug.20	Aug.21	Aug.22	Aug.23
22	23	24	25	26	27	28
Aug.24	Aug.25	Aug.26	Aug.27	Aug.28	Aug.29	Aug.30
29	30					
Aug.31	Sept.1					

JULY

1	2	3	4	5	6	7
Sept.2	Sept.3	Sept.4	Sept.5	Sept.6	Sept.7	Sept.8
8	9	10	11	12	13	14
Sept.9	Sept.10	Sept.11	Sept.12	Sept.13	Sept.14	Sept.15
15	16	17	18	19	20	21
Sept.16	Sept.17	Sept.18	Sept.19	Sept.20	Sept.21	Sept.22
22	23	24	25	26	27	28
Sept.23	Sept.24	Sept.25	Sept.26	Sept.27	Sept.28	Sept.29
29	30	31				
Sept.30	Oct.1	Oct.2				

AUGUST

1	2	3	4	5	6	7
Oct.3	Oct.4	Oct.5	Oct.6	Oct.7	Oct.8	Oct.9
8	9	10	11	12	13	14
Oct.10	Oct.11	Oct.12	Oct.13	Oct.14	Oct.15	Oct.16
15	16	17	18	19	20	21
Oct.17	Oct.18	Oct.19	Oct.20	Oct.21	Oct.22	Oct.23
22	23	24	25	26	27	28
Oct.24	Oct.25	Oct.26	Oct.27	Oct.28	Oct.29	Oct.30
29	30	31				
Oct.31	Nov.1	Nov.2				

SEPTEMBER

1	2	3	4	5	6	7
Nov.3	Nov.4	Nov.5	Nov.6	Nov.7	Nov.8	Nov.9
8	9	10	11	12	13	14
Nov.10	Nov.11	Nov.12	Nov.13	Nov.14	Nov.15	Nov.16
15	16	17	18	19	20	21
Nov.17	Nov.18	Nov.19	Nov.20	Nov.21	Nov.22	Nov.23
22	23	24	25	26	27	28
Nov.24	Nov.25	Nov.26	Nov.27	Nov.28	Nov.29	Nov.30
29	30					
Dec.1	Dec.2					

OCTOBER

1	2	3	4	5	6	7
Dec.3	Dec.4	Dec.5	Dec.6	Dec.7	Dec.8	Dec.9
8	9	10	11	12	13	14
Dec.10	Dec.11	Dec.12	Dec.13	Dec.14	Dec.15	Dec.16
15	16	17	18	19	20	21
Dec.17	Dec.18	Dec.19	Dec.20	Dec.21	Dec.22	Dec.23
22	23	24	25	26	27	28
Dec.24	Dec.25	Dec.26	Dec.27	Dec.28	Dec.29	Dec.30
29	30	31				
Dec.31	Jan.1	Jan.2				

NOVEMBER

1	2	3	4	5	6	7
Jan.3	Jan.4	Jan.5	Jan.6	Jan.7	Jan.8	Jan.9
8	9	10	11	12	13	14
Jan.10	Jan.11	Jan.12	Jan.13	Jan.14	Jan.15	Jan.16
15	16	17	18	19	20	21
Jan.17	Jan.18	Jan.19	Jan.20	Jan.21	Jan.22	Jan.23
22	23	24	25	26	27	28
Jan.24	Jan.25	Jan.26	Jan.27	Jan.28	Jan.29	Jan.30
29	30					
Jan.31	Feb.1					

DECEMBER

1	2	3	4	5	6	7
Feb.2	Feb.3	Feb.4	Feb.5	Feb.6	Feb.7	Feb.8
8	9	10	11	12	13	14
Feb.9	Feb.10	Feb.11	Feb.12	Feb.13	Feb.14	Feb.15
15	16	17	18	19	20	21
Feb.16	Feb.17	Feb.18	Feb.19	Feb.20	Feb.21	Feb.22
22	23	24	25	26	27	28
Feb.23	Feb.24	Feb.25	Feb.26	Feb.27	Feb.28	Mar.1
29	30	31				
Mar.2	Mar.3	Mar.4				

On the whelping chart the large type shows date bitch was bred, and she will be due to whelp on the date shown in small type immediately below. Dates are based on the normal gestation period of sixty-three days. Variations in date of birth of two or three days either way are not unusual.

The sixty-three day gestation period is the usual time given for bitches and is based on the bitch being bred on the twelfth day after color shows, or the second day after the bitch will stand for the stud. The actual gestation period, however, is from the time of ovulation, so that sixty-one days rather than sixty-three days is more nearly the true gestation period. The bitch usually gives a warning that she will whelp soon by refusing her usual meal.

There is an almost universal belief that if a bitch is bred on her first season it will stunt her development and prevent her from ever attaining her otherwise maximum size. On the other hand, it is also believed by many that breeding a bitch at her first season will develop her spring of rib. Data on height at shoulder vs. age unfortunately is insufficient to show at just what age a bitch reaches her maximum height. The chart on page 101 shows that a bitch reaches her optimum weight at about eighteen months, at which age she will have been in season once or twice. Weight alone, however, is not a sufficient measure for a bitch's growth as she will continue to gain weight for some months after she has attained her final height. We are now collecting data on height at shoulder vs. age for both dogs and bitches, so after a few years we should have a definite answer as to whether breeding a bitch on her first season will stunt her growth or not. For instance, how can we say a bitch was stunted because she was bred on her first season? How do we know she would have grown any larger if she had not been bred on her first season?

It has been well established that additional quantities of certain vitamins in a bitch's diet are essential before her season and until the puppies are weaned. These are vitamins A, B, B_2, D, and E. These vitamins are better assimilated or utilized through natural sources than from the drug store bottle. Alfalfa leaf meal, animal organs, cooked eggs, irradiated yeast, and wheat germ will supply all of the necessary

216

vitamins. It has recently been reported that cod liver oil is toxic to some dogs, and it would seem best, until more is known on the subject, to use oleum percomorphum, alfalfa leaf meal or irradiated yeast for the necessary additional supply of vitamins A and D.

When bitches are shipped considerable distances for breeding to a desirable stud, I believe that the owner of the bitch often does not give enough serious thought to the project and that this lack of interest is the main reason for bitches so shipped failing to conceive. It is assumed that the stud is potent, as will be indicated by his other recent litters. The bitch sent to him should not be fat but rather on the lean side, e.g., a bitch who in show bloom will weigh fifty-five pounds should be thinned down by exercise to about fifty pounds before she comes in season. She should be given the extra supplement of vitamins. You should **know** and not guess or estimate the day she starts to show color, and so advise the owner of the stud so that he can breed her on the fourteenth day after color started to show, or on the third day after the bitch will stand for the stud. She should arrive at the stud's kennel three or four days before the estimated time of service so that the stud owner can make the proper observations to determine the correct time for service. She should remain at the stud's kennel for two or three days after service.

Breeders who are trying to improve the breed and raise above-average specimens must make up their mind to try for quality and not quantity. A litter of English Setters numbering over five presents a problem to the breeder. Either the puppies in excess of five should be taken entirely away from the mother after the second day and fed from a bottle or a foster-mother, or destroyed. Puppies in large litters will, as a rule, not develop as well as those of a small litter. The problem then is to decide which five puppies of the larger litter are to be left with the mother.

In making this choice it is suggested that the litter be first divided into two lots: (1) those well marked and (2) those mismarked. The next division would be (3) the largest and (4) the smallest. We will then have four groups. The groups can then be looked over carefully for any other desirable or undesirable features. Any malformation should be eliminated at once. The navels should be examined for rupture. The ear set and head shape should be studied. After you have finally decided on the five who are to stay with the mother, mark them with a drop of tincture of Gentian Violet. If possible it is well to call in another breeder whose opinion you respect, and have him also look them over and make his choice of the two batches; and where he does not agree with you, the case should be argued out.

Two-day-old puppies can be bottle fed, using a formula or canned simulated bitch's milk (formula preferred), and they will do just about as well as those that are left with the mother if you are willing and able to be careful and punctual about their care and feeding. There is one important difference between the two groups in that those who stay with the mother are usually immune to diseases while they are nursing, while those fed on the bottle are not. It is therefore advisable not to let outsiders handle the bottle-fed puppies, and you should wash your hands and face thoroughly and change your shoes and clothes before feeding, especially if you have been with your other dogs. The bottle-fed puppies should be kept in the home away from the kennel to prevent spread of infectious disease and should be massaged gently after each feeding to encourage elimination.

A whelping box is a necessity for English Setter bitches to have their puppies in. The box is built with a recess all around so that the puppies have a chance of getting out of the way when the bitch lies down to nurse them, and in this way many puppies are saved from being crushed. It is best to leave the boards on the bottom uncovered, because if paper is used, the bitch will tear it up, and the puppies will get covered up so that she cannot see them. Carpet or burlap tacked on the bottom has the same disadvantage, and in addition it is difficult to keep clean. After the puppies start climbing out of the whelping box, it should be removed and thoroughly scrubbed, aired, and sunned, and put away for the next use. The accompanying photograph shows a whelping box for an English Setter bitch.

Whelping box for English Setters. Size 33 inches by 33 inches, depth 6½ inches, width of overhang 3½ inches.

A great deal has been written* about the science of breeding dogs which may be included under the general classification of genetics. We read about Mendel's law, the phenotype and the genotype, chromosomes and genes, dominant and recessive factors. Scientists are still trying to unravel and understand nature's laws, but **life** is still a secret. Their studies are interesting to the dog breeder (though somewhat bewildering and depressing because there is still so much to learn and so little time is left of our life span) because they give him a general idea of the intricate and complex pattern that is behind their efforts to breed good dogs. Most dog breeders, however, are doctors, lawyers, engineers, artists, bankers,

* *How to Breed Dogs*, Leon F. Whitney, Howell Book House, New York.
The New Art of Breeding Better Dogs, Kyle Onstott, Howell Book House Inc., 845 Third Avenue, New York, N. Y. 10022

farmers—business men and women in general—who have a very hazy picture of genetics, and in the long run breed better dogs than do the scientists who know and understand genetics.

Breeding good bench type English Setters by the use of the principles of genetics is almost hopelessly involved. We breed cows for maximum milk or butter fat production; we breed race horses for speed; chickens for maximum egg production; pigs for lard or bacon types; field trial English Setters for nose. To secure these end results we sacrifice everything else. As soon as we try to breed chickens not only to produce the maximum number of eggs but also to make up to broiler size in the least possible time, we run into difficulties. As soon as we try to breed a cow that not only will give the maximum quantity of milk but also give the finest quality of beef, we strike a snag.

Successful breeding of dairy cows, race horses, chickens, pigs, or field trial type English Setters is quite simple in comparison to the Herculean task that we have set ourselves in breeding good bench type English Setters. We want everything and are unwilling to sacrifice anything. We want, for instance, good heads, low set ears, good mouth, dark eyes, long square muzzle, mild pleasing expression, pigmented eyelids, long arched neck, lack of throatiness, deep chest, good spring of rib, short loin, no dip in the back, not high behind, correct height at shoulder, good tail set, short tail, straight tail carriage, good front, good shoulders, good feet, good toes, good angulation, strong thighs and rear legs, good bone, stylish movement, good texture and length of coat, correct color, well marked, good disposition, good health, resistant to disease, normal from a breeding standpoint, a good nose and willing to hunt. We are trying to breed a SUPER dog.

We learn from genetics that all of these desirable qualities are controlled by genes or combinations of genes, but we have no way of looking at these genes in the particular dog. To make the problem a little simpler, let's imagine that the stud and the brood bitch each have a good and a bad gene for each of the desirable qualities. Our chances then of having all of the desirable genes of the stud combine with all of the desirable genes of the bitch, and all of the undesirable ones rejected, are just about the same as shaking up fifty pennies in a hat and having them all come up heads.

Our problem is terrifically complicated, and no breeder has yet been able to call his shots. I can say without fear of contradiction that every great bench type English Setter that was ever raised was purely the result of accident, and that no credit can be claimed by the breeder for his astuteness. To indicate that my viewpoint is shared by others, I quote from Leon Whitney* (past executive Secretary of the American Eugenics Society) : "Probably the greatest breeders are those who have a great variety in type to begin with and constantly breed a very large number of puppies and have a much wider selection from which to choose."

To quote again from Whitney, "The real secret of any great breeder's success lies in breeding just as many puppies as he possibly can. If there is only one good puppy in one hundred, even when the best is considered, then the breeder who raises one thousand puppies from good stock stands just twenty times the chance of getting that one than the breeder who raises only fifty puppies a year. The greatest breeders are not those who raise a litter a year. They understand somehow that they have a better statistical chance of breeding great dogs, and they resort to numbers, for after all, heredity in dogs is what counts and the way you feed does not greatly change the appearance of the dog, so long as both are well done. Therefore the way to fame in any breed is to breed and show plenty of dogs, and the more of both you do, the better are your chances to attain fame for your dog and yourself."

That breeding bench type English Setters is largely a gamble is the secret of why the confirmed breeder keeps on. He knows the odds are all against him but he keeps on putting in the dimes hoping his will be the luck of hitting the jackpot. Knowing full well that the dogs he exhibits are not his ideal and that they have shortcomings, he shows them at the bench shows so that he can see by comparison with others if he is doing better or worse than his friends.

Because of lack of genetic data on studs and bitches of the past and the loose nomenclature used in describing the ani-

---

* *How to Breed Dogs*, op. cit.

mals, we cannot depend very much from a practical standpoint on Mendelian color inheritance for determining accurately the color to be expected for a litter of puppies. Some generalization can be made, however, that is of some, if doubtful, value.

Our English Setter studs and bitches have been so mixed up by breeding blue to blue, blue to orange, blue to tricolor, orange to orange, orange to tricolor, and tricolor to tricolor, each of which were not genetically true in color, that it is extremely difficult to predict with any degree of accuracy the color of puppies resulting from any given mating.

In general, an orange belton stud bred to an orange belton bitch will produce oranges, although occasionally you will find a blue belton puppy from such a mating. Orange belton puppies are, as a rule, more evenly marked than either blue beltons or tricolors.

Blue belton studs bred to blue belton bitches usually produce blue belton puppies, although it is not uncommon to find some orange beltons and tricolors with such a mating. Of course, the reason for this variety of colors is that the stud or bitch or both were not real genetic blues and had orange and tricolor genes. I have noticed that blue beltons who are not genetic blues have some dark hairs that take on a copper tinge when the light is right, and that these studs and bitches throw mixed colored litters. I am not positive that I am correct on this conclusion as my opportunity for observation has been limited to five animals. One of the disappointing results of breeding blue belton studs to blue belton bitches is the large number of poorly marked puppies resulting, which in effect reduces the size or value of the litter. Of course a black patch is not a disqualification, and, if otherwise excellent, the dog can go to the top of the shows, e.g., Ch. Blue Dan of Happy Valley, Ch. Pilot of Crombie, and Ch. Stylish Black Cock of Bromley were all blue beltons with black head patches.

A tricolor bitch bred to an orange belton stud will give a mixed litter of orange beltons and tricolors and sometimes a blue belton. A tricolor bitch bred to a blue belton dog will produce blue beltons, tricolors, and oranges. A tricolor stud bred to a tricolor bitch will usually produce all tricolor puppies. Like blue beltons, the size or value of a tricolor litter is reduced because of the large percentage of poorly marked puppies. The above explains in part, at least, the popularity of the orange belton.

It is to be noted that in this discussion the designation blue belton, orange belton, and tricolor relates to the color of the individual and not to the genetic color, and it is understood that any of these colors may, and usually do, carry color inheritance other than their own individual color.

These mixed inheritance factors are one of the reasons it is so difficult to filter out much of practical breeding value from the so-called science of breeding. Eye color inheritance factors are in the same scrambled condition. To state that a dark-eyed stud bred to a dark-eyed bitch can but result in dark-eyed puppies is not true, because these dark-eyed parents are supposed to be genetically dark-eyed, and we know that our present studs and bitches, although as individuals may be dark-eyed, are not usually genetically dark-eyed. Further to complicate our problem the dark-eyed stud, although most desirable from the eye point of view, may have nothing much else to recommend him, so we are forced, not by choice but by common sense, to use a lighter-eyed stud. In other words, if we were breeding for dark-eyed dogs only, our path would indeed seem to be a rosy one and we might conclude that in a short time we could have all of our English Setters with dark eyes. Unfortunately the law of variation steps in, and color of eyes being a continuous type of variation, some puppies, even from parents having genetic dark eyes, will have lighter eyes than the parents.

Exceptions to general rules always exist. These exceptions, however, in no way detract from the truth or practical acceptance of the general rule. In fact, these exceptions to the general rule point out the danger in trying to form a general opinion from too few observations. For any practical work we must accept the general rules and then treat with the exceptional cases as they arise. English Setters, from a breeding standpoint, conform very closely to the general rules, and it may be good practice to weed out exceptions when they are on the undesirable side by careful selection. For instance, if you actually have a bitch that can conceive only when bred on the eighth day, she is an exception, but she in no way disproves that the optimum time for breeding is on the fourteenth day, and it may be advisable, from hereditary considerations, not to breed her. It has been noted that pilots practicing instrument landings usually are above the proper glide angle because they are overly cautious, and afraid they will contact the ground before they reach the paved runway. In the same way many dog breeders are over-cautious about waiting until the proper time for breeding, as they are afraid it will be too late if they wait another day.

There are a few truths, proven by long practice, that may well be a primer for English Setter breeders:

In selecting a stud, do not look at his show record and pedigree alone. Rather find out how many of his get have been able to make the grade at the shows. The questions that should be answered are: 1. Is he a good specimen? 2. Is he able to reproduce his good points in his get? 3. Is he only fairly good but has the proven ability to sire outstanding specimens? Obviously (3) and (2) would make a better stud than (1). An outstanding example of (3) was Rummey Stagboro who never finished his championship but was responsible for a large number of outstanding dogs and bitches. In fact so good was he as a stud that his strain was the winning strain for years. You will be surprised to see how many of yesterday's top winners had Rummey Stagboro as a grandsire.

When buying a bitch for breeding purposes, it is not necessary to buy a top flight show specimen. A large bitch with a few outstanding faults of the type that are not common in English Setters, from a uniform litter that were all as good or better than she, is a better buy from a breeding standpoint that an outstanding bitch who is the pick of a poor litter. It would be much better to buy the poorest in an outstanding litter. Leon Whitney* states: "The finest bit of common sense ever produced by any method for studying heredity is that which is so ably summed up by the Norwegian proverb. It gets at the very root and the very truth of the whole matter. 'Marry not the maid who is the only good maid in the clan.' "

---

* *How to Breed Dogs*, op. cit.

It is also desirable to buy breeding stock from a kennel located in a climate more severe than your own, and where environmental conditions are poorer than your own.

If we were to breed the very best English Setter bitch in the country to the very best English Setter dog, none of the get would be as good as either of the parents. They represent the very apex of improvement and any change will be downward—they degenerate. This is a most important consideration for a breeder; he must realize that he must continue climbing the ladder, for if he ever reaches the top he can go no further. There is never a static condition in breeding but rather one of flux—we must go up or down, and can never stand still. If you accidentally breed a hot one, just make up your mind that the get from it will be poorer. It is not necessary to start at the bottom of the ladder each time, as a good breeder will usually be found somewhere about the last three-quarters of the way up the ladder. This is a healthy condition because it gives everyone a chance to be the first to reach the top of the ladder. Do not confuse the breeder with the professional handler who for many years has shown winning dogs; the professional handler often represents the maximum effort of many breeders. He is the jockey who rides the winning horse, but he does not breed the horses.

The law of the drag of the breed is constantly operating. It may be the breeder's best friend or his worst enemy, depending upon whether you make it work for you or you work for it. All English Setters tend toward an average of the breed. Thus, if the average height of English Setter bitches is twenty-four inches, then there must be about as many under twenty-four inches as there are above twenty-four inches, and if you breed a twenty-five inch bitch, her get will average less than twenty-five inches. So it is for most of the desirable points. The only way that we can raise the height of an English Setter bitch as a breed from an average of twenty-four to an average of twenty-five inches (if it is desirable to do this) is by selective breeding. Of course there is a limit in this direction, and the more nearly we approach this limit the more difficult it becomes to force the average upward. There is a tendency in breeding English Setters toward increasing their size. This tendency is an unhealthy one for the breed and should be closely watched by the English Setter Association, as its long continued practice could eventually harm the breed structurally.

Any breeder, to be successful in the long run, must co-operate with nature and not try to go contrary to her laws or improve on them. In his egotism, man may think he can improve on God, but sooner or later he will find that he is wrong. Chemicals, machines, money cannot improve on or replace nature. The whole dog is not merely the integration of parts, nor can the parts be mixed, as salt and water, to get the desired concentration, but rather it is an organism with laws of a higher order than the physio-chemical—it is LIFE.

Do not let your kennel get stocked up with poor specimens of the English Setter. Destroy all but the very best. If you look hard enough you can always find some good points in almost any well-bred English Setter. Here again we should go along with nature who, by her law of the survival of the fittest, is constantly destroying the weaklings and the misfits. Do not sell or give away undesirable specimens, for by so doing you are helping the drag of the breed to bring down the degree of excellence that you are striving to bring up. For example, take eye color alone. If there are 100,000 English Setters in the world having eye color varying from yellow to dark brown and the average of all eyes is hazel in color, then if all the English Setters with lighter eyes than hazel were destroyed, leaving only those with hazel to dark brown eyes to breed from, it is easy to follow that if this selection were continued long enough the average eye color would be pushed from hazel toward the dark brown. These probability curves are commonly used for establishing the mean of continuous variations and are mathematically expressed as $y = Ex^{-2}$, where $E = 2.713$.

From a practical standpoint, the law of variation is the drag of the breed which tends to bring all English Setters up or down to the average of the breed. This makes rigid selection of puppies, bitches, and studs necessary if real improvement is desired.

226

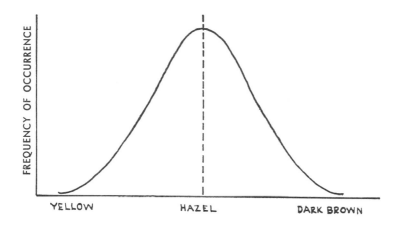

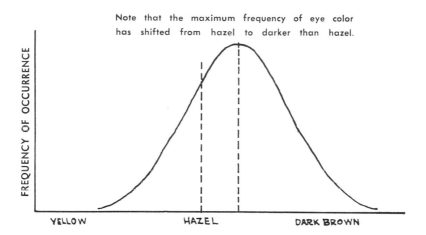

Note that the maximum frequency of eye color has shifted from hazel to darker than hazel.

Typical curves showing variations from the average, and illustrating how by long selection the average color of eyes may be pushed from hazel toward dark brown.

In factory work, inspectors throw out over- and under-sized pieces and other defective products at an early stage in the process of manufacture, so that hidden defects in the finished assembled product will not show up later and be costly because so much time and money had already been put in the finished piece. Factories have "go" and "no go" gauges to indicate which products should be thrown out. Usually these defectives are scrapped, but when they are sold they are plainly marked "Seconds," so that the good name of the firm will not suffer. We should do the same with our dogs. As breeders we also need certain gauges so that puppies can be scrapped or sold as "Seconds" before too much costly feeding, training, and other items of expense are put into them. The age-weight chart (page 101) is such a gauge. Others are needed but data for making them is not currently available. The English Setter Association of America might well establish certain gauges and ask its members to submit information periodically for review, analysis and updating. Today, many breeders are concerned about oversized dogs, and this is one important area which needs exhaustive statistics and analysis.

It is doubtful if there are very many litters of English Setters having uniformly good quality. An occasional litter may produce several champions, but this happy development is rare. Most puppies from most litters should be sold as pets. Since experienced fanciers and breeders will not risk acquiring a show prospect under six to twelve months of age, the market for young show puppies is thin, and selling them to beginners as show prospects is unpardonable. English Setters mature slowly, and some faults do not show up in early puppyhood.

A serious English Setter breeder cannot make a profit on his dogs, any more than can a breeder of high-class dairy cows, and if he goes into breeding with the profit motive in mind he should stop before he starts. Profits from puppies are best left to the pet shops which, as the name implies, deal in pets for profit.

An examination of the cost of raising a litter of six English Setter puppies to the age of six months will make it clear that a profit cannot be made on the sale of puppies.

Cost of Raising a Litter of Six English Setter Puppies to Six Months of Age

Cost of a good brood bitch at $250 (amortized over 5 years) ....$	50.00
Stud service to a good stud ($75 plus shipping expense)	100.00
Feeding bitch for one year (including special feeding) 40c per day .:........................	146.00
Inoculation against distemper	36.00
Worming (Four times @ 25c per puppy)	6.00
Feeding	225.00
Veterinarian fees and medicine	10.00
Labor—feeding, cleaning, some training (3 hours @ $1.50 an hour)	810.00
Interest on investment (Bitch, kennel, equipment, 6% of $500)	30.00
Dog license on bitch (in Connecticut)	10.00
Advertising puppies in local paper	4.00
Miscellaneous (Phone calls, electricity, stamps, etc.)	2.00
TOTAL ....$	1,429.00

Thus the six puppies at six months would cost approximately $238.00 each. There are no customers for a litter of English Setters at $238.00 each. One in the litter may be worth $250.00 at six months, and the other five perhaps $150.00 each, so that all you could hope for, even if they all lived and you could find customers for them, would be $1,000.00 out of a cash expense of $1,429.00. I have purposely made this cost estimate low and have omitted many items—taxes, general auto expense, entertaining the prospective customer, etc.— but trim my estimate as you will, you will find that you cannot break even selling purebred English Setter puppies, if you are a breeder and trying to raise the best ones possible.

From the tabulation of cost it will be noted that the stud fee is a relatively small item, compared with the cost of food for the bitch and the puppies. It follows, therefore, that it is false economy to try to save money on the stud service at the risk of using an inferior stud. The best is none too good.

The English Setter breeder who tries to make his kennel pay a profit or break even will never become one of our top breeders because he is tempted to sacrifice the ideal for dollars. You will find such a profit-minded man drifting from one breed to another, trying to cash in on the popular breed of the day. He will never stick at one breed long enough to accomplish anything, yet he is unwilling to quit and sacrifice his equipment and the cost of the knowledge he has gained. He is usually the chronic griper who wants the breed standard changed to suit his dogs, and who continually sounds off that dog show judges look at the wrong end of the lead.

Anyone who wishes to breed English Setters with the ideal of improving the breed must have certain personal characteristics. I have listed them as follows, and unless you are strong on the ones marked (*), you had better stay out of English Setters.

*Self-control.	Don't take it out on your dogs.
*Perseverance.	Don't quit in the face of adversity, hard luck, sickness in your dogs, etc.
*A good sport.	Don't crab when you lose. If your dog is good, he will win eventually.
Good natured.	A smile does not cost anything.
*Love for animals.	All kinds, and have an eye for them.
*Energetic.	Not lazy.
*Early riser.	Not a late sleeper. Do it now. Don't procrastinate and invent excuses.
*Honest.	
*Truthful.	Don't lie about your own or the other fellow's dog.
Helpful.	Try to help the other breeder.

Breeders may be divided into three classes: (a) the small breeder who has one or two bitches and breeds one or two litters a year, (b) the medium breeder who keeps two to four bitches and raises two or three litters a year, and (c) the large breeder who keeps more than four bitches and raises more than three litters a year.

The small breeder should certainly not maintain a stud except under very unusual circumstances. He can breed to the best studs in the country for less than it costs to feed one, and the chance that he would have the best stud in the country for his particular bitch is remote. He should concentrate on bitches and show and improve them; and if he is diligent and smart he will usually gravitate to the (b) class of intermediate breeders. The small breeder has a distinct advantage over the (b) and (c) classes in that he can give each litter his personal attention to feeding and sanitation, and after the puppies are weaned he can give them individual attention for exercise and training. This individual attention is so important, and the puppies develop so nicely, that to call it beginner's luck is erroneous. The small breeders are the backbone of the English Setter group. They should be respected, helped, encouraged, and given all the credit due them. After all, breeding good English Setters requires ordinary common sense, and I have often met larger breeders who talk a good game but do not follow through nearly as well as the small breeder. After all is said and done, a small breeder with two bitches who raises one good English Setter every five years deserves more acknowledgment than a large breeder with ten bitches who raises one good one every two years.

Some may say that the small breeder is handicapped by not having enough money to show consistently. I do not think that this is a factor, for where there's a will there's a way. I was out to dinner at a small breeder's home not long ago and they were complaining about the high cost of meat. The pot roast cost about three dollars, yet they did not complain about the cost of the bottle of Scotch that cost about six dollars. So it is with the dog shows. If you want to go you will cut down on some other pleasure so that you can afford it. Several of the large breeders do not get around to the shows because of social duties, so the small and large breeders are in the same position for different reasons. The medium and large breeder should never underestimate the small breeder. Selling the small breeder or the beginner an inferior puppy for show or breeding stock is sharp practice, to put it mildly. The small breeder and beginner of today may well be a top breeder of English Setters tomorrow, so if the small breeder can't afford the price of a top show prospect or breeding stock, then the large breeder should let him have a top animal for a low price that he can afford to pay, or even make him a present of it.

The large breeder has a heavy responsibility on his shoulders and should carry it ungrudgingly and with enthusiasm. On his shoulders falls the work of The English Setter Association: publicity in the newspapers and dog magazines, the routine work of organizing and conducting the local dog shows, selecting judges for the shows who will treat everyone fairly; donating prizes, money, and trophies, planning and executing match shows and gun dog stakes, maintaining a good dog at public stud, and last but not least, raising good English Setters.

Inbreeding

It is often stated by the uninformed that pedigreed, thoroughbred, or purebred dogs have been so long inbred that they are high strung, nervous, more susceptible to disease, and less smart than mutts. The only difference between a pedigreed dog and a mutt is that the ancestors of a pedigreed dog are known while those of a mutt are not known, and a mutt may very well be an inbred animal. A thoroughbred is a variety of horse and has no connection with a dog. A purebred dog is one whose ancestors for many generations have been of the same breed. The only real inbreeding is the mating of father and daughter, mother and son, and brother and sister. Half-brother and sister mating is the primary cross for line breeding. It will readily be seen that brother and sister mating is much closer inbreeding than father and daughter when the daughter's mother is not also the father's sister.

Assuming that the sire and dam of an inbred mating are good physical and mental specimens, there is no reason why such matings should not be used. In fact, inbreeding is the surest way to fix desirable characteristics in a strain—but it should be kept well in mind that any undesirable characteristics of the sire or dam are also fixed.

The revulsion against inbreeding, to many, is no doubt the effect of long prohibition of human marriages too closely in the same family and the terrible consequences are cited, e.g.,

232

the Jukes family, etc. On the other hand there may be cited the Ptolemy family of Egypt, of which Cleopatra was the end of a long line of brother-sister marriages. History tells us that Cleopatra was intelligent and good to look upon. Her morals should be judged by the standards of her time.

In this defense of inbreeding I am not advocating inbreeding as the best way to breed good English Setters, but am only trying to destroy the popular misconception that inbreeding is the cause of monstrosities.

The Winning Strain

It is an established fact that in most breeds an examination of the show records of the breed over a ten-year period will show a "winning strain." This means that there are usually one or two dogs who have been able to transmit good qualities to their get, and that these good qualities are more or less passed on from generation to generation to at least the great-great-grandchildren, provided they are not out-crossed too much on the bitch's side. Such a sire is often referred to as a prepotent sire because he definitely leaves his mark on his get. Due to this prepotent sire, improvement in the breed can be secured by breeding his closely related get without ever actually using the prepotent sire. For example, by mating half-brother and half-sister, both of whom were sired by the prepotent sire, or, even once again removed, by breeding half-brother and half-sister who were sired by a son of the prepotent sire, the unmistakable stamp of the prepotent sire can be observed.

(In the earlier edition of this book, Mr. Tuck wrote that the winning strain of English Setters for the decade of the 1940's was strong in the influence of Rummey Stagboro. As proof he cited the winners of the Westminster and Morris and Essex Kennel Clubs for those years. Among them were Maro of Maridor, Daro of Maridor, End O' Maine Sorry, Prune's Own Palmer, Rip of Blue Bar, Silvermine Wagabond, Sturdy

Max II, Dean of Blue Bar, Mary of Blue Bar and Rock Falls Cavalier. In every case Rummey Stagboro was either the grandfather, great-grandfather, or great-great-grandfather of the winner. Mr. Tuck also listed thirty-three champion sons and daughters sired by Rummey Stagboro. Prior to Rummey, the prepotent sire was listed as Int. Ch. Rackets Rummey, great-grandfather of Rummey Stagboro. Rummey Stagboro's most famous son, and for a time second only to his father in his ability to transmit excellent qualities to his get, was the great Ch. Sturdy Max.

As we shall see in a later chapter, the Rummey Stagboro influence continued into more recent history, though attenuated by time, through various Rock Falls, Ludar of Blue Bar and Mike of Meadboro lines.—E.S.H.)

There are still some breeders who disregard nature's laws and work out some elaborate system of breeding that in their mind will produce flyers with mathematical precision. Just because they may accidentally get one or two good ones does not prove that their system works. Where are the many other puppies that were sold cheap or destroyed? If we will assume that Rummey Stagboro was one of the greatest English Setter studs, our faith even in his prepotency may be shaken when we consider that he served one hundred forty-five bitches, and if the average litter were five, then he would have sired seven hundred twenty-five puppies. His owner's records show that of these seven hundred twenty-five puppies only thirty-three, or 4.5 per cent, made their championships.

Following this line of reasoning your chances of producing a flyer, even when you have a super stud like Rummey Stagboro, are only about 5 per cent, and you can make your own guess what your chances are without another Rummy Stagboro. The chances that the popular idol of the day in the show ring will sire a dog as good as himself are remote. Where are his brothers and sisters? Where are his many champion sons and daughters?

These ideas are not written to be discouraging or derogatory of any particular breeder, as the general quality of English Setters is, in my opinion, the best of all times. This high quality is the result of many serious breeders striving constantly to improve the breed. It is this monthly deposit in the savings bank that builds up a reserve and not the nickels, dimes, and quarters dropped in the slot machines, trying for the jackpot.

The only means known of improving the breed of English Setters is to practice selective line breeding which is made possible by nature's laws of variation, which in turn is preponderantly the result of reduction in the germ cells of both dog and bitch at time of breeding.

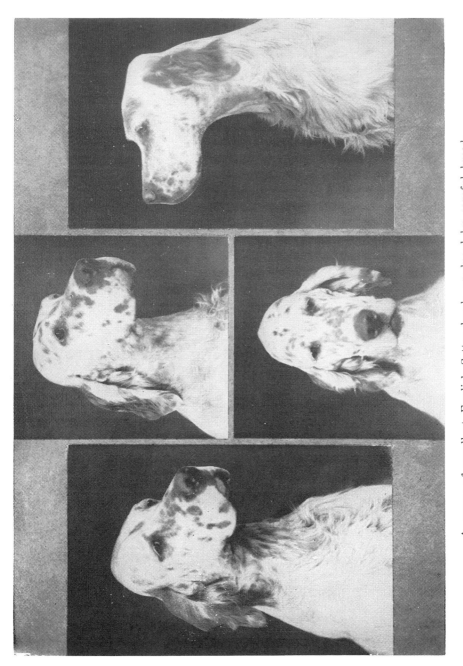

A group of excellent English Setter heads produced by careful breeding having in mind head improvement as being of major importance.

11

Laverack Type
in America

THE Laverack type English Setters in America, including Canada, are, as we know them, a relatively recent strain dating back to about 1900, or some seventy years ago. Our modern Laverack type English Setter's breeding stock was, for the most part, imported from the Mallwyd, Maesydd, Stylish, Shiplake, Rummey, and Crombie kennels from the United Kingdom, and around 1920 from Swedish imports.

The Mallwyd imports have been by far the greatest influence on our modern Laverack type English Setters, because the imports from the other kennels of the United Kingdom were strong in Mallwyd bloodlines. The introduction of Swedish blood, coming when it did, had an excellent influence by introducing hybrid vigor into the Mallwyd strain without the usual adverse characteristics of out-crossing. Rummey Stagboro was the outstanding result of this Mallwyd-Swedish outcross. A few other outcrosses were also made to the Llewellin strain, of which Mallhawk Jeff and Blue Dan of Happy Valley are the best known.

A word of caution at this point is not amiss, lest the reader confuse and take too literally the descriptive words "Laverack" and "Llewellin." As already pointed out, these names that have been tacked on to English Setters, were poorly chosen. Llewellin actually originated the Mallwyd strain, and Statter and others originated the so-called Llewellin strain (so-called in America, but not in England). Regardless of the actual facts, however, common usage in America has placed the Laverack English Setter as the Bench Show type, and the Llewellin English Setter as the Field Trial type, both representing a kind of spectacle in the Dog Show and Field Trial, and having little or no connection with the original purpose for which the English Setter was developed: a facility in the procurement of game birds for meat. (Note the title of the often quoted book, "Hunger's Prevention, or the Whole Art of Fowling, by Water and Land," 1661.)

The Mallwyd strain of English Setters was the property of Thomas Steadman of Merionitshire, Wales, and the very height of his success is exemplified in Ch. Mallwyd Albert in 1916. Mallwyd Albert was genetically sound and prepotent. The Selkirk, Grayland, Southboro, Rowland, Crombie, Shiplake, Happy Valley and other English Setter kennels, were founded on the prepotency of Mallwyd Albert, as were the Maesydd Kennels of D. K. Steadman, the son of Thomas Steadman.

The Mallwyd influence on English Setters of some 20 years ago, which predominated as will be seen by a study of the pedigree section, was due largely to such outstanding and prepotent sires as Ch. Rummey Racket, owned by H. A. Belcher of Somerville, Mass.; Ch. Racket's Rummey, bred by Rees James and owned by Erik Bergishagen of Birmingham, Mich.; and the greatest sire of his time, Rummey Stagboro, bred and owned by H. F. Steigerwald of Auburn, N. Y. Rummey Stagboro traces back to Mallwyd Albert on his dam's side, and was a direct outcross to Swedish blood on the maternal side of his sire.

238

We cannot breed to dead studs nor to bitches who have long since passed away. We can, however, continue their bloodlines, although it is more difficult to do because of the terrific discount brought to bear by "the drag of the breed."

The major credit for bringing the 20th century English Setter, Laverack type, to its present state of excellence, belongs, more or less, in the order named, to Thomas Steadman, Dr. L. Thurston Price, N. P. McConnell, A. J. Kruger, Wallace Wilgress, Dr. J. F. Daw, J. J. Sinclair, Erik Bergishagen, William F. Gilroy, Richard Jennings, Henry J. Hunt, Dr. A. A. Mitten, J. Raymond Hurley, William M. Crull, Philip Schwartz, Henry D. Myers, E. E. Elderd, C. N. Myers, Charles Palmer, Priscilla Ryan, C. H. Allen, Noah Burfoot, Henry Steigerwald, Ward C. Green, Davis H. Tuck, Mary Ann Wadsworth, Wm. T. Holt, Mr. and Mrs. John Ward Brady, Jr., Joseph Rotella, Mead Hanes, Claude and Ethel (now White) Decker, William Sears, Rachael Van Buren, Mr. and R. I. Pusey, Jr., Mrs. John Chambers, Mr. and Mrs. Peter Polley, Mr. and Mrs. Andrew Hawn, Commander Thomas W. Hall and family, Mr. and Mrs. Earl Zamarchi, John A. Stocker, Dorothy Reiter, Mr. and Mrs. James Wallace, Dr. and Mrs. George Rosen, Warren Brewbaker, Jeanne Millet, Jeanne and Lynne Smith, Mr. and Mrs. Robert Ellen, Joan Stainer, Mr. and Mrs. J. Brooks Emory, Susan Maire, Mr. and Mrs. Richard Howe, Harry Kurzrock, Mary Beth Nichol, Mr. and Mrs. Robert Ellen, Mrs. Frank Vertulia, Mr. and Mrs. Ray Parsons and Mr. and Mrs. Neal Weinstein. There are a great many others who have given freely of their time, brains and money to advance the breed, and credit is due them also. Time and perspective will add new names to the list from the generation now carrying on old bloodlines and establishing new ones. The list of great producers and pedigrees in the next chapters will write the future of the breed.

12

Great Winners and Producers of the 1930's and 1940's

IN the first edition of this book, Davis Tuck included the pictures and pedigrees of 78 English Setters that had shone in the show ring and/or produced great progeny.

As time passes, any such large compilation as 78 needs to be sifted down to the truly great dogs of the past. Space must be provided for the newcomers, some of which greatly excel their predecessors in performance.

In the reviser's judgment, 37 of the dogs appearing in the first edition merit continuation in this new edition. Unfortunately, we had no statistician in the 1930's and 1940's to compile the breeding records which appear in the next chapter for the leading winners and sires and dams of the 1950's and 1960's. However, the following list of those retained from the previous edition is representative of the best English Setters of their day. It is historically interesting because many of the dogs pictured in this chapter are the ancestors of the producers pictured in the next chapter titled "The Leading Winners, Sires and Dams of the 1950's and 1960's."

240

Ch. Blue Dan of Happy Valley
Ch. Cedric of Delwed
Ch. Corking Credit of
   Armsworth
Ch. Daro of Maridor
Ch. Dean of Blue Bar
Int. Ch. Gilroy's Chief Topic
Ch. Grayland Racket's Boy
Kanandarque Rackets Boy
Ch. Lakelands Yuba
Ch. Lancelot of Blue Bar
Ch. Lem of Blue Bar
Ch. Mallhawk's Jeff
Ch. Mallhawk's Rackets Boy
Ch. Maro of Maridor
Ch. Mary of Blue Bar
Ch. Max of Dixmont
Ch. Pat II
Ch. Pilot of Crombie of
   Happy Valley

Ch. Prune's Own Palmer
Rackets Rummey
Ch. Rip of Blue Bar
Ch. Rhett Butler of
   Silvermine
Rummey Stagboro
Ch. Rummey Sam of Stagboro
Ch. Samantha of Scyld
Ch. San Marino P.S.
Int. Ch. Silvermine Waga-
   bond
Ch. Sir Herbert of Kennel-
   worth
Ch. The Snark of Scyld
Int. Ch. Spiron
Ch. Sturdy Max
Int. Ch. Tula II of Jagersboro

(*Note:* The following dogs also appeared in the original edition: Ch. Agene's Colonel Gilbert, Ch. Rock Falls Cavalier, Ch. Rock Falls Colonel, Ch. Rock Falls Racket and Ch. Vigil of Vilmar. Since they were outstanding sires in the 1950's, their pictures, pedigrees and lists of progeny appear in the next chapter.)

CH. BLUE DAN OF HAPPY VALLEY

AKC No. 762757   Whelped April 10, 1926   Dog
Height - 24 inches   Weight - 60 pounds   Color - Blue Belton
Owner: Happy Valley Kennels, Roxborough, Philadelphia, Pa.
Breeder: D. B. LeCompte

		Leonidas of Ware	Massycromer Mallwyd
	Heather Shot Over		Ch. Primley Hesse
		Peg O' My Heart	Ch. Bachelor Racket
Gores Blue Pal			Rowlands Sparkling Beauty
		Leonidas of Ware	Massycromer Mallwyd
	Monte Carlo Topsy		Ch. Primley Hesse
		Keatings Nellie	Ch. Bachelor Racket
			Keatings Molly
		Island Count	Berkeley Rocket
	Simmon's Count Jack		Shaw's Lady Rose
		Yadkin Diana	Dobel B
LeCompte's Queen			Baldwins Princess
		Dock	Dock's Ghost
	Jones Trixie		Lady's Speedy Ghost
		Belle's Ghost	Eugene's Ghost
			Bell Benstone

242

CH. CEDRIC OF DELWED

AKC No. A-278647   Whelped February 23, 1938   Dog
Height - 26 inches   Weight - 65 pounds   Color - Orange Belton
Breeder - Owner: George F. Wedel, DeWitt, Michigan

		Spiron Jagersbo	Int. Ch. Spiron
	Rummey Stagboro		Arbu Lala B
		Selkirk Snooksie	Int. Ch. McConnell's Nori
Ch. Sturdy Max			Int. Ch. Selkirk Juliet
		Ch. Pat TT	Mountain Top Tony
	Rummey Girl of Stagboro		Ch. Lady Rowland
		Selkirk Snooksie	Int. Ch. McConnell's Nori
			Int. Ch. Selkirk Juliet
			Ch. Fernbank Blue Rock of Inglehurst
		Inglehurst Rock	Ch. Inglehurst Patches
	Ch. Rock of Stagboro		Int. Ch. McConnell's Nori
		Selkirk Snooksie	Int. Ch. Selkirk Juliet
Lutta of Delwed			Mallwyd Roy
		Ch. Pennine Patron	Misty of Coity
	Princess of Debonair		Albert's McAllister
		Kanandarque Dixie Lady	Ch. Dixie Corene

CH. CORKING CREDIT OF ARMSWORTH

AKC No. S-84422   Whelped June 19, 1945   Dog
Height - 25 inches   Weight - 63 pounds   Color - Orange Belton
Owner: Luther M. Otto, III, Armsworth Kennels, Westminster, Mass.
Breeder: Michael Murnik

```
                          Rummey Stagboro            Spiron Jagersbo
              Ch. Sturdy Max                         Selkirk Snooksie
                          Rummey Girl of Stagboro    Ch. Pat II
Ch. Daro of Maridor                                  Selkirk Snooksie
                          Rummey Stagboro            Spiron Jagersbo
              Ch. Lakeland's Dawn                    Selkirk Snooksie
                          Lakeland's Nymph           Ch. Racket's Rummey
                                                     Lakeland's Fascination
                          Ch. Sturdy Max             Rummey Stagboro
              Prune's Own Maxon                      Rummey Girl of Stagboro
                          Ch. Desire of Maridor      Rummey Stagboro
Ch. Corking Candy                                    Lakeland's Nymph
                          Ch. Sir Orkney Racket      Ch. Sir Orkney Willgress
              Corking Chloe                          Ch. Lady Molly O
                          Red Rose Suzanne           Ch. Red Rose Tim
                                                     Red Rose Winnie Winkle
```

CH. DARO OF MARIDOR

AKC No. A-231570   Whelped March 18, 1937   Dog
Height - 25 1/4 inches   Weight - 63 pounds   Color - Orange Belton
Owner: Charles Grayson Diamon, Roxbury, Conn.
Breeder: Maridor Kennels

		Spiron Jagersbo	Int. Ch. Spiron
	Rummey Stagboro		Arbu Lala B
		Selkirk Snooksie	Int. Ch. McConnell's Nori
Ch. Sturdy Max			Int. Ch. Selkirk Juliet
		Ch. Pat II	Mountain Top Tony
	Rummey Girl of Stagboro		Ch. Lady Rowland
		Selkirk Snooksie	Int. Ch. McConnell's Nori
			Int. Ch. Selkirk Juliet
		Spiron Jagersbo	Int. Ch. Spiron
	Rummey Stagboro		Arbu Lala B
		Selkirk Snooksie	Int. Ch. McConnell's Nori
Ch. Lakelands Dawn			Int. Ch. Selkirk Juliet
		Ch. Rackets Rummey	Ch. Mallwyd Ralph
	Lakelands Nymph		Stylish Pretty Polly
		Lakelands Fascination	Meadowdale Mallwyd Count
			Myers' Blue Bird

245

CH. DEAN OF BLUE BAR

AKC No. 4311325   Whelped July 14, 1938   Dog
Height - 24 3/4 inches   Weight - 55 pounds   Color - Orange Belton
Breeder-Owner: C. N. Myers, Blue Bar Kennels, Hanover, Pa.

		Int. Ch. Rackets Rummey	Ch. Mallwyd Ralph
	Ch. Mallhawk Rackets Boy		Stylish Pretty Polly
		Lady Rowland Racket	Ch. Rowlands Pathfinder
Ch. Mallhawk Jeff			Rackets Belle
		Int. Ch. Mallhawk Banker	Ch. Mallhawk Rackets Boy
	Flora Mallhawk		Patsy What
		Selkirk Mallhawk Juliet	Int. Ch. McConnell's Nori
			Int. Ch. Selkirk Juliet
		Spiron Jagersboro	Int. Ch. Spiron
	Rummey Stagboro		Arbu Lala B
		Selkirk Snooksie	Int. Ch. McConnell's Nori
Ch. Lakeland's Peaches			Int. Ch. Selkirk Juliet
		Ch. Rackets Rummey	Ch. Mallwyd Ralph
	Lakeland's Nymph		Stylish Pretty Polly
		Lakeland Fascination	Meadowdale Mallwyd Count
			Myers' Blue Bird

246

INT. CH. GILROY'S CHIEF TOPIC

AKC No. 799365   Whelped June 30, 1930   Dog
Height - 24 inches   Weight - 58 pounds   Color - Blue Belton
Owner: Mrs. Allan Ryan, Rhinebeck, N. Y.
Breeder: W. F. Gilroy

```
                                          Beachley Haig
                    Ch. Primley Nebo      Primley Hesse
        Ch. Gilroy's Speckled Chief       Ch. Gilroy's Chase
                    Clover Ridge Dottie    Ch. Clover Ridge Maid
Gilroy's Speckled Chief II                Alberts Sir Allister
                    Ch. Cole's Guess Again Dix Girl
            Clover Ridge Jane             Sir Roger's Emma
                    Ch. Clover Ridge Rose  Brown's Queen B

                                          Chase
                    Ch. Gilroy's Chase    Brown's Colo
        Ch. Gilroy's Pal                  Ch. Cole's Guess Again
                    Ch. Clover Ridge Maid  Ch. Sis Boom
Gilroy's Lady Doris                       Alberts Sir Allister
                    Ch. Cole's Guess Again Dix Girl
            Clover Ridge Jane             Sir Roger's Emma
                    Ch. Clover Ridge Rose  Brown's Queen B
```

247

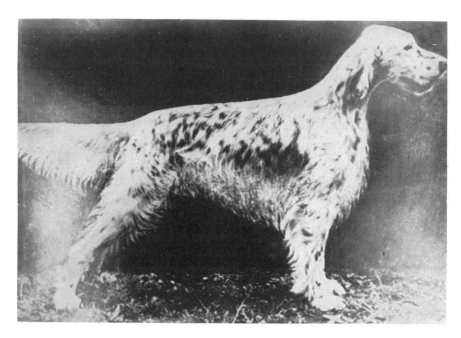

CH. GRAYLAND RACKET'S BOY

AKC No. A-310961   Whelped February 16, 1937   Dog
Height - 24 1/2 inches   Weight - 61 pounds   Color - Orange Belton
Owners: Mr. and Mrs. W. T. Holt, Rock Falls Kennel, Richmond, Va.
Breeder: Frank A. Bily

	Int. Ch. Spiron	Ch. Pluto Horridoh
Spiron Jagersbo		Tonny
	Arbu Lala B	Quip Cadillac
Rummey Stagboro		Ch. Gloria's Peggy B
	Int. Ch. McConnell's Nori	Int. Ch. Racket's Rummey
Selkirk Snooksie		Ch. Grayland Snowbird
	Int. Ch. Selkirk Juliet	Ch. Rowlands Pathfinder
		Ch. Grayland Snowbird
	Ch. Mallwyd Ralph	Ch. Mallwyd Albert
Int. Ch. Racket's Rummey		Kell View Nell
	Stylish Pretty Polly	Ch. Bachelor Racket
Bleheim Violet		Stylish Kate
	Snowden Ralph	Ch. Mallwyd Ralph
Principe Bonnie		Ch. Grayland June
	Graylands Belle	Overland Superfine
		Grayland Lassie

248

KANANDARQUE RACKETS BOY

AKC No. 920907   Whelped December 7, 1932   Dog
Height - 25 1/2 inches   Weight - 65 pounds   Color - Orange Belton
Owner: C. N. Myers, Blue Bar Kennels, Hanover, Pa.
Breeder: A. J. Krueger

	Ch. Mallwyd Ralph	Ch. Mallwyd Albert
Int. Ch. Rackets Rummey		Kell View Nell
	Stylish Pretty Polly	Ch. Bachelor Racket
Ch. Mallhawk Racket's Boy		Stylish Kate
	Ch. Rowl ands Pathfinder	Ch. Rowlands Credential
Imp. Lady Rowland Racket		Ch. Lady Rowland Sensation
	Rackets Belle	Ch. Bachelor Racket
		Kettings Molly
	Int. Ch. Rackets Rummey	Ch. Mallwyd Ralph
Int. Ch. McConnell's Nori		Stylish Pretty Polly
	Grayland Snowbird	Ch. Mallwyd Ralph
Selkirks Mallhawk Juliet		Ch. Grayland June
	Ch. Rowlands Pathfinder	Ch. Rowlands Credential
Int. Ch. Selkirks Juliet		Ch. Lady Rowland Sensation
	Grayland Snowbird	Ch. Mallwyd Ralph
		Ch. Grayland June

249

CH. LAKELANDS YUBA

AKC No. 880734   Whelped March 27, 1932   Dog
Height - 25 1/2 inches   Weight - 64 1/2 pounds   Color - Blue Belton
Owner: Charles Palmer, East Longmeadow, Mass.
Breeder: Henry D. Meyers

```
                                          Ch. Pluto Horridoh
                   Int. Ch. Spiron        Tonny
        Spiron Jagersbo                   Quip Cadillac
                   Arbu Lala B            Ch. Gloria's Peggy B
Rummey Stagboro                           Int. Ch. Racket's Rummey
                   Int. Ch. McConnell's Nori  Ch. Grayland Snowbird
        Selkirk Snooksie                  Ch. Rowlands Pathfinder
                   Int. Ch. Selkirk Juliet    Ch. Grayland Snowbird

                                          Ch. Mallwyd Albert
                   Ch. Mallwyd Ralph      Kell View Nell
        Ch. Rackets Rummey                Ch. Bachelor Racket
                   Stylish Pretty Polly   Stylish Katie
Lakeland's Nymph                          Junedale Prince
                   Meadowdale Mallwyd Count    May Fairbanks
        Lakeland Fascination              Cook's Blue Prince
                   Myers' Blue Bird       Lad Rodney's Doll
```

250

CH. LANCELOT OF BLUE BAR

AKC No. A-963950   Whelped July 12, 1945   Dog
Height - 25 1/4 inches   Weight - 70 pounds   Color - Orange Belton
Owners: Mr. and Mrs. Davis H. Tuck, Silvermine Kennels, Redding Ridge, Conn.
Breeder: C. N. Myers

```
                    Ch. Mallhawk Jeff          Ch. Mallhawk Rackets Boy
            Roy of Blue Bar                    Flora Mallhawk
                    Kanandarque Lovelyness     Kanadarque Rackets Boy
  Ch. Jesse of Blue Bar                        Dawn of Stagboro
                    Rummey Stagboro            Spiron Jagersbo
            Ch. Lovely Lady of Stucile         Selkirk Snooksie
                    Ch. Modern Maid of Stucile Ch. Sir Orkney Wilgress, Jr.
                                               Wilgress Lady Luck

                    Ch. Mallhawk Rackets Boy   Int. Ch. Rackets Rummey
            Ch. Mallhawk Jeff                  Lady Rowland Racket
                    Flora Mallhawk             Int. Ch. Mallhawk Banker
  Mag of Blue Bar                              Selkirk's Mallhawk Juliet
                    Rummey Stagboro            Spiron Jagersbo
            Ch. Lakeland's Peaches             Selkirk Snooksie
                    Lakeland's Nymph           Int. Ch. Rackets Rummey
                                               Lakeland Fascination
```

CH. LEM OF BLUE BAR

AKC No. A-495250   Whelped May 19, 1941   Dog
Height - 25 1/4 inches   Weight - 62 pounds   Color - Orange Belton
Owner: C. N. Myers, Blue Bar Kennels, Hanover, Pa.
Breeder: J. Raymond Hurley

	Ch. Mallhawk Rackets Boy	Int. Ch. Rackets Rummey
Ch. Mallhawks Jeff		Lady Rowland Racket
	Flora Mallhawk	Int. Ch. Mallhawk Banker
Lone Ace of Kanandarque		Selkirk Mallhawk Juliet
	Ch. Esterada Blue Haze	Rackets Rummey
Esterada's White Flyer		Keatings Belle
	Miss Whitey Flyer	Ch. Kanandarque Chief
		Ch. Miss Grey Flyer
	Ch. Mallhawk Rackets Boy	Int. Ch. Rackets Rummey
Kanandarque Racket Boy		Lady Rowland Racket
	Selkirks Mallhawk Juliet	Int. Ch. McConnell's Nori
Lovely Dawn of Kanandarque		Int. Ch. Selkirk Juliet
	Ch. Mallhawk Banker	Ch. Mallhawk Rackets Boy
Dawn of Stagboro		Int. Ch. Patsy What
	Ch. Fly of Stagboro	Inglehurst Rock
		Selkirk Snooksie

252

CH. MALLHAWK'S JEFF

AKC No. A-1910   Whelped May 22, 1935   Dog
Height - 25 1/2 inches   Weight - 60 pounds   Color - Orange Belton
Owner: C. N. Myers, Blue Bar Kennels, Hanover, Pa.
Breeder: Earl C. Kruger

```
                                              Ch. Mallwyd Albert
                    Ch. Mallwyd Ralph         Kell View Nell
        Int. Ch. Rackets Rummey               Ch. Bachelor Racket
                    Stylish Pretty Polly       Stylish Katie
Ch. Mallhawk Rackets Boy                      Ch. Rowland Credential
                    Ch. Rowlands Pathfinder   Ch. Lady Rowland Sensation
        Lady Rowland Racket                   Ch. Bachelor Racket
                    Rackets Belle             Keatings Molly

                                              Int. Ch. Rackets Rummey
                    Ch. Mallhawk Rackets Boy  Lady Rowland Racket
        Int. Ch. Mallhawk Banker             Leonidas of Ware
                    Int. Ch. Patsy What       Queen Mohawk Girl
Flora Mallhawk                                Int. Ch. Rackets Rummey
                    Int. Ch. McConnell's Nori Grayland Snowbird
        Selkirk Mallhawk Juliet              Ch. Rowlands Pathfinder
                    Int. Ch. Selkirk's Juliet Grayland Snowbird
```

CH. MALLHAWKS RACKETS BOY

AKC No. 595867   Whelped March 26, 1926   Dog
Height - 26 inches   Weight - 73 pounds   Color - Orange Belton
Owner: A. J. Kruger, Mallhawk Kennels, Troutdale, Oregon
Breeder: G. Vanaken

		Mallwyd Markham
	Ch. Mallwyd Albert	Mallwyd Violet
	Ch. Mallwyd Ralph	Smut of Hest
	Kell View Nell	Bob White Killview Meg
Int. Ch. Rackets Rummey		Prince Charming II
	Ch. Bachelor Racket	Stylish Katie
	Stylish Pretty Polly	Mallwyd Prince
	Stylish Katie	Gypsy Girl II
		Ch. Mallwyd Rowland
	Ch. Rowlands Credential	Woodsmore Peggy
	Ch. Rowlands Pathfinder	Ch. Bachelor Racket
	Ch. Lady Rowland Sensation	Snowden Lady Rowland
Lady Rowland Racket		Prince Charming II
	Ch. Bachelor Racket	Stylish Katie
	Rackets Belle	Arbutus Sirdar
	Keatings Molly	Count's Molly Whitestone

CH. MARO OF MARIDOR

AKC No. A-231572   Whelped March 18, 1937   Dog
Height - 25 inches   Weight - 60 pounds   Color - Orange Belton
Owner: Wilfred Kennedy, Detroit, Mich.
Breeder:: Maridor Kennels

```
                              Spiron Jagersbo          Int. Ch. Spiron
                  Rummey Stagboro                      Arbu Lala B
                              Selkirk Snooksie         Int. Ch. McConnell's Nori
Ch. Sturdy Max                                         Int. Ch. Selkirk Juliet
                              Ch. Pat II               Mountain Top Tony
                  Rummey Girl of Stagboro              Ch. Lady Rowland
                              Selkirk Snooksie         Int. Ch. McConnell's Nori
                                                       Int. Ch. Selkirk Juliet

                              Spiron Jagersbo          Int. Ch. Spiron
                  Rummey Stagboro                      Arbu Lala B
                              Selkirk Snooksie         Int. Ch. McConnell's Nori
Ch. Lakeland's Dawn                                    Int. Ch. Selkirk Juliet
                              Ch. Rackets Rummey       Ch. Mallwyd Ralph
                  Lakeland's Nymph                     Stylish Pretty Polly
                              Lakelands Fascination    Meadowdale Mallwyd Count
                                                       Myers' Blue Bird
```

CH. MARY OF BLUE BAR

AKC No. S-109320   Whelped November 13, 1946   Bitch
Height - 24 inches   Weight - 54 pounds   Color - Orange Belton
Breeder-Owner : C. N. Myers, Blue Bar Kennels, Hanover, Pa.

```
                                              Ch. Mallhawk Rackets Boy
                    Ch. Mallhawk's Jeff       Flora Mallhawk
           Ray of Blue Bar                    Kanandarque Rackets Boy
                    Kanandarque Lovelyness    Dawn of Stagboro
  Ch. Jesse of Blue Bar                       Spiron Jagersbo
                    Rummey Stagboro           Selkirk Snooksie
           Ch. Lovely Lady of Stucile         Ch. Sir Orkney Wilgress, Jr.
                    Ch. Modern Maid of Stucile  Wilgress Lady Luck
                                              Ch. Mallhawk Rackets Boy
                    Ch. Mallhawk's Jeff       Flora Mallhawk
           Sammy of Blue Bar                  Kanandarque Rackets Boy
                    Kanandarque Lovelyness    Dawn of Stagboro
  Ch. Lola of Blue Bar                        Ch. Mallhawk Rackets Boy
                    Kanandarque Rackets Boy   Selkirk Mallhawk Juliet
           Faith of Blue Bar                  Ch. Rackets Rummey
                    Saga Oakholm II           Ch. Mallhawk Sister
```

256

CH. MAX OF DIXMONT

AKC no. A-387325   Whelped March 17, 1939   Dog
Height - 25 inches   Weight - 68 pounds   Color - Orange Belton
Owner: James S. Haring, Jr., Sundridge Kennels, Ridgewood, N. J.
Breeder: Neil E. Wakeman

	Spiron Jagersbo	Int. Ch. Spiron
Rummey Stagboro		Arbu Lala B
	Selkirk Snooksie	Int. Ch. McConnell's Nori
Ch. Lakeland's Yuba		Int. Ch. Selkirk Juliet
	Int. Ch. Rackets Rummey	Ch. Mallwyd Ralph
Lakeland's Nymph		Stylish Pretty Polly
	Lakeland's Fascination	Meadowdale Mallwyd Count
		Myer's Blue Bird
	Rummey Stagboro	Spiron Jagersbo
Ch. Sturdy Max		Selkirk Snooksie
	Rummey Girl of Stagboro	Ch. Pat II
Dutchess of Dixmont		Selkirk Snooksie
	Int. Ch. Rackets Rummey	Ch. Mallwyd Ralph
Lakeland's Nymph		Stylish Pretty Polly
	Lakeland's Fascination	Meadowdale Mallwyd Count
		Myer's Blue Bird

CH. PAT II

AKC No. 609965   Whelped September 7, 1926   Dog
Height - 25 inches   Weight - 63 pounds   Color - Orange Belton
Owner: Captain Thomas W. Reilly, Newfoundland, N. J.
Breeder: C. H. Stewart

	Bob Lynk	Mallwyd Edward
Thorn Lake Tony		Rodger Blue Bell
	Lady Lemon Molly	Meadowview Bob Roy
Mountain Top Tony		Meadowview Vassar
	Ch. Sir Roger de Coverly II	Sir Roger de Coverly
Cute of Playmore		Blue Girl Janie
	Beck's Peg O' My Heart	Mallwyd Invader
		Wyoming Valley Valma
		Mallwyd John
	Ch. Mallwyd Rowland	Mallwyd Rose
Ch. Rowland's Credential		Ch. Mallwyd Albert
	Woodsmore Peggy	Mallwyd Margot
Ch. Lady Rowland		Prince Charming II
	Ch. Bachelor Racket	Stylish Katie
Ch. Lady Rowland's Sensation		Ch. Mallwyd Rowland
	Snowden Lady Rowland	Woodsmore Peggy

CH. PILOT OF CROMBIE OF HAPPY VALLEY

AKC No. 881743   Whelped February 21, 1930   Dog
Height - 25 1/2 inches   Weight - 60 pounds   Color - Blue Belton
Owner: Happy Valley Kennels, Roxborough, Philadelphia, Pa.
Breeder: Prof. L. Turton Price, Dundee, Scotland

			Fosters Double
		O' By Jingo	Fleda
	Maesydd Poy of Ardagh		Beachley Haig
		Maesydd Pansy	Rufflyn Fickle
Albert of Crombie			Tarnside Major
		Ch. Crossfell	Grouse of Crossfell
	Maesydd Monica		Rufflyn Clansman
		Nan of Crombie	Glaisnock Kate
			Mallwyd Foster
		Fosters Double	Myrtle Connie
	O' By Jingo		Glaisnock Haig
		Fleda	Glaisnock Nannie
Patch of Crombie			Glaisnock Jim
		Beachley Haig	Craigielands Madge
	Maesydd Pansy		Ch. Mallwyd Albert
		Rufflyn Fickle	Rufflyn Fanela

259

CH. PRUNE'S OWN PALMER

AKC No. A-853935   Whelped July 4, 1944   Dog
Height -26 inches   Weight - 70 pounds   Color - Lemon Belton
Owner: N. Burfoot, Elizabeth City, N. C.
Breeder: Albert K. Thommen

```
                                           Rummey Stagboro
                      Ch. Sturdy Max        Rummey Girl of Stagboro
          Ch. Prune's Own Sensation         Rummey Stagboro
                      Ch. Desire of Maridor  Lakeland Nymph
Ch. San Marino P. S.                         Ch. Sir Orkney Willgress
                      Orkney Master Key      Orkney Masterpiece
          Fern Hill Trigger P. S.            Ch. Sturdy Max
                      Fern Hill Gee Gee      Hi Nellie P. S.

                                           Rummey Stagboro
                      Ch. Sturdy Max        Rummey Girl of Stagboro
          Ch. Maro of Maridor               Rummey Stagboro
                      Ch. Lakeland Dawn      Lakeland's Nymph
Prune's Own Duchess                          Ch. Spiron Jagersbo
                      Rummey Stagboro        Selkirk Snooksie
          Ch. Roger Dale Flirtation          Ch. Kanandarque Chief
                      Queen of Stagboro      Ch. Smile of Stagboro
```

RACKETS RUMMEY

AKC - No. 428961   Whelped December, 1922   Dog
Height - 26 inches   Weight - 70 pounds   Color - Orange Belton
Owner: Erik Bergishagen, Birmingham, Mich.
Breeder: Rees Jones

```
                                    Mallwyd Markham    Mallwyd Major
                    Ch. Mallwyd Albert                 Mallwyd Evelyn
                                    Mallwyd Violet     Ch. Mallwyd Diamond
Ch. Mallwyd Ralph                                      Mallwyd Rose
                                    Smut of Hest       Bolton Simon
                    Kell View Nell                     Bolton Katie
                                    Kell View Meg      Mallwyd Blue Prince
                                                       Juno
                                    Prince Charming II Ch. Mallwyd Bob
                    Ch. Bachelor Racket                Rockline Ladybird
                                    Stylish Katie      Mallwyd Prince
Stylish Pretty Polly                                   Gypsy Girl II
                                    Mallwyd Prince     Mallwyd Bob
                    Stylish Katie                      Victoria
                                    Gypsy Girl II      Mallwyd Major
                                                       Arbutus Pearl
```

CH. RIP OF BLUE BAR

AKC No. A-749742   Whelped July 1, 1943   Dog
Height - 26 inches   Weight - 68 pounds   Color - Orange Belton
Breeder-Owner: C. N. Myers, Blue Bar Kennels, Hanover, Pa.

		Ch. Mallhawk Rackets Boy	Int. Ch. Rackets Rummey
	Ch. Mallhawk Jeff		Lady Rowland Racket
		Flora Mallhawk	Int. Ch. Mallhawk Banker
Ch. Dean of Blue Bar			Selkirk Mallhawk Juliet
		Rummey Stagboro	Spiron Jagersbo
	Ch. Lakeland's Peaches		Selkirk Snooksie
		Lakeland's Nymph	Ch. Rackets Rummey
			Lakeland's Fascination
		Ch. Mallhawk Jeff	Ch. Mallhawk Rackets Boy
	Roy of Blue Bar		Flora Mallhawk
		Kanandarque Lovelyness	Kanandarque Rackets Boy
Ina of Blue Bar			Dawn of Stagboro
		Inglehurst Rock	Ch. Fernbank Blue Rock
	Ch. Fly of Stagboro		Inglehurst Patches
		Selkirk Snooksie	Int. Ch. McConnell's Nori
			Int. Ch. Selkirk Juliet

262

CH. RHETT BUTLER OF SILVERMINE

AKC No. A-236797   Whelped, January 26, 1938   Dog
Height - 25 1/2 inches Weight - 70 pounds   Color - Orange Belton
Breeder-Owner: Davis H. Tuck, Silvermine, Redding Ridge, Conn.

		Int. Ch. Spiron	Ch. Pluto Horridoh
	Spiron Jagersbo		Tonny
		Arbu Lala B	Quip Cadillac
Rummey Stagboro			Ch. Gloria's Peggy B
		Int. Ch. McConnell's Nori	Int. Ch. Racket's Rummey
	Selkirk Snooksie		Ch. Grayland Snowbird
		Int. Ch. Selkirk Juliet	Ch. Rowlands Pathfinder
			Ch. Grayland Snowbird
		Gilroy's Speckled Chief II	Ch. Gilroy's Speckled Chief
	Int. Ch. Gilroy's Chief Topic		Clover Ridge Jane
		Gilroy's Lady Doris	Ch. Gilroy's Pal
Lady Dian of Silvermine			Clover Ridge Jane
		Int. Ch. Racket's Rummey	Ch. Mallwyd Ralph
	Racket's Nell		Stylish Pretty Polly
		Keating's Nellie	Ch. Bachelor Racket
			Keating's Mollie

RUMMEY STAGBORO

AKC No. 746120   Whelped, August 31, 1929   Dog
Height - 26 inches   Weight - 65 pounds   Color - Orange Belton
Breeder-Owner: Henry F. Steigerwald, Stagboro Kennels, Auburn, N. Y.

```
                    Ch. Pluto Horridoh        Brush
        Int. Ch. Spiron                       Ch. Hera
                    Tonny                     Ch. White Noirhat
    Spiron Jagersbo                           Sussan
                    Quip Cadillac             Ch. A Real Beau
        Arbu Lala B                           Brightfield Good Fairy
                    Ch. Gloria's Peggy B      Linwood Spot
                                              Ch. Watlands Gloria
                                              Ch. Mallwyd Ralph
                    Int. Ch. Racket's Rummey  Stylish Pretty Polly
        Int. Ch. McConnell's Nori             Ch. Mallwyd Ralph
                    Ch. Grayland Snowbird      Grayland June
    Selkirk Snooksie                          Ch. Rowlands Credential
                    Ch. Rowlands Pathfinder   Ch. Lady Rowlands Sensation
        Int. Ch. Selkirk Juliet               Ch. Mallwyd Ralph
                    Ch. Grayland Snowbird      Grayland June
```

264

CH. RUMMEY SAM OF STAGBORO

AKC No. A-411011   Whelped February 20, 1939   Dog
Height - 25 1/4 inches   Weight - 65 pounds   Color - Orange Belton
Owner: M. L. Hanes, Buffalo, N. Y.
Breeder: Stagboro Kennels

```
                        Spiron Jagersbo          Int. Ch. Spiron
            Rummey Stagboro                       Arbu Lala B.
                        Selkirk Snooksie         Int. Ch. McConnell's Nori
Rummey II Stagboro                                Int. Ch. Selkirk Juliet
                        Kanandarque Racket's Boy  Ch. Mallhawk Racket's Boy
            Ch. Ladybelle of Stagboro             Selkirk Mallhawk Juliet
                        Ch. Fly of Stagboro       Ch. Inglehurst Rock
                                                  Selkirk Snooksie
                        Kanandarque Racket's Boy  Ch. Mallhawk Racket's Boy
            Ch. Mark of Stagboro                  Selkirk Mallhawk Juliet
                        Ch. Fly of Stagboro       Ch. Inglehurst Rock
Kate of Stagboro                                  Selkirk Snooksie
                        Rummey Stagboro           Spiron Jagersbo
            Racket Mary Ann                       Selkirk Snooksie
                        Lakeland Nymph            Int. Ch. Racket's Rummey
                                                  Lakeland Fascination
```

CH. SAMANTHA OF SCYLD

AKC No. A-408376　　　Whelped March 27, 1940　　　　　Bitch
Height - 25 3/4 inches　　Weight - 51 pounds　　Color - Orange Belton
Breeder-Owner:　Ward C. Green, South Norwalk, Connecticut

	Int. Ch. Spiron	Ch. Pluto Horridoh
Spiron Jagersbo		Tony
	Arbu Lala B.	Quip Cadillac
Rummey Stagboro		Ch. Gloria's Peggy B.
	Int. Ch. McConnell's Nori	Int. Ch. Racket's Rummey
Selkirk Snooksie		Ch. Grayland's Snowbird
	Ch. Selkirk Juliet	Ch. Rowland's Pathfinder
		Ch. Grayland's Snowbird
	Rummey Stagboro	Spiron Jagersbo
Ch. Sturdy Max		Selkirk Snooksie
	Rummey Girl of Stagboro	Ch. Pat II
Jane of Maridor		Selkirk Snooksie
	Ch. Phar Lap P. S.	Ch. Gilroy's Speckled Chief
Hi Nellie P. S.		Double Bronx P. S.
	Ch. Highlight Lady	Ch. Highlight P. S.
		Ch. Post Road Peggie

266

CH. SAN MARINO P.S.

AKC No. A-722842   Whelped June 17, 1942   Dog
Height - 24 1/4 inches   Weight - 61 pounds   Color - Blue Belton
Breeder-Owner : Philip Schwartz, Brookside, Suffield, Connecticut

```
                    Rummey Stagboro           Spiron Jagersbo
          Ch. Sturdy Max                      Selkirk Snooksie
                    Rummey Girl of Stagboro   Ch. Pat II
Ch. Prune's Own Sensation                     Selkirk Snooksie
                    Rummey Stagboro           Spiron Jagersbo
          Ch. Desire of Maridor               Selkirk Snooksie
                    Lakeland's Nymph          Rackets Rummey
                                              Lakeland's Fascination
                    Ch. Bachelor Rocket       Prince Charming II
          Ch. Sir Orkney Willgress            Stylish Katie
                    Coate's Lady Gravell      Ch. Mallwyd Rowland
Fern Hill Trigger P. S.                       Woodsmoor Peggy
                    Ch. Sturdy Max            Rummey Stagboro
          Fern Hill Gee Gee                   Rummey Girl of Stagboro
                    Hi Nellie P. S.           Ch. Phar Lap P. S.
                                              Ch. Highlight Lady
```

267

INT. CH. SILVERMINE WAGABOND

AKC No. A-837082   Whelped August 14, 1944   Dog
Height - 26 inches   Weight - 70 pounds   Color - Blue Belton
Owner: Davis H. Tuck, Silvermine, Redding Ridge, Conn.
Breeder: Augustus Kellog

                    Spiron Jagersbo   Int. Ch. Spiron
            Rummey Stagboro   Arbu Lala B
                    Selkirk Snooksie   Int. Ch. McConnell's Nori
    Ch. Rhett Butler of Silvermine   Int. Ch. Selkirk Juliet
                    Int. Ch. Gilroy's Chief Topic   Gilroy's Speckled Chief II
            Lady Dian of Silvermine   Gilroy's Lady Doris
                    Racket's Nell   Int. Ch. Racket's Rummey
                                              Keating's Nellie
                                              Rummey Stagboro
                    Ch. Lakeland Yuba   Lakeland's Nymph
            Fox Flame   Ch. Sturdy Max
                    Duchess of Dixmont   Lakeland's Nymph
    Keyfield Judy   Spiron Jagersbo
                    Rummey Stagboro   Selkirk Snooksie
            Lavender Lady   Dusty D
                    Blue Diana   Betsy D

CH. SIR HERBERT OF KENNELWORTH

AKC No. S-242571   Whelped October 12, 1947   Dog
Height - 26 inches   Weight - 65 pounds   Color - Orange Belton
Owner: C. N. Myers, Hanover, Pa.
Breeder: David Ross Scott

```
                 Ch. Mallhawk Jeff              Ch. Mallhawk Racket's Boy
          Ch. Dean of Blue Bar                  Flora Mallhawk
                 Ch. Lakeland Peaches           Rummey Stagboro
    Ch. Rip of Blue Bar                         Lakeland Nymph
                 Roy of Blue Bar                Ch. Mallhawk's Jeff
          Ina of Blue Bar                       Kanandarque Loveliness
                 Ch. Fly of Stagboro            Inglehurst Rock
                                                Selkirk Snooksie
                                                Rummey Stagboro
                 Int. Ch. Maxie of Stagboro     Kate of Stagboro
          Banker of Fallondale                  Rummey Stagboro
                 Ch. Grayland Orange Blossom    Mallhawks Lady Daine
    Vivacious Doll of Vilmar                    Rummey Stagboro
                 Ch. Sturdy Max                 Rummey Girl of Stagboro
          Delta of Larana                       Rummey Stagboro
                 Ch. Lakeland Dawn              Lakeland's Nymph
```

CH. THE SNARK OF SCYLD

AKC No. A-687708   Whelped June 15, 1943   Dog
Height - 25 3/4 inches   Weight - 61 pounds   Color - Orange Belton
Breeder-Owner: Ward C. Green, South Norwalk, Connecticut

		Int. Ch. Spiron
	Spiron Jagersbo	Arbu Lala B
Rummey Stagboro		Int. Ch. McConnell's Nori
	Selkirk Snooksie	Ch. Selkirk Juliet
Ch. Sturdy Max		Mountain Top Tony
	Ch. Pat II	Ch. Lady Rowland
Rummey Girl of Stagboro		Int. Ch. McConnell's Nori
	Selkirk Snooksie	Ch. Selkirk Juliet
		Int. Ch. Spiron
	Spiron Jagersbo	Arbu Lala B
Rummey Stagboro		Int. Ch. McConnell's Nori
	Selkirk Snooksie	Ch. Selkirk Juliet
Ch. Samantha of Scyld		Rummey Stagboro
	Ch. Sturdy Max	Rummey Girl of Stagboro
Jane of Maridor		Ch. Phar Lap P. S.
	Hi Nellie P. S.	Ch. Highlight Lady

INT. CH. SPIRON

AKC No. 509949   Whelped April 19, 1916   Dog
Height - 26 inches   Weight - 70 pounds   Color - Blue Belton
Owner: Eric Bergishagen, Birmingham, Michigan
Breeder: Herr Wilhelm Carlberg

```
                          Dan
             Brush
                          Windi
Ch. Pluto Horridoh
                          Boy                 Ponto
             Ch. Hera Jaegerhus               Bella av Marndrup
                          Dora av Jaegerhus   Ponto
                                              Cora
                          Ch. Noirhat Monk II Blue Monk
             Ch. White Noirhat                Lize
                          White Frigg         Odd
                                              Beauty E
Tonny
                          Leader of Salop     Duke
             Sussan                           Belle
                          Gitta               Compton Ben
                                              Gerda av Stavanger
```

CH. STURDY MAX

AKC No. 944324   Whelped October 12, 1932   Dog
Height - 25 3/4 inches   Weight - 65 pounds   Color - Orange Belton
Owner: Dr. L. T. Rogers, Roger Dale Kennels, Stamford, Conn.
Breeder: Sturdy Dog Food Company

<pre>
                Int. Ch. Spiron   Ch. Pluto Horridoh
          Spiron Jagersbo   Tony
                Arbu Lala B   Quip Cadillac
    Rummey Stagboro   Ch. Gloria's Peggy B.
                Int. Ch. McConnell's Nori Int. Ch. Racket's Rummey
          Selkirk Snooksie   Ch. Grayland Snowbird
                Int. Ch. Selkirk Juliet Ch. Rowland's Pathfinder
                                         Ch. Grayland Snowbird

                Mountain Top Tony   Thorn Lake Tony
          Ch. Pat II   Cute of Playmore
                Ch. Lady Rowland   Ch. Rowland's Credentials
    Rummey Girl of Stagboro   Ch. Lady Rowland's Sensation
                Int. Ch. McConnell's Nori Int. Ch. Racket's Rummey
          Selkirk Snooksie   Ch. Grayland Snowbird
                Int. Ch. Selkirk Juliet Ch. Rowland's Pathfinder
                                         Ch. Grayland Snowbird
</pre>

272

INT. CH. TULA II OF JAGERSBO

AKC No. 781052   Whelped March 14, 1930   Bitch
Height - 23 3/4 inches   Weight - 57 pounds   Color - Orange Belton
Breeder-Owner: Erik Bergishagen, Birmingham, Michigan

```
                              Ch. Mallwyd Albert      Mallwyd Marksman
                Ch. Mallwyd Ralph                     Mallwyd Violet
                              Kell View Nell          Smut of Hest
Int. Ch. Rackets Rummey                               Kell View Meg
                              Ch. Bachelor Racket     Prince Charming II
                Stylish Pretty Polly                  Stylish Katie
                              Stylish Katie           Mallwyd Prince
                                                      Gypsy Girl II
                              Pluto Horridoh          Brush
                Ch. Spiron                            Ch. Hera Jagerhus
                              Tonny                   Ch. White Noirhat
Int. Ch. Tula Jagerhem                                Sussan

                Ch. Kally Jagerhem
```

13

The Leading Sires and
Dams of the
1950's and 1960's

———————————————

THE following compilation represents an unequalled contribution to the future of the English Setter. It is the labor of love of Mrs. Peter C. Polley and Mrs. John Dillon, former secretaries of the English Setter Association of America and two of the greatest benefactors the breed will ever know.

They poured thousands of hours of painstaking effort into this list. It is priceless because it offers the breeders of today and tomorrow a **blueprint for breeding** unique in the annals of pure-bred dog lore. From it, any breeder may prepare and accumulate a chart of interesting combinations to research and plan his own breeding program.

To qualify for entry herein, the minimum number of champions produced was set at three. The reader may extend this compilation by adding new champions as produced by the listed dogs. The champion progeny listed are up to date as of the February 1970 issue of **Pure-bred Dogs—The American**

Kennel Gazette, published monthly by the American Kennel Club, 51 Madison Avenue, New York, N. Y. Reference to later issues of this publication will extend and amplify this listing as long as the official AKC magazine publishes the names of new champions. These continuing studies can be a pleasurable, creative and rewarding activity.

The wise breeder will keep in mind that sheer numbers of champions produced are not necessarily the only criteria for considering a sire or dam a "great" producer. Frequency of matings, outstanding show records, accessibility to certain sires and dams, and other factors often have a bearing on the records. A sire or dam may produce several champions from only one litter, and never produce another champion; or it may "nick" successfully with one mate but not others. Even repeated matings of the same sire and dam may not duplicate the high quality of progeny born of the first mating; gene influences may vary from mating to mating of the same parents. The **quality** of champions, preferably from more than one mate, is the best measure of a stud or dam.

The reader is strongly advised to temper his statistical study with a sound knowledge of breeding principles, good judgment and the fruits of his own experience.

As an author, editor and publisher, the reviser of this book is painfully aware of the occasional error that inevitably creeps into any such complex compilation as follows. While every effort has been made to insure accuracy—even to the point of correcting an owner's information by reference to AKC records—the publisher will welcome notice of errors providing, however, that the correction has been verified by the AKC. The publisher hereby absolves the compilers from any errors which may appear. They have the most meticulous minds he has ever encountered. But several other minds—of editors, typesetters, proofreaders and the reviser himself— have worked on the compilation since it was prepared.

(IMPORTANT!—The following abbreviations, designations and information should be reviewed by the reader for proper understanding of the compilation.)

Am. & Can. Ch. indicates dog has been awarded championship certificates by the American and Canadian Kennel Clubs.

If **Am.** does not appear before **Ch.**, dog is an American champion only. If **Can.** only appears before **Ch.**, dog is a Canadian champion only.

Ch. is omitted before names of American champion progeny of listed sires and dams, to save space and eliminate needless repetition.

Numbers following dogs' names, such as **S-454627**, represent registrations in the American or Canadian Kennel Clubs.

Numbers in parentheses, such as **(2)**, represent number of champions sired by or out of progeny listed.

Pedigrees are given for the most outstanding sires and dams. In some cases, where pedigrees appear elsewhere for sires and dams of outstanding producers, no pedigrees are shown for the latter, and the reader may construct such pedigrees to the fifth generation. In fact, the reader will find the construction of pedigrees, from the data given herein, to be a fascinating exercise, all the more informative because he is doing it himself. The influence of such studs as Rummey Stagboro, Sturdy Max, Rock Falls Cavalier, Dean of Blue Bar, Rip of Blue Bar, Rock Falls Colonel, Rock Falls Racket, Ludar of Blue Bar, Margand Lord Baltimore, Ben-Dar's Winning Stride and The Rock of Stone Gables can be readily traced by analysis of the pedigrees in this and the preceding chapters. An absorbing game may be played by predicting the prepotent and winning lines of the future from the backgrounds of living champions listed under the leading sires and dams of the 1950's and 1960's.

Note that pictures of champion progeny often appear after their respective sires or dams. In other cases, the progeny themselves have produced sufficient champions to warrant special listings of their own.

CH. AGENE'S COLONEL GILBERT, S-108277

			Ch. Mallhawk Rackets Boy
Ch. Rip of Blue Bar	Ch. Dean of Blue Bar	Ch. Mallhawk Jeff	Flora Mallhawk
		Ch. Lakeland's Peaches	Rummey Stagboro
			Lakeland's Nymph
	Ina of Blue Bar	Roy of Blue Bar	Ch. Mallhawk Jeff
			Kanandarque Loveliness
		Ch. Fly of Stagboro	Inglehurst Rock
			Selkirk Snooksie
			Int. Ch. Spiron
Ch. Blossom of Stagboro	Rummey Stagboro	Spiron Jagersbo	Arbu Lala B
		Selkirk Snooksie	Int. Ch. McConnell's Nori
			Int. Ch. Selkirk Juliet
	Nancy Girl of Stagboro	Rummey Stagboro	Spiron Jagersbo
			Selkirk Snooksie
		Ch. Knoll Croft Nancy Lou	Ch. Knoll Croft Prince
			Ch. Nellie of Stagboro

<u>Sire of 5 Champions</u>:   <u>Out of</u>:

Agene's Blue Colonel   S-502697   ⎫
Agene's Ladybird   S-502700   ⎪
Agene's Colonel Jack G   S-555647   ⎬   Agene's Texas Blue Bonnet
Agene's Dixie Jubilee   S-355770   ⎪
Agene's Holli-Jo   S-355771   ⎭

CH. ASPETUCK'S DIANA, S-622274

	Rummey Stagboro	Spiron Jagersbo
	Ch. Lakeland's Yuba	Selkirk Snooksie
	Lakeland's Nymph	Can. & Am. Ch. Rackets Rummey
Sturdy Max II		Lakeland's Fascination
	Ch. Sturdy Max	Rummey Stagboro
	Ch. Dora of Maridor	Rummey Girl of Stagboro
	Ch. Lakeland's Dawn	Rummey Stagboro
		Lakeland's Nymph
	Ch. The Snark of Scyld	Ch. Sturdy Max
	Ch. Silvermine Showman	Ch. Samantha of Scyld
	Silvermine Story	Can. & Am. Ch. Maro of Maridor
Aspetuck's Red Sumac		Melanie of Silvermine
	Can. & Am. Ch. Sig of Blue Bar	Kanandarque Rackets Boy
	Ch. Suzette of Setterfield	Inglehurst Matchless
	Trim of Blue Bar	Int. Ch. Pilot of Crombie of Happy Valley
		Inglehurst Matchless

<u>Dam of 7 Champions:</u>   <u>Sired by:</u>

Chatterwood Hot Toddy (2)	S-696509	⎫
Chatterwood on the Rocks (2)	S-696508	⎬
Chatterwood Lyric	S-824737	
Aspetuck's Golden Touch	S-696515	Ch. Rock Falls Racket
Chatterwood Marmalade	S-824735	
Aspetuck's Shadow (8)	S-957593	
Aspetuck's Red Satin, C.D.	S-915777	⎭

ASPETUCK'S RED SUMAC, S-543458

	Ch. Sturdy Max	Rummey Stagboro
	Ch. The Snark of Scyld	Rummey Girl of Stagboro
	Ch. Samantha of Scyld	Rummey Stagboro
Int. Ch. Silvermine Showman		Jane of Maridor
	Ch. Maro of Maridor	Ch. Sturdy Max
	Silvermine Story	Ch. Lakeland Dawn
	Melanie of Silvermine	Ch. Rhett Butler of Silvermine
		Nellie Flagg
	Kanandarque Rackets Boy	Ch. Mallhawks Rackets Boy
	Int. Ch. Sig of Blue Bar	Selkirks Mallhawks Juliet
	Inglehurst Matchless	Ch. Sir Orkney of Willgress
Ch. Suzette of Setterfield		Inglehurst Mary
	Int. Ch. Pilot of Crombie	Albert of Crombie
	Trim of Blue Bar	Patch of Crombie
	Inglehurst Matchless	Ch. Sir Orkney of Willgress
		Inglehurst Mary

<u>Dam of 5 Champions:</u>   <u>Sired by:</u>

Aspetuck's Diana (7)	S-622274	⎫
Aspetuck's Feather (3)	S-584358	⎰ Sturdy Max 2nd
Aspetuck's Red Letter (1)	S-648297	Ch. Rock Falls Racket
Aspetuck's Red Robin	S-569092	Sturdy Max 2nd
Betsworth Gold Flake (4)	S-601825	Ch. Rock Falls Racket

278

Aspetuck's Red Sumac

CH. ASPETUCK'S SHADOW, S-957593
(Ch. Rock Falls Racket x Ch. Aspetuck's Diana)
See their pedigrees.

Sire of 8 Champions:		Out of:
Canberra Blue Shadow (4)	SA-167332	Blue Mist of Stone Gables
Canberra Miss-Conduct	SA-209007	
Canberra Sunburst	SA-209006	Ch. Valley Run's Miss Cassandra
Valley Run's Upland Traveler	SA-325116	
Valley Run's Uncle Ben	SA-243656	
Gilroy's Shadow	SA-328934	Gilroy's Dixie
Canberra's Legend (1)	SA-167332	
Sukarla's Serendipity	SA-403013	Ch. Chandelle's Bambi

AM. & CAN. CH. BEN-DAR'S ADVANCE NOTICE, S-568625
(Am. & Can. Ch. Ludar of Blue Bar x Ch. Silvermine Chambray)
See their pedigrees.

Sire of 6 Champions: Out of:

Am. & Can. Ch. Skidby's
    Sturdy Tyke (2)   S-825073   Am. & Can. Ch. Hillsdale Susan
Top O' Tarnina (1)   S-820754 }
Top O' Tarnock (1)   S-820753 } Flecka's Hush Puppy
Ben-Dar's Shiny Dime   S-696410   Black Imp of Caryland
Top O' Tamerlaine (5)   S-820752 }
Top O' Sagi (3)   S-820755 } Flecka's Hush Puppy

Ch. Skidby's Sturdy Tyke (Ch. Ben-Dar's
Advance Notice—Ch. Hillsdale Susan)

AM. & CAN. CH. BEN-DAR'S CARBON COPY, S-655200
(Am. & Can. Ch. Ludar of Blue Bar x Ch. Silvermine Chambray)
See their pedigrees.

Sire of 7 Champions:		Out of:
Hidden Lane's Green Briar Rap	SA-19198	Ch. Hidden Lane's Penelope
Heldon's Rocky Nimrod (2)	SA-27767	Robbie's Saucy Tammy
Jet's Royal Rogue (1)	S-982894	Hidden Lane's High Tide
Sue-Lin's Golden Spur	SA-17686	Sue-Lin's Shooting Star
Darbella's Topaz	SA-139173	
Can. & Am. Ch. Camelot Candace	SA-140366	Ch. Cynthia Darbella
Gay Dawn of Darbella	SA-128007	

CAN. & AM. CH. BEN-DAR'S REPLICA, S-689328
(Can. & Am. Ch. Ludar of Blue Bar x Yorkley's Wisp O' Heather)
See their pedigrees.

Sire of 5 Champions:		Out of:
Can. & Am. Ch. Krisquier's Lone Eagle (4)	S-881155	Can. & Am. Ch. Hillsdale Susan
Can. Ch. Skidby's Deborah (1)	385715	Rock Falls Fay-Don Tillie
Can. & Am. Ch. Wragge Run's Roulette (4)	SA-186604	
Can. Ch. Wragge Run's Pride of Replica	544020	Can. & Am. Ch. Ludar's Ludette
Can. Ch. Wragge Run's Michael V (1)	544019	

282

Can. Ch. Wragge Run's Pride of Replica

AM. & CAN. CH. BEN-DAR'S WINNING STRIDE, S-689327

		Ch. Rip of Blue Bar	Ch. Dean of Blue Bar
	Ch. Sir Herbert of Kennelworth		Ina of Blue Bar
		Vivacious Doll of Vilmar	Banker of Fallondale
Can. & Am. Ch. Ludar of Blue Bar			Delta of Larana
		Ch. Dean of Blue Bar	Ch. Mallhawk's Jeff
	Ch. Manlove's Goldie		Ch. Lakeland's Peaches
		Ch. Manlove's Goldie of Stagboro	Ch. Rummey Boy of Stagboro
			Viola of Stagboro
			Can. & Am. Ch. Maro of Maridor
		Ch. Commander Rickey	Meadow's Penny
	Ch. Sunny Jim		Ch. Dean of Blue Bar
		Prune's Own Patricia	Ch. Prune's Own Sunbeam
Yorkley Wisp O' Heather			Rummey Stagboro
		Tom of Merrie Sherwood	Lady Bell of Stagboro
	Ch. Southern Lady of Aragon		Ch. Sturdy Max
		Orange Empress of Aragon	Ch. Pride of Arthurlie

284

AM. & CAN. CH. BEN-DAR'S WINNING STRIDE, S-689327

Sire of 22 Champions:		Out of:
Oaklynn's Top Brass (2)	S-922031	Oaklynn's Lakeland Robby
Hidden Lane's Penelope (1)	S-834221 ⎫	Notice-Me of Carylane
Hidden Lane's Winning Pride (1)	S-834219 ⎬	
Am. & Can. Ch. Winifred of Cherry Lane	S-957334	Bunnydale's Daisy Belle
Hidden Lane's Bridget (1)	SA-35451	Linda
Susie Chubb (1)	S-893365	Dag Mar Little Lady
Can. Ch. Hidden Lane's Blue Symphony (1)	409644	Notice-Me of Carylane
Windsor of Cherry Lane (3)	S-967333	Bunnydale's Daisy Belle
Hidden Lane's Sindy-Lou	S-943135	Ch. Lady Marco
Wallis of Cherry Lane (4)	S-957332	Bunnydale's Daisy Belle
End O' Maine White Rock (8)	SA-35816	Notice-Me of Carylane
Anne of Sherwood	SA-101993	Ch. Manlove's Anna Lee
Cynthia Darbella (3)	S-967392	Linda
Goldie of Meadboro	SA-83374	Hasty Miss of Meadboro
Chandelle's Folly (1)	S-996226	Ch. Parpoint Precarious
Flirtation of Meadboro (3)	SA-83375	Hasty Miss of Meadboro
Hidden Lane's Barnstormer (1)	SA-117113	Enid of Cherry Lane
Hidden Lane's Mark Me (4)	SA-122414	Enid of Cherry Lane
Saber of Mardego	SA-976776	Ch. Lady Marco
Buff's Pride (10)	SA-68293	Bunnydale's Daisy Belle
Brandy of Bloomfield	SA-65743	Bambi of Bloomfield
James of Cherry Lane	SA-312329	Ch. Pretty Maid of Cherry Lane

Am. & Can. Ch. Winifred of Cherry Lane

CH. BETA OF DEER RUN, S-936402
(Ch. Zamitz Jumpin' Jack x Ch. Silvermine Connie)

Dam of 5 Chapions: Sired by:

Barnaby of Berriwood (1)   SA-157946 ⎫
Sir Featherston of Berriwood   SA-81476 ⎪
Popcorn of Berriwood (5)   SA-81478 ⎬ Ch. Waseeka's Ace High
Haleridge Poppy of Berriwood (3)   SA-83511 ⎪
Sir John Bull of Berriwood   SA-81477 ⎭

CH. BLUE CINDERS OF BLUE BAR, S-750228
(Ch. Trump of Blue Bar x Ch. Grail of Blue Bar)

Dam of 5 Champions: Sired by:

Am. & Can. Ch. Madame Hi-Tone
    of Rocky Nevada (7)   S-980585 ⎫
Am. & Can. Ch. Desert Sage of   ⎪
    Rocky Nevada   SA-1669   ⎬ Ch. Rocky Nevada
My Fair Blue Lady from Nevada   S-980583 ⎪
Truckee Triumph   S-979286 ⎪
Rocky Nevada's White Gold   S-980582 ⎭

CAN. CH. BLUE DIAMOND OF SPRUCE
(Can. Ch. Banner of Spruce x Spruce Sapphire)

Sire of 5 Champions: Out of:

Can. Ch. Spruce Sweet William   537111   Spruce Blossom
Can. Ch. Goldenacres Blue Lady (2)   548149   Spruce Wavely
Can. Ch. Lord Timothy of Sethaven   537120   Can. Ch. Spruce Bandanna
Can. Ch. Helen's Pride (4)   537765   Spruce Blossom
Can. Ch. Sethaven Blue Prince   537956   Can. Ch. Spruce Bandanna

286

BRETT OF LONESOME LANE, SA-347779
(Ch. Phantom Brook's Blue Spruce x Ch. Frenessa of Calamity Lane)

Sire of 5 Champions: Out of:

Sis of Lonesome Lane	SA-347778	Cathy of Sherwood
Son of Lonesome Lane	SA-347779	
Faith of Lonesome Lane	SA-421996	Old Vicks Juliet of Mayhew
Fred of Lonesome Lane	SA-438683	
Sunswift Brettson	SA-524160	Gun Moll of Calamity Lane

CH. BUFF'S PRIDE, SA-68293
(Can. & Am. Ch. Ben-Dar's Winning Stride x Bunnydale's Daisy Belle)

Sire of 10 Champions: Out of:

Vicar of Cherry Lane	SA-289885	
Can. & Am. Ch. Viking of Cherry Lane	SA-289882	Enid of Cherry Lane
Viscount of Cherry Lane (1)	SA-289884	
Bayonet Point Preakness (2)	SA-272218	Heljax Black Eyed Susan
Yankee Clipper of Makepeace	SA-397049	Valley Run Dinah's Damoselle
Can. Ch. Browning of Cherry Lane	SA-351094	Enid of Cherry Lane
Bridget of Cherry Lane	SA-351090	
Valley Run's Beau Barbu	SA-369688	Ch. Valley Run Dixie Barbu
Manlove's All American (1)	SA-435974	Ch. Manlove's Cover Girl
Heljax Just Call Me Mister	SA-332431	Heljax Black Eyed Susan

CH. BULLET OF CALAMITY LANE, S-664399
(Ch. Yorkley Ensign Roberts x Ch. Candy of Blue Bar)

Sire of 8 Champions:

Out of:

Carbine of Calamity Lane	S-792626	⎫
Confetti of Calamity Lane (10)	S-792633	
Clementine of Calamity Lane (1)	S-792636	⎬ Ch. Rock Candy of
Cocoa of Calamity Lane (2)	S-792634	Calamity Lane
Calamity of Calamity Lane (2)	S-792635	
Cinnamon of Calamity Lane	S-792629	⎭
Gingham of Calamity Lane	SA-233445	Ch. Belle of Calamity Lane
Wesley The Whip of Scotchmoor	SA-387547	Ch. Blessed By Lonesome Lane

CH. CHANDELLE'S ANCHOR MAN, SA-95127
(Ch. Margand Lord Baltimore x Ch. Chandelle Lady)
See their pedigrees.

Sire of 12 Champions:

Out of:

Gypsy Lane's Big Joe (1)	SA-248247 ⎫	
Redstone's Gypsy Lane Gerry	SA-243524 ⎬	Zip of Hi-Flight
Excalibrette of Gypsy Lane (1)	SA-221694 ⎭	
Black Oak's Brett of Tel-Mo	SA-313786	Ch. Lynda's Melynda of Tel-Mo
Sudrok's Honey of Pine Park	SA-379538	Karamel of Berriwood
Chandelle's City Slicker	SA-391403	Ch. Chandelle Lady
Pollyanna's Penelope	SA-255200	Ch. Lieutenant's Pollyanna
Plum Creek's Hot Toddy	SA-457453	Ch. Cecily of High Moon
Tel-Mo's Lady Debora	SA-348217	Ch. Lynda's Melynda of Tel-Mo
Michigan Slim By Law	SA-433004	Ch. Hidden Lane's Scheherazade
Excalibur's Anchors Aweigh	SA-395307	Ch. Lynda's Melynda of Tel-Mo
Gal's Gay Debut of Tel-Mo	SA-542015	Ch. Lynda's Melynda of Tel-Mo

Ch. Chandelle's Anchor Man (at 8 years)

CH. CHANDELLE LADY, S-925916

			Ch. Grayland Rackets Boy
	Ch. Rock Falls Cavalier		Ch. Linda Lou of Blue Bar
	Ch. Rock Falls Colonel		Ch. Grayland Rackets Boy
		Ch. Rock Falls Belle	Nocturne of Crowlcroft
Ch. Rock Falls Lieutenant			Ch. Grayland Rackets Boy
		Ch. Jack O' Rackets	Ch. Linda Lou of Blue Bar
	Jacklin O' Rackets		Ch. Cedric of Delwed
		Tyronne Farm Belle	Blondie Bell

			Thelma Sir Rocklyn
	Ch. Mike of Meadboro		Lady McBeth
	Rugged Boy		Ch. Captain Jenks
		Ch. Gloria	My True Blue
Duchess Rugger Honey			Ch. Prunes Own Yukon
		Ch. Samboaux Rik	Dusk of Devon
	Rubin's Honey Maid		Ch. Prunes Own Yukon
		Ch. Betty Grable of Aragon	Prunes Own New Moon

Dam of 11 Champions:

Sired by:

Chandelle's Anchor Man (12)	SA-95127	
Chandelle's Air Mail, C.D.	SA-95126	
Chandelle's Allspice	SA-95130	Ch. Margand Lord Baltimore
Chandelle's Littlest Angel (1)	SA-95128	
Chandelle's Bambi (1)	SA-250902	
Chandelle's Bittersweet	SA-250905	
Chandelle's Billet Doux	SA-250904	Ch. Margand Lord Baltimore
Chandelle's Butterscotch	SA-250903	
Chandelle's City Slicker	SA-391403	
Chandelle's Charmin	SA-391405	Ch. Chandelle's Anchor Man
Chandelle's Chambray	SA-391404	

CH. CONFETTI OF CALAMITY LANE, S-792633
(Ch. Bullet of Calamity Lane x Ch. Rock Candy of Calamity Lane)

Dam of 10 Champions: Sired by:

Dover's Wall Street	S-946627	
Dover's Replica of Ludar	S-949336	
Dover's Ticker Tape (1)	S-924006	Am. & Can. Ch. Ludar of Blue Bar
Dover's Par Value (1)	S-939358	
Dover's Sir-Plus, C.D. (1)	S-925080	
Dover's Robert E. Lee	SA-82716	Ch. Derringer of Calamity Lane
Dover's Molly Pitcher	SA-253022	Can. Ch. Wamlay's Mike Chism
Can. Ch. Dover's Betsy Ross	609235	
Dover's Blue Sky (5)	SA-187369	Mt. Mansfield's Spruce Peak
Dover's Blue Velvet	SA-195052	

Ch. Dover's Ticker Tape

292

AM. & CAN. CH. CRAWFIE OF BLUE BAR, S-461515

				Ch. Mallhawk's Jeff
		Ch. Rip of Blue Bar	Ch. Dean of Blue Bar	Ch. Lakeland's Peaches
			Ina of Blue Bar	Roy of Blue Bar
	Ch. Sir Herbert of Kennelworth		Banker of Fallondale	Ch. Fly of Stagboro
		Vivacious Doll of Vilmar		Can. & Am. Ch. Maxie of Stagboro
			Delta of Larana	Ch. Grayland Orange Blossom
				Ch. Sturdy Max
				Ch. Lakeland's Dawn
		Ch. Jesse of Blue Bar	Roy of Blue Bar	Ch. Mallhawk's Jeff
			Ch. Lovely Lady of Stucile	Kanandarque Lovelyness
	Ch. Enid of Blue Bar			Rummey Stagboro
		Ch. Lola of Blue Bar	Sammy of Blue Bar	Ch. Modern Maid of Stucile
			Faith of Blue Bar	Ch. Mallhawk's Jeff
				Kanandarque Lovelyness
				Kanandarque Rackets Boy
				Saga Oakholm II

Dam of 6 Champions:

Sundridge Antiphon (3)   S-883546
Halfback of Button Ball   S-832549
Javelin of Button Ball   S-868833
Vaulter of Button Ball (3)   S-868839
Discus of Button Ball (1)   S-868838
Al-Kay's Sky Watch   S-868836

Sired by:

Ch. Rock Falls King Charles
Al-Kay's Lar Sonny

Ch. Thelan Mark of Distinction

293

CH. DIONE DUTCHESS OF DOGSTAR, SA-198187
(Ch. Faneal's Blue Danube x Ch. Golden Dawn of Dogstar)

Dam of 8 Champions:

Sired by:

Gemody's Danny Boy	SA-457261	
Gemody's Star Dust	SA-457263	
Gemody's Gidget Goes Hawaiian	SA-457266	
Gemody's Ina Darling	SA-457267	Ch. Margand Meteor
Gemody's Barbara Gal	SA-457270	of Dogstar
Gemody's Rambling Laddie	SA-457260	
Gemody's Gemini of Dogstar	SA-460394	
Gemody's Sophisticated Lady	SA-457268	

CH. DOVER'S BLUE SKY, SA-187369
(Mt. Mansfield's Spruce Peak x Ch. Confetti of Calamity Lane)

Sire of 5 Champions:

Out of:

Blue Diamond's Abner Yokum	SA-344912	
Blue Diamond's Alice Blue Gown	SA-344915	Ch. Blue Diamond Mist
Blue Diamond's Abbigirl, C.D.	SA-344913	
Kaynor's Aces Over	SA-383418	Ch. Kaynor's Samantha of Mayhew
Blue Lupine of Beriwood	SA-346028	Kopper Penny of Berriwood

CH. EARL OF ELM KNOLL, S-310586
(Ch. Case's General Jackson x Reba of Blue Bar)

Sire of 6 Champions:

Out of:

Eadie of Elm Knoll (3)	S-637788	
Fusilier of Elm Knoll	S-637793	
Emilie of Elm Knoll	S-637787	
Lancer of Elm Knoll	S-637797	Mallhawk Mallie of Elm Knoll
Elaine of Elm Knoll (5)	S-737790	
Ellen of Elm Knoll	S-637791	

CH. ELTON OF BLUE BAR, S-603623
(Ch. Gus du Hameau x Ch. Norma of Blue Bar)

Sire of 6 Champions: Out of:

Lo-Erls Country Gentleman	SA-87294	Lo-Erls Sensation at Dusk
Fleck of Fillmore, C.D.	S-858286	
Quinn's Golden Dawn Lady (2)	SA-216747	
Lo-Erls Country Squire	SA-244241	
Kiba's Rowdy	SA-59922	Rebel Roc's Blue Dinah
Scott The Striking Cavalier	SA-79122	

CH. END O'MAINE WHITE ROCK, SA-35816
(Am. & Can. Ch. Ben-Dar's Winning Stride x Notice-Me of Carylane)

Sire of 8 Champions:		Out of:
Rip of Cherry Lane	SA-183529	
White Cap of Cherry Lane	SA-219126	
Rebecca of Cherry Lane (2)	SA-183528	Enid of Cherry Lane
Douglas of Cherry Lane	SA-243094	
Kaynor's Samantha of Mayhew (1)	SA-150046	
Mayhew's Game Girl (4)	SA-156282	Ch. Wallis of Cherry Lane
Mayhew's Stormy Knight (1)	SA-156283	
Mirock's Missy	SA-252311	Honey Jill's Memory

CH. ENGLISH ACCENT OF VALLEY RUN, S-893847

			Rummey Stagboro
	Ch. Grayland Rackets Boy		Blenheim Violet
	Ch. Rock Falls Cavalier		Ch. Blue Bar Limited
		Ch. Linda Lou of Blue Bar	Gretta of Blue Bar
Ch. Rock Falls Racket			Rummey Stagboro
		Ch. Grayland Rackets Boy	Blenheim Violet
	Ch. Rock Falls Belle		Ch. Blaze of Fallondale
		Nocturne of Crowlcroft	Romance of Crowlcroft
			Rummey Stagboro
		Ch. Lakeland's Yuba	Lakeland's Nymph
	Sturdy Max II		Ch. Sturdy Max
		Ch. Dora of Maridor	Ch. Lakeland's Dawn
Ch. Starbright of Valley Run			Ch. Mallhawk's Jett
		Ch. Dean of Blue Bar	Ch. Lakeland's Peaches
	Silvermine Confection		Int. Ch. Silvermine Wagabond
		Silvermine Wanita	Ch. Rackets Gene of Silvermine

Sire of 10 Champions: Out of:

Gentleman Jim of Valley Run	SA-86980	⎫	
Valley Run's Miss Cassandra (2)	SA-119254	⎬	Posie of Blue Bar
Prince Charlie of Valley Run (1)	SA-104105		
Valley Run Dixie Barbu (1)	SA-58256	⎭	
Merry Rover of Valley Run (18)	SA-116098		Wamlay's Merry Minx
Phantom Brook's Oliver	SA-129431	⎱	
Betsworth Judy Van Buren	SA-142534	⎰	Ch. Phantom Brook's Pinafore
Valley Run's Accent's Finale	SA-163061	⎱	
Valley Run's Cinnamon Cindy	SA-88582	⎬	Posie of Blue Bar
Valley Run's Sabrina Fair (1)	SA-119253	⎭	

Ch. Gentleman Jim of Valley Run

Ch. Prince Charlie of Valley Run

ENID OF CHERRY LANE, SA-3878

	Ernford Easter Parade	Fluellen of Fermara
Ernford Apollo		Celandine of Haverbrack
	Ernford Cilldara Silver	Grouse of Capard
Ch. Ernford Highflier		Minx of Medeshamstede
	Ensign of Remor	Irish Ch. Banner of Crombie
Teal of Yaresyde		Pretty Maid of Ketree
	Tarnock Fiona of Remor	Irish Ch. Banner of Crombie
		Penelope of Ketree
	Ch. Rip of Blue Bar	Ch. Dean of Blue Bar
Dill of Blue Bar		Ina of Blue Bar
	Schoolgirl Sue of Havertown	Banker of Fallondale
Bunnydale's Daisy Belle		Belle's Queen
	Ch. Rummey Sam of Stagboro	Rummey II of Stagboro
Martie of Blue Bar		Kate of Stagboro
	Kanandarque **Goldie**	Ch. Dean of Blue Bar
		Ch. Gem of Blue Bar

Dam of 14 Champions:		Sired by:
Pretty Maid of Cherry Lane (3)	SA-159968	Ch. Bunnydale's Orange Vulcan
Rip of Cherry Lane	SA-183529	Ch. End O'Maine White Rock
Hidden Lane's Barnstormer (1)	SA-117113	Can. & Am. Cn. Ben-Dar's Winning Stride
Hidden Lane's Mark Me (4)	SA-122414	
White Cap of Cherry Lane	SA-219126	Ch. End O'Maine White Rock
Can. & Am. Ch. Viking of Cherry Lane	SA-289882	
Vicar of Cherry Lane	SA-289885	Ch. Buff's Pride
Viscount of Cherry Lane (1)	SA-289884	
Can. & Am. Ch. Pilot of Cherry Lane	SA-380969	Ch. Bayonet Point Preakness
Portia of Cherry Lane	SA-380973	
Douglas of Cherry Lane	SA-243094	Ch. End O'Maine White Rock
Can. Ch. Browning of Cherry Lane	SA-351094	Ch. Buff's Pride
Rebecca of Cherry Lane (2)	SA-183528	Ch. End O'Maine White Rock
Bridget of Cherry Lane	SA-351090	Ch. Buff's Pride

299

CH. ERNFORD ORIOLE, S-997572

Sh. Ch. Ripleygae Mallory	Archdale Corncrake of Haverbrack
Kirket Kerryboy	Heatherdrake Diane
Kirket Karmina	Sh. Ch. Rombalds Sentinal
Ernford Kingfisher	Sh. Ch. Kirket Marinette
Ernford Easter Parade	Fluellen of Fermanar
Ch. Ernford Evening Flight	Celandine of Haverbrack
Teal of Yarsyde	Ensign of Remor
	Tarnock Fiona of Remor
Ir. Ch. Peter of Beechmount	Balmuto Gamble
Grouse of Capard	Leonora of Langlea
Nan of Beechmount	Ir. Ch. Banner of Crombie
Ch. Ernford Cilldara Felicity	Poppy of Beechmount
Rombalds Furious	Bayldone Breeze
Minx of Medeshamstede	Rombalds Rovigo
Blue Belle	Rombalds Tempest
	Dolly Daydreams

Sire of 10 Champions: Out of:

Margand Wildcatter (6)	SA-77804	⎫	
Margand Captain Dan (1)	SA-85616	⎪	Ch. Margand Mary Jane
Margand Man About Town (2)	SA-77803	⎪	
Par-point Pretti-Tri (3)	SA-118747	⎬	Ch. Parpoint Precarious
Margand Magnolia Blossom	SA-132797	⎪	Ch. Margand Mary Jane
Robinwood's Freckles	SA-208831	⎪	
Candy Chips of Hathaway	SA-197092	⎪	Ch. Robinwood's Dot
Adam of Lonesome Lane (3)	SA-124846	⎪	Ch. Clementine of Calamity La
Chandelle's Sixpence, C.D.	SA-208754	⎪	Ch. Chandelle's Folly
Blue Diamond Mist (4)	SA-234932	⎭	Ch. Parpoint Precarious

CH. FRENCHTOWN CALICO BUTTON, S-334742

Ch. Mallhawk's Jeff	Ch. Mallhawk's Rackets Boy
Roy of Blue Bar	Flora Hallhawk
Kanandarque Lovelyness	Kanandarque Rackets Boy
Ch. Jesse of Blue Bar	Dawn of Stagboro
Rummey Stagboro	Spiron of Jagersbo
Ch. Lovely Lady of Stucile	Selkirk Snooksie
Ch. Modern Maid of Stucile	Ch. Sir Orkney Willgress, Jr.
	Willgress Lady Luck
Bickerton's Monarch	Explorer of Stucile
Pendlemar Dan	Bickerton's Lady Gene
Squirrel Run Speckled Rose	Can. & Am. Ch. Gilroy's Chief Topic
Frenchtown Blue Feather	Gilroy's Queen B
Clown of Barleymill	Happy Valley Helmsman
Brandy's Barmaid	Happy Valley Colleen Chloe
Brandy D	Brookloo D (C.D.)
	Autumn's Lady Betty

Dam of 6 Champions: Sired by:

Frenchtown Calico Flower	S-550935	⎫
Frenchtown April Dawn	S-507100	
Frenchtown Main Copy (2)	S-579153	
Frenchtown Peter Paul (2)	S-550934	⎬ Ch. Frenchtown
Frenchtown Topaz	S-579152	Main Topic
Can. Ch. Frenchtown		
Chocolate Soldier		⎭

CH. FRENCHTOWN MAIN TOPIC, S-154104

	Ch. Mallhawk's Jeff	Ch. Mallhawk's Rackets Boy
Ch. Dean of Blue Bar		Flora Mallhawk
	Ch. Lakeland's Peaches	Rummey Stagboro
Ch. Rip of Blue Bar		Lakeland's Nymph
	Roy of Blue Bar	Ch. Mallhawk's Jeff
Ina of Blue Bar		Kanandarque Lovelyness
	Ch. Fly of Stagboro	Inglehurst Rock
		Selkirk Snooksie
	Bickerton's Monarch	Explorer of Stucile
Pendelmar Dan		Bickerton's Lady Gene
	Squirrel Run Speckled Rose	Can. & Am. Ch. Gilroy's Chief Topic
Frenchtown Blue Feather		Gilroy's Queen B
	Clown of Barleymill	Happy Valley Helmsman
Brandy's Barmaid		Happy Valley Colleen Chloe
	Brandy D	Freckles D (C.D.)
		Autumn's Lady Betty

Sire of 8 Champions: Out of:

Frenchtown Calico Flower	S-550935	
Frenchtown April Dawn	S-507100	
Frenchtown Main Copy (2)	S-579153	
Frenchtown Peter Paul (2)	S-550934	Ch. Frenchtown
Frenchtown Topaz	S-579152	Calico Button
Can. Ch. Frenchtown		
Chocolate Soldier		
Pencader Judy Anne	S-296695	Nan of Pencader
Pencader Sammy K	S-396694	

CH. FLECKA'S FLASH OF CABIN HILL, SA-3977
(Ch. Manlove's Colonel x Ch. Princessa de Rancho Tranquilo)

Sire of 5 Champions:

Out of:

Manlove's Grenadier	SA-226348	
Cabin Hill Tom Tom (2)	SA-208439	Manlove's Nancy Lee
Bayonet Point Amber Flash	SA-324457	Dunwick's Dixie of Riscot
Cabin Hill Flashlight	SA-144334	Ch. Waseeka's Memphis Belle
Lady Guenevere of High Tor	SA-315445	Brunhilda of High Tor

CH. FRENESSA OF CALAMITY LANE, SA-122679
(Dover's Doc Holiday x Ch. Calamity of Calamity Lane)

Dam of 7 Champions:

Sired by:

Brooks of Lonesome Lane	SA-248024	
Beloved of Lonesome Lane	SA-201597	Ch. Phantom Brook's
Blessed By Lonesome Lane (1)	SA-201596	Blue Spruce
Bradley of Lonesome Lane	SA-220074	
Dolly of Lonesome Lane	SA-312928	Ch. Adam of Lonesome Lane
Raybar Wisp of Lonesome Lane	SA-418085	Ch. Spark 2nd of
Raybar's Ain't She Sweet	SA-408241	Cherry Lane

CH. GILROY'S CHANCELLOR, SA-186767
(Gilroy's Spot x Gilroy's Dixie)

Sire of 5 Champions:

Out of:

Penmaen's Meg of Gypsy Lane	SA-512960	Can. & Am. Ch. Skidby's Cambridge Miss
Mr. Pym of Polperro	SA-415461	
Can. and Am. Ch. Galahad of Polperro	SA-415462	Ch. Lady Jane of Polperro
Piper of Polperro	SA-415460	
Penmaen Blue Cambric	SA-510511	Can. & Am. Ch. Skidby's Cambridge Miss

GORGEOUS GOLDIE OF ORKNEY, S-461808
(Special Agent of Orkney x Sperry's Happy Landing)

Dam of 6 Champions:		Out of: Sired by:
Iverlee Fortune Hunter (2)	S-690255 ⎫	
Orkney Bob	S-709645 ⎪	
Memory of Orkney (1)	S-658281 ⎬	Ch. Rock Falls Troubadour
Laguna Honda Gold Flake	S-701933 ⎭	
Bem's Sir Christopher	S-740421 ⎫	
Bem's Sir James	S-845480 ⎭	Ch. Flecka's Andy

Ch. Iverlee Fortune Hunter

CH. GUYS 'N DOLLS BRIDGET O'SHEA, C.D. - SA-119962
(Ch. Sir Guy of Ellendale x Lady Jill of Ellendale)

Dam of 5 Champions:

		Sired by:
Guys 'N Dolls Miss Adelaide (3)	SA-342336	
Guys 'N Dolls Shalimar Duke	SA-342335	
Guys 'N Dolls Dave the Dude	SA-342333	Am. & Can. Ch.
Guys 'N Dolls Good Time Charlie	SA-342334	Hillsdale Sentinel
Guys 'N Dolls Sarah Brown	SA-342337	

CAN. & AM. CH. HILLSDALE SENTINEL, SA-68549
(Can. & Am. Ch. Skidby's Sturdy Tyke x Can. & Am. Ch. Hillsdale Susan)

Sire of 9 Champions:

		Out of:
Faneal's Glendale Sentinel (1)	SA-218286	Faneal's Lindell Lady
Faneal's Royal Queen	SA-198204	Rebel Roc's Song Leader
Ellendale's Royal Feather	SA-325218	Rebecca of Ellendale
Guys 'N Dolls Miss Adelaide (3)	SA-342336	
Guys 'N Dolls Shalimar Duke	SA-342335	
Guys 'N Dolls Dave the Dude	SA-342333	Ch. Guys 'N Dolls
Guys 'N Dolls Good Time Charlie	SA-342334	Bridget O'Shea, C.D.
Guys 'N Dolls Sarah Brown	SA-342337	
Guys 'N Dolls Mr. Prendergast	SA-360013	Ch. Lady Dana of Ellendale

CH. IKE OF BLUE BAR, S-586365
(Ch. Rock Falls Racket x Ch. Rip Tide of Blue Bar)

Sire of 6 Champions: Out of:

Glenmary Penny Ante (1)	S-787222	Schoettle's Moontide
Candlewood Distinction (3)	SA-3229	Ch. Candlewood Flirtation
Day Money of Calamity Lane	SA-54844 ⎫	Ch. Rock Candy of
Derringer of Calamity Lane (1)	SA-281194 ⎭	Calamity Lane
Tirvelda Solitaire	SA-91896	Can. & Am. Ch. Hillsdale Susan
Candlewood Elusive	SA-3228	Ch. Candlewood Flirtation

JEFF OF BLUE BAR
(Ch. Gus du Hameau x Ch. Flower of Blue Bar)

Sire of 6 Champions: Out of:

Can. & Am. Ch. Lulu Bill of Richmond	SA-577	Ch. Rock Falls Tar-Heel Tilly
Fancy Feathers (2)	S-818526	Flecka's Fancy
Duke of Lulu Island	SA-181221	Flecka's Powder Dixie
Orange Princess of Richmond (1)	SA-60074	Ch. Rock Falls Tar-Heel Tilly
Can. Ch. Sheila of Lulu Island (1)	546346	Flecka's Powder Dixie
Can. Ch. Inglewood Orange Prince	616388	Spruce Periwinkle

AM., CAN. & MEX. CH. LA MAY'S PLAYMATE'S GUNNER, SA-58910
(Ch. La May's Jim Dan Dee x Manlove's Judy)

Sire of 10 Champions:

		Out of:
Quiet Hills Brotherly Love	SA-101371	Ch. La May's Playmate
Farthest North Heather (1)	SA-152351	Farthest North Patches, C.D.
Can. Ch. Quiet Hills Gun Butt	743078	Ch. Farthest North Heather
Bret Harte of Rocky Nevada	SA-133369	
Mark Twain of Rocky Nevada	SA-133371	
Rocky Nevada's Reno Girl	SA-133366	
Rocky Nevada's Shoshone Belle	SA-133368	Can. & Am. Ch. Madame Hi-Tone of Rocky Nevada
Kit Carson of Rocky Nevada	SA-133372	
Pogonip of Rocky Nevada	SA-133373	
Toiyabe of Rocky Nevada	SA-133367	

AM. & CAN. CH. LUDAR OF BLUE BAR, S-454627

	Ch. Dean of Blue Bar	Ch. Mallhawk's Jeff
	Ch. Rip of Blue Bar	Ch. Lakeland's Peaches
	Ina of Blue Bar	Roy of Blue Bar
Ch. Sir Herbert of Kennelworth		Ch. Fly of Stagboro
	Banker of Fallondale	Can. & Am. Ch. Maxie of Stagboro
	Vivacious Doll of Vilmar	Ch. Grayland Orange Blossom
	Delta of Larana	Ch. Sturdy Max
		Ch. Lakeland's Dawn
	Ch. Mallhawk's Jeff	Ch. Mallhawk's Rackets Boy
	Ch. Dean of Blue Bar	Flora Mallhawk
	Ch. Lakeland's Peaches	Rummey Stagboro
Ch. Manlove's Goldie		Lakeland's Nymph
	Ch. Rummey Boy of Stagboro	Rummey Stagboro
	Ch. Manlove's Goldie of Stagboro	Ch. Rose of Stagboro
	Viola of Stagboro	Rummey Stagboro
		Winsome of Stagboro

Sire of 26 Champions: Out of:

Can. & Am. Ch. Ben-Dar's Replica (5)   S-689328 ⎤
Can. Ch. Ben-Dar's Special Edition   S-689329 ⎥
Yorkley's Statesman (2)   S-689326 ⎬ Yorkley Wisp O'Heather
Can. & Am. Ch. Ben-Dar's   ⎥
    Winning Stride (22)   S-689327 ⎦

Ludar (continued)

Can. & Am. Ch. Hillsdale Susan (4)	S-747434	
Can. & Am. Ch. Hillsdale Betty	S-663940	Can. Ch. Pollyanna
Hillsdale Surprise (1)	S-689350	
Can. Ch. Hillsdale Sparkle (2)	347752	
Can. & Am. Ch. Ben-Dar's Advance Notice (6)	S-568625	Ch. Silvermine Chambray
Sir Gallant of Panthorn (2)	S-761457	Ch. Silvermine Decal
Tioga Wild Honey (3)	S-688128	Ch. Tioga Dotted Swiss
Dover's Wall Street	S-946627	Ch. Confetti of Calamity Lane
Can. & Am. Ch. Krisquier's Flambeau O'Ludar	S-801138	Can. & Am. Ch. Hillsdale Susan
Can. & Am. Ch. Darby of Carylane (1)	S-660482	Ch. Silvermine Chambray
Lady of Carylane	S-776704	Ch. Silvermine Matchless
Can. & Am. Ch. Ben-Dar's Carbon Copy (7)	S-655200	Ch. Silvermine Chambray
Ben-Dar's Sweet Sue (2)	S-689331	Yorkley Wisp O'Heather
Dover's Replica of Ludar	S-949336	Ch. Confetti of Calamity Lane
Can. & Am. Ch. Ludar's Ludette (3)	451838	Ch. Lady Marco
Dover's Ticker Tape (1)	S-924006	Ch. Confetti of Calamity Lane
Can. Ch. Ben-Dar's Little Slam	340693	Ch. Silvermine Chambray
Can. Ch. Wendy of Algoma (2)	365333	Jill of Algoma
Lady Lark of Panthorn (2)	S-761460	Ch. Silvermine Decal
Dover's Par Value (1)	S-939358	Ch. Confetti of Calamity Lane
Dover's Sir-Plus, C.D. (1)	S-925080	
Sir Lance of Panthorn	S-761458	Ch. Silvermine Decal

Can. and Am. Ch. Ludar's Ludette

AM. & CAN. CH. MADAM HI-TONE OF ROCKY NEVADA, S-980585
(Ch. Rocky Nevada x Ch. Blue Cinders of Blue Bar)

Dam of 7 Champions:

Sired by:

Rocky Nevada's Shoshone Belle	SA-133368	
Kit Carson of Rocky Nevada	SA-133372	
Bret Harte of Rocky Nevada	SA-133369	Am. & Can. Ch. La May's
Mark Twain of Rocky Nevada	SA-133371	Playmate's Gunner
Rocky Nevada's Reno Girl	SA-133366	
Pogonip of Rocky Nevada	SA-133373	
Toiyabe of Rocky Nevada	SA-133367	

MALLHAWK MALLIE OF ELM KNOLL, S-538880
(Mallhawk Heather Grouse x Mallhawk Quail)

Dam of 6 Champions:

Sired by:

Eadie of Elm Knoll (3)	S-637788	
Fusilier of Elm Knoll	S-637793	
Emilie of Elm Knoll	S-637787	
Lancer of Elm Knoll	S-637797	Ch. Earl of Elm Knoll
Elaine of Elm Knoll (5)	S-637790	
Ellen of Elm Knoll	S-637791	

CH. MANLOVE'S COLONEL, S-740461
(Am., Can. & Cuban Ch. Rock Falls Colonel x Ch. Manlove's Patsy Lee)

Sire of 10 Champions:

Out of:

Cabin Hill Blue Belle	S-977764	Ch. Waseeka's Memphis Belle
Flecka's Dutchess of Dunwick	S-991236	
Flecka's Flash of Cabin Hill (5)	SA-3977	Ch. Princessa de
Flecka's Charlie (2)	S-989553	Rancho Tranquilo
Kerry of Berriwood (4)	SA-219087	
Sir Kippford of Berriwood	SA-216002	
Krackerjack of Berriwood	SA-217268	Ch. Popcorn of Berriwood
Koko of Berriwood (1)	SA-219088	
Kernel of Berriwood	SA-220647	
Dover's Dawn of Scotchmoor	SA-242297	Ch. Dover's Ticker Tape

310

Ch. Manlove's Colonel

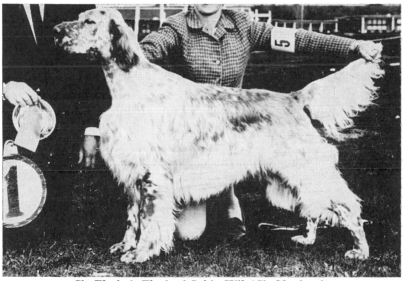

Ch. Flecka's Flash of Cabin Hill (Ch. Manlove's
Colonel—Ch. Princess de Rancho Tranquila)

CH. MANLOVE'S DUKE OF HIGHRIDGE, S-620732
(Ch. Rock Falls Blue Baron x Manlove's Rose Dee)

Sire of 5 Champions:

Out of:

Rebel Roc's Queen of Avalon (1)	S-931948	Ch. Rock Falls Dixie Darling
Rebel Roc's Rebel (1)	S-856766	Rock Falls Libby
Rebel Roc's Prince of Avalon	S-931949 ⎫	
Avalon's Sir Pert of Roads End	S-922560 ⎬	Ch. Rock Falls Dixie Darling
Aspetuck's Lucky Duke	S-960961	Ch. Aspetuck's Feather

Ch. Rebel Roc's Queen of Avalon

AM. & CAN. CH. MANLOVE'S MAX, 310266
(Ch. Rip of Rockboro x Ch. Manlove's Goldie)

Sire of 5 Champions: Out of:

Can. Ch. Milroy's Blue Sage
     of Roncliff (2)   377692   Can. Ch. Wendy of Algoma
Can. Ch. Best Friend's
     Blue Knight (2)   440817
Can. Ch. Best Friend's
     Court Jester (1)   377727
Can. Ch. Best Friend's   Can. Ch. Royalty's Princess
     Miss Debutant   366872   Patricia
Can. Ch. Best Friend's
     Happy Melody   392421

CH. MANLOVE'S PATSY GIRL, S-468759
(Ch. Rock Falls Cavalier x Manlove's Rose Dee)

Dam of 5 Champions: Sired by:

Manlove's Colonel (10)   S-740461
Manlove's Anna Lee (2)   S-740464   Can., Cuban & Am.
Manlove's Belle   S-810216   Ch. Rock Falls Colonel
Colonel Robert E. Lee   S-838435
Devoncote's Betsy Boo (2)   SA-67069   Ch. Squire of Blue Bar

MARGAND BROWN GIRL, SA-34858
(Ch. Margand Lord Calvert x Margand Lily Ann)

Dam of 5 Champions:

Sired by:

Margand Alexandra (1)	SA-208001	⎫ Ch. Margand Lord Baltimore
Margand Duke of Baltimore	SA-188370	⎬
Margand Dan Cupid	SA-263091	⎫
Margand Valentina	SA-246127	⎬ Ch. Margand Wildcatter
Margand King of Hearts	SA-263092	⎭

Ch. Margand Lord Baltimore

CH. MARGAND LORD BALTIMORE, S-846454

```
                          Ch. Buzz of Haon          Rummey Stagboro
              Margand El Capitan                     Ch. Knollcroft Nancy Lou
                          Dutchess"s Blue Artemis    Prediction's Test Pilot
Ch. Margand Lord Calvert                             Rummey Ann's Blue Duchess
                          Ch. Els-Har Jake           Ch. Marbar's Little John
              Margand Princess Anne                  Ch. Merry Sunshine of Maple Lawn
                          Ch. Talphant Lady Elizabeth Ch. Mallhawk Orange Lad
                                                     Mid-Oak Pride
                          Ch. Rock Falls Cavalier    Ch. Grayland Rackets Boy
              Ch. Rock Falls Colonel                 Ch. Linda Lou of Blue Bar
                          Rock Falls Belle           Ch. Grayland Rackets Boy
Ch. Phantom Brook's Petticoat                        Nocturne of Crowlcroft
                          Ch. Ken of Blue Bar        Ch. Jesse of Blue Bar
              Ch. Phantom Brook's Deductible         Ora of Blue Bar
                          Ch. Babe of Blue Bar II    Ch. Rip of Blue Bar
                                                     Bette of Blue Bar
```

Sire of 24 Champions: Out of:

Margand Mary Jane (5)	S-964786	Ch. Stagmore's Lady Jane
Chandelle's Anchor Man (12)	SA-95127	
Chandelle's Air Mail, C.D.	SA-95126	Ch. Chandelle Lady
Chandelle's Allspice (1)	SA-95130	
Chandelle's Littlest Angel	SA-95128	
Robinwood's Angel (1)	SA-143364	
Robinwood's Big Hunter	SA-157723	Ch. Robinwood's Dot
Margand Meteor of Dogstar (9)	SA-234567	Ch. Margand Mary Jane
Stellaire Debute of Ramar	SA-215559	Mary of Haleridge
Chandelle's Bambi (1)	SA-250902	
Chandelle's Bittersweet	SA-250905	Ch. Chandelle Lady
Chandelle's Butterscotch	SA-250903	
Chandelle's Billet-Doux	SA-250904	
Margand Alexandra (1)	SA-208001	
Margand Duke of Baltimore	SA-188370	Margand Brown Girl
Jaccard Hill Alastaire	SA-317411	Ch. Top O' Yankee Doodle
Jaccard Hill Amelia (1)	SA-317412	Candace
Margand Masquerader	SA-363373	
Margand Jennifer	SA-348398	Margand Jacquelyne
Lo-Erls Golden Girl of Golden Q	SA-405891	Ch. Quinn's Golden Dawn Lady
Margand King of Golden Q (1)	SA-363365	
Lady Meg of Shallegan	SA-432211	Ch. Parpoint Pretti-Tri
Fedric's Lord Pepper Jaccard	SA-325189	Ch. Top O' Yankee Doodle Candace
Margand Artemis	SA-363370	Margand Jacquelyne

CH. MARGAND MARY JANE, S-964786
(Ch. Margand Lord Baltimore x Ch. Stagmore's Lady Jane)

Dam of 5 Champions: Sired by:

Margand Wildcatter (6)	SA-77804	
Margand Man About Town (2)	SA-77803	Ch. Ernford Oriole
Margand Magnolia Blossom	SA-132797	
Margand Captain Dan (1)	SA-85616	
Margand Meteor of Dogstar (9)	SA-234567	Ch. Margand Lord Baltimore

CH. MARGAND METEOR OF DOGSTAR, SA-234567
(Ch. Margand Lord Baltimore x Ch. Margand Mary Jane)

Sire of 9 Champions: Out of:

Merry Meteor of Dogstar	SA-404752	Quiet Hills White Cloud
Gemody's Danny Boy	SA-457261	
Gemody's Star Dust	SA-457263	
Gemody's Gidget Goes Hawaiian	SA-457266	
Gemody's Ina Darling	SA-457267	Ch. Dione Dutchess
Gemody's Barbara Gal	SA-457270	of Dogstar
Gemody's Rambling Laddie	SA-457260	
Gemody's Gemini of Dogstar	SA-460394	
Gemody's Sophisticated Lady	SA-457268	

CH. MARGAND WILDCATTER, SA-77804
(Ch. Ernford Oriole x Ch. Margand Mary Jane)

Sire of 6 Champions: Out of:

Margand Dan Cupid	SA-263091	
Margand Valentina	SA-246127	Margand Brown Girl
Margand King of Hearts	SA-263092	
Margand Roustabout	SA-316378	Margand Zsa Zsa
Boelle of Shallegan	SA-515169	
Parpoint Placater	SA-484561	Ch. Parpoint Pretti-Tri

CH. MERRY ROVER OF VALLEY RUN, SA-116098

Ch. Rock Falls Cavalier
Ch. Rock Falls Racket
Ch. Rock Falls Belle
Ch. English Accent of Valley Run
Sturdy Max II
Ch. Starbright of Valley Run
Silvermine Confection

Thelan Sir Rockland
Ch. Mike of Meadboro
Lady MacBeth
Wamlay's Merry Minx
Ch. Sharoc's Monty of Oak Valley
Cinderella of Oak Valley
Gold Dust of Oak Valley

Ch. Grayland Rackets Boy
Ch. Linda Lou of Blue Bar
Ch. Grayland Rackets Boy
Nocturne of Crowlcroft
Ch. Lakeland's Yuba
Ch. Dora of Maridor
Ch. Dean of Blue Bar
Silvermine Wanita
Ch. Jack O'Racket
Rock Falls Lady Marilyn
Ch. Honor's Even Marksman
Royal Whirl
Sturdy Max II
Ch. Sharoc Dolly Madison
Ch. Golden Boy of Fairlawn
Judy of Stoughton

CH. MERRY ROVER OF VALLEY RUN, SA-116098

Sire of 18 Champions:

Out of:

Can. & Am. Ch. Stan The Man of Valley Run	SA-24088	Ch. Valley Run Dinah-Mite
Meadowset's Polly Flinders	SA-292913 ⎫	Blue Serenade of
Valley Run's Windfall	SA-307697 ⎭	Stone Gables
Judy's Gingersnap	SA-345161	Ch. Rebecca of Cherry Lane
Bold Bidder of Bloomfield	SA-405530	Ch. Hidden Lane's Broker's Tip
Sir Timothy of Valley Run	SA-259096	Ch. Valley Run Dinah-Mite
Can. & Am. Ch. Top Man of Meadboro	SA-395038	Ch. Flirtation of Meadboro
Pinney Page of Valley Run	SA-454463	Ch. Valley Run's Sabrina Fair
Guys 'N Dolls Lady Eliza	SA-493240	Ch. Guys 'N Dolls Miss Adelaide
Thenderin Merry Belle O'Delta	SA-436794 ⎫	Ch. Thenderin Golden Dream
Thenderin Jessabelle O'Delta	SA-505716 ⎭	
Guys 'N Dolls Society Max	SA-493235 ⎫	Ch. Guys 'N Dolls Miss Adelaide
Guys 'N Dolls Honey Grove	SA-493239 ⎭	
Bambi-Two of Bloomfield	SA-405529	Ch. Bambi of Bloomfield
Valley Run's English Muffin	SA-346590	Ch. Rebecca of Cherry Lane
Thenderin Revor of Delta	SA-413620 ⎫	Ch. Thenderin Golden Dream
Bem's Sir Anthony of Delta	SA-400906 ⎬	
Thenderin Headliner of Delta	SA-461548 ⎭	

Ch. Stan The Man of Valley Run

CH. MIKE OF MEADBORO, S-415928

	Ch. Grayland Rackets Boy	Rummey Stagboro
Ch. Jack O'Rackets		Blenheim Violet
	Ch. Linda of Blue Bar	Ch. Blue Bar Limited
Thelan Sir Rocklyn		Gretta of Blue Bar
	Ch. Grayland Rackets Boy	Rummey Stagboro
Ch. Rock Falls Lady Marilyn		Blenheim Violet
	Nocturne of Crowlcroft	Ch. Blaze of Fallondale
		Romance of Crowlcroft
	Ch. Maro of Maridor	Ch. Sturdy Max
Ch. Honor's Even Marksman		Ch. Lakelands Dawn
	Ch. Rodger Dale Dean	Ch. Sturdy Max
Lady McBeth		Ch. Nellie of Stagboro
	Ch. Rummey Sam of Stagboro	Rummey 2nd of Stagboro
Royal Whirl		Kate of Stagboro
	End O' Maine Tangerine	Ch. Cedric of Delwed
		Margarine Penelope

<u>Sire of 19 Champions:</u>   Out of:

Sir Rellim of Stone Gables	S-717651	Ch. Prize Par-Sal of Stone Gables
Mt. Mansfield's Smuggler (1)	S-670594	Reveille's Pandora
The Rock of Stone Gables, C.D. (12)	S-770432	Ch. Vivacious Sally of Vilmar
Weloset Yankee Boy	S-729866	Cinderella of Oak Valley
Weloset Silver Ripple (1)	S-706319	Wamlay Snow White
Phantom Brook's Thunderbolt (6)	S-819203	Ch. Phantom Brook's Popcorn
Chism's Cherokee Mike	S-812186	Chism's Queenie
Pretty Romper of Panthorn	S-847494	Ch. Silvermine Decal
Kings Ransom Timberdoodle	S-804912	Ch. Hillsdale Surprise

Can. Ch. Wamlay's Mike Chism (8)	S-812817	Chism's Queenie
Agene's Mi-Bo	S-591977	Ch. Agene's Holli-Jo
Thelan Memory of Nocturne (1)	S-507406	Ch. Rock Falls Lady Marilyn
Wamlay's Lollypop (1)	S-749782	Ch. Vivacious Sally of Vilmar
Phantom Brook's Blizzard	S-819202	Ch. Phantom Brook's Popcorn
Thelan Mark of Distinction (5)	S-507401	Ch. Rock Falls Lady Marilyn
Pheasant Point Hottentot	S-782526	Ch. Rock Falls Virginia Dare
Jean's Pearl Buttons	S-832852	Breezy Acres Spitfire
Robin Roy of Stone Gables (2)	S-877442	Ch. Prize Par-Sal of Stone Gables
Jean's Eldorado	S-884871	Breezy Acres Spitfire

MISTER MAR-JON, SA-113375
(Can. & Am. Ch. Ben-Dar's Carbon Copy x Notice-Me of Carylane)

Sire of 5 Champions:

Out of:

Bucket O'Bolts By Law (1)	SA-290280 ⎫	Ch. Hidden Lane's
Hidden Lane's Broker's Tip (2)	SA-264681 ⎭	Scheherazade
Hidden Lane's Busy Imp (1)	SA-296968 ⎫	
Hidden Lane's Samantha	SA-308373 ⎭	Dutchess of Westfield
Can. & Am. Ch. Hidden Lane's Merry Max	SA-507784	Ch. Hidden Lane's Nelle

CH. MT. MANSFIELD TEAR DROP, S-582157
(Ch. Prune's Own Parade x Reveille's Pandora)

Dam of 6 Champions: Sired by:

Mt. Mansfield Spring Song	S-928030	Ch. Ulysses of Blue Bar
Mt. Mansfield Rum Runner	S-866758	Ch. Mt. Mansfield Smuggler
Mt. Mansfield Sugar Bush	S-928028	Ch. Ulysses of Blue Bar
Mt. Mansfield Flanders Field (1)	S-981024	Ch. Yorkley Statesman
Mt. Mansfield Moonbeam	SA-60161	Ch. Ulysses of Blue Bar
Can. Ch. Mt. Mansfield Hill Billy (3)	513636	

CH. PANTHORN VALLEY RUN SAMANTHA, S-956900
(Silvermine Sky Chief x Ch. Panthorn's Gold-of-Pleasure)

Dam of 6 Champions: Sired by:

Lady Jane of Polperro (3)	SA-154899	
Valley Run Dinah-Mite (2)	SA-163052	Ch. Pirate of Polperro
Lynda's Melynda of Tel-Mo (3)	SA-155316	
Puck of Polperro	SA-154898	
Valley Run Samantha's Birdie	SA-350122	Ch. Flecka's Charlie
Misty Sample of Valley Run	SA-370858	

CH. PHANTOM BROOK'S DEDUCTIBLE, S-482279

		Roy of Blue Bar	Ch. Mallhawk's Jeff
	Ch. Jesse of Blue Bar		Kanandarque Lovelyness
		Ch. Lovely Lady of Stucile	Rummey Stagboro
Ch. Ken of Blue Bar			Ch. Modern Maid of Stucile
		Ch. Dean of Blue Bar	Ch. Mallhawk's Jeff
	Ora of Blue Bar		Ch. Lakeland's Peaches
		Ch. Gem of Blue Bar	Kanandarque Rackets Boy
			Inglehurst Matchless
		Ch. Dean of Blue Bar	Ch. Mallhawk's Jeff
	Ch. Rip of Blue Bar		Ch. Lakeland's Peaches
		Ina of Blue Bar	Roy of Blue Bar
Babe of Blue Bar II			Ch. Fly of Stagboro
		Ch. Rummey Sam of Stagboro	Rummey II of Stagboro
	Bette of Blue Bar		Kate of Stagboro
		Kanandarque Goldie	Ch. Dean of Blue Bar
			Ch. Gem of Blue Bar

Dam of 8 Champions:

Sired by:

Phantom Brook's Petticoat (1)	S-607395	⎫
Phantom Brook's Capital Gains (1)	S-865996	⎬ Can., Am. & Cuban
Phantom Brook's Popcorn (5)	S-607396	⎭ Ch. Rock Falls Colonel
Phantom Brook's Frolic (1)	S-658352	Ch. Phantom Brook's Crown
Phantom Brook's Excess Profit	S-865997	⎫ Can., Am. & Cuban
Phantom Brook's Gold Digger	S-866000	⎭ Ch. Rock Falls Colonel
Phantom Brook's Chip	S-989999	⎫
Phantom Brook's Dale	S-990000	⎭ Phantom Brook's Cholmondley

Ch. Phantom Brook's Capital Gains

PHANTOM BROOK'S FOREVER YOURS, SA-87976
(Mt. Mansfield's Spruce Peak x Ch. Phantom Brook's Popcorn)

Dam of 6 Champions:

Sired by:

Raybar's Orange Blossom	SA-346878	
Raybar's Brandy	SA-344333	
Raybar's Champagne Velvet	SA-345008	Ch. Spark 2nd
Raybar's Boilermaker	SA-345782	of Cherry Lane
Raybar's Mai Tai of Taporcan	SA-410686	
Raybar's Early Times	SA-357836	

CH. PHANTOM BROOK'S POPCORN, S-607396
Am., Can. & Cuban Ch. Rock Falls Colonel x Ch. Phantom Brook's Deductible)
See their pedigrees.

Dam of 5 Champions:

Sired by:

Phantom Brook's Bufferin (1)	S-729844	Phantom Brook's Cholmondley
Phantom Brook's Pidgeon	S-729846	
Phantom Brook's Thunderbolt (6)	S-819203	Ch. Mike of Meadboro
Phantom Brook's Blizzard	S-819202	
Phantom Brook's Blue Spruce (4)	SA-87977	Mt. Mansfield Spruce Peak

CH. PHANTOM BROOK'S THUNDERBOLT, S-819203
(Ch. Mike of Meadboro x Ch. Phantom Brook's Popcorn)

Sire of 6 Champions: Out of:

Phantom Brooks Pinafore (3)   SA-38121   Ch. Phantom Brooks
                                                          Peppercorn
Phantom Brooks Jeeves, C.D.   SA-25110   Phantom Brooks Bambi
Phantom Brooks VIP   SA-56679   Phantom Brooks HiFi
Phantom Brooks Captain Blye (1) SA-156603   Ch. Sweet Suzanna
Phantom Brooks Breeze   SA-300577 ⎫   Ch. Pretty Maid of
Phantom Brooks Gale   SA-300580 ⎭   Cherry Lane

CH. POPCORN OF BERRIWOOD, SA-81478
(Ch. Waseeka's Ace High x Ch. Beta of Deer Run)

Dam of 5 Champions: Sired by:

Kerry of Berriwood (4)   SA-219087 ⎫
Sir Kippford of Berriwood   SA-216002 ⎪
Krackerjack of Berriwood   SA-217268 ⎬   Ch. Manlove's Colonel
Koko of Berriwood (1)   SA-219088 ⎪
Kernel of Berriwood   SA-220647 ⎭

POSIE OF BLUE BAR, S-738432
(Ch. Lep of Blue Bar x Ginny of Blue Bar)

Dam of 7 Champions: Sired by:

Gentleman Jim of Valley Run   SA-86980 ⎫
Prince Charlie of Valley Run (1) SA-104105   ⎪
Valley Run Dixie Barbu (1)   SA-58256 ⎬   Ch. English Accent
Valley Run Cinnamon Cindy   SA-88582 ⎪   of Valley Run
Valley Run's Miss Cassandra (2) SA-119254   ⎪
Valley Run's Sabrina Fair (1)   SA-119253   ⎭
Quiambaugh Scotch Lassie   S-884701   Ch. Rock Falls Cavalier

CAN. CH. POLLYANNA, S-273231
(Rummey Sun Beau of Stagboro x Pamela)

Dam of 5 Champions:		Sired by:
Can. & Am. Ch. Hillsdale Susan (4)	S-747434	
Can. & Am. Ch. Hillsdale Betty	S-663940	Can. & Am. Ch. Ludar of Blue Bar
Hillsdale Surprise (1)	S-689350	
Can. Ch. Hillsdale Sparkle (2)	347752	
Can. Ch. Hillsdale Bob	304115	Happy of Howland

Am. and Can. Ch. Hillsdale Betty

CH. PRINCE OF DEERFIELD, SA-55588

(Ch. The Rock of Stone Gables, C.D. x Ch. Frosty of Stone Gables)

Sire of 9 Champions:

Out of:

Ranger of Stone Gables	SA-341925	Roxanne of Stone Gables
Blue Talisman of Stone Gables	SA-295904	Blue Ecstasy of Stone Gables
Duke of Whittenton	SA-287087	
Clariho Pym of Stone Gables	SA-292346	Candy of Clariho
Peppermint of Clariho	SA-279557	
Clariho Fieldstone Carousel	SA-430994	Ch. Tiffany of Clariho
Raff's Replica of Stone Gables	SA-495782	Blue Ecstasy of Stone Gables
Clariho Blossom Slosson	SA-429885	Ch. Tiffany of Clariho
Can. Ch. Blue Charm of Stone Gables	756601	Kruczek's Lady

CH. REMITTANCE MAN OF LAZY F, SA-111558

(Ch. Windsor of Cherry Lane x Ch. Lady Lark of Panthorn)

Sire of 5 Champions:

Out of:

Mayhew's Dauntless of Lazy F	SA-269540	Ch. Mayhew's Game Girl
Mayhew's Deb of Lazy F	SA-273648	
Mayhew's Brown Sugar	SA-428911	
Walker's Briggs of Mayhew, C.D.	SA-253341	
Can. Ch. Spruce Pirate of Lazy F		Spruce Diamete

326

CH. ROCK FALLS CAVALIER, S-131384

	Spiron Jagersbo	Int. Ch. Spiron
Rummey Stagboro		Arbu Lala B
	Selkirk Snooksie	Int. Ch. McConnell's Nori
Ch. Grayland Rackets Boy		Int. Ch. Selkirk Juliet
	Int. Ch. Rackets Rummey	Ch. Mallwyd Ralph
Bleheim Violet		Stylish Pretty Polly
	Principe Bonnie	Snowdon Ralph
		Graylands Belle
		Ch. Mallhawk Rackets Boy
	Kanandarque Rackets Boy	Selkirk's Mallhawk Juliet
Ch. Blue Bar Limited		Ch. Sir Orkney Willgress
	Inglehurst Matchless	Inglehurst Mary
Ch. Linda Lou of Blue Bar		Ch. Mallhawk Rackets Boy
	Ch. Mallhawk Jeff	Flora Mallhawk
Gretta of Blue Bar		Rummey Stagboro
	Ch. Lakeland's Peaches	Lakeland's Nymph

Sire of 21 Champions:

Out of:

Can., Am. & Cuban Ch.		
Rock Falls Colonel (30)	S-329961	Ch. Rock Falls Belle
Rock Falls Racket (29)	S-254264	
Winbert's Snooksie	S-709092	Hyde's Kip
Rock Falls Troubadour (6)	S-370334	Ch. Manlove's Goldie
		of Stagboro

Cavalier (continued)

Rock Falls King Charles (4)	S-446142	Ch. Rip's Miss Dusky of Havertown
Rock Falls Rhett Butler	S-804176	Rock Falls Libby
Carolina's Adorable Lady (1)	S-360849	Prune's Own Sweetheart
Kings Ransom Bufflehead	S-477791	Ch. Suave of Scyld
Rock Falls Virginia Dare (2)	S-504564	Ch. Rock Falls Belle
Hadceda Jewel 2nd	S-461501	Ch. Rip's Miss Dusky of Havertown
Flush of Blue Bar	S-524585	Ch. Mary of Blue Bar
Rock Falls Blue Baron (3)	S-402086	Ch. Manlove's Goldie of Stagboro
Rocky Nevada (5)	S-504146	Ch. Miss Tilly of Blue Bar
Al-Kay's Gold Fever	S-625813	Ch. Thelon Memory of Nocturne
Kings Ransom Lord Jeff	S-477790	Ch. Suave of Scyld
Manlove's Patsy Girl (5)	S-468759	Manlove's Rose Dee
Hadceda Cavalier	S-461499	Ch. Rip's Miss Dusky of Havertown
Rock Falls Crystal	S-850903	Ch. Rock Falls Mamie
Rock Falls Lancelot	S-370333	Ch. Manlove's Goldie of Stagboro
Rock Falls Galahad	S-256844	Ch. Rock Falls Belle
Quiambaugh Scotch Lassie	S-884701	Posie of Blue Bar

The great Ch. Rock Falls Colonel, son of Cavalier and winner of 101 Bests in Show, with his owners.

AM., CAN. & CUBAN CH. ROCK FALLS COLONEL, S-329961

		Spiron Jagersbo
	Rummey Stagboro	Selkirk Snooksie
	Ch. Grayland Rackets Boy	Int. Ch. Rackets Rummey
	Bleheim Violet	Principe Bonnie
Ch. Rock Falls Cavalier		Kanandarque Rackets Boy
	Ch. Blue Bar Limited	Inglehurst Matchless
	Ch. Linda of Blue Bar	Ch. Mallhawk Jeff
	Gretta of Blue Bar	Ch. Lakeland's Peaches
		Spiron Jagersbo
	Rummey Stagboro	Selkirk Snooksie
	Ch. Grayland Rackets Boy	Int. Ch. Racket's Rummey
	Bleheim Violet	Principe Bonnie
Ch. Rock Falls Belle		Ch. Mark of Stagboro
	Ch. Blaze of Fallondale	Ch. Grayland Orange Blossom
	Nocturne of Crowlcroft	Ch. Ladysman of Jagersbo
	Romance of Crowlcroft	Patrician Lady of Jagersbo

Sire of 30 Champions: Out of:

Manlove's Colonel (10)	S-740461	Ch. Manlove's Patsy Girl
Phantom Brook's Capital Gains (1)	S-865996	Ch. Phantom Brook's Deductible
Manlove's Lady Wolfscroft	S-855790	Manlove's Jenny Lee
Cabin Hill Sensation	S-880887	Rock Falls Amber

329

Sig of Snowfeather	S-545355	Ch. Dame Bonny of Snowfeather
Phantom Brook's Petticoat (1)	S-607395	Ch. Phantom Brook's Deductible
Heljax Sweet Lady (2)	S-642275	Heljax Rebecca
Phantom Brook's Popcorn (5)	S-607396	Ch. Phantom Brook's Deductible
Can. & Am. Ch. Rock Falls Manlove Peter Pan (1)	S-581673	Alliene of Blue Bar
Rock Falls Mamie (1)	S-623498	Rock Falls Eve
Rock Falls Dixie Darling (3)	S-614218	Rock Falls Amber
Destiny's Small Talk (4)	S-541769	Jubalee's Destiny
Manlove's Dawn (2)	S-581239	Ch. Manlove's Goldie
Phantom Brook's Lyric	S-665384	Ch. Phantom Brook's Fortune
Craiglare's Major's Command	S-681766	Bolton Rebound
Can. & Am. Ch. Manlove's Ike (1)	S-621883	Rock Falls Eve
Rolling Greens Marysam	S-714231	Ch. Caroline's Adorable Lady
Rock Falls Sky Way (9)	S-585551	Rock Falls Peggy
Bishop of Highbridge Acres	S-654228	Blue Lady of Highbridge Acres
Manlove's Anna Lee (2)	S-740464	Ch. Manlove's Patsy Girl
Rock Falls Lieutenant (8)	S-519226	Jacklinn-O-Rackets
Rock Falls Daisy Mae (2)	S-614213	Rock Falls Eve
Phantom Brook's Gold Digger	S-866000	Ch. Phantom Brook's Deductible
Manlove of Ellendale (2)	S-907448	Ch. Manlove's Dawn
Phantom Brook's Excess Profit	S-865997	Ch. Phantom Brook's Deductible
Cabin Hill Hostess (1)	S-880889	Rock Falls Amber
Manlove's Mona (3)	S-810218	Ch. Rip's Miss Dusky of Havertown

Manlove's Belle	S-810216	} Ch. Manlove's Patsy Girl
Colonel Robert E. Lee	S-838435	
Manlove's Lovely Lady (3)	S-987652	Manlove's Lady Juliet

CH. ROCK FALLS LIEUTENANT, S-519226
(Am., Can. & Cuban Ch. Rock Falls Colonel x Jacklinn-O-Rackets)

Sire of 8 Champions:		Out of:
Rock Candy of Calamity Jane (8)	S-635750	Ch. Candy of Blue Bar
Chandelle Lady (9)	S-925916	Duchess Rugger Honey
Robinswood Dot (4)	SA-9423	Miss Freckles of Devon
Tioga Symphony	S-621766	Ch. Yorkley Cover Girl
Freckles of Devonshire	SA-10000	Miss Freckles of Devon
Brynnestone Orange Crumpet, C.D.	SA-39194	} Kennelquest Spring Delight
Willow's Stanley	SA-103777	
Lieutenant's Pollyanna (1)	SA-86489	

330

CH. ROCK FALLS RACKET, S-254264

		Spiron Jagersbo
	Rummey Stagboro	Selkirk Snooksie
	Ch. Grayland Rackets Boy	Int. Ch. Rackets Rummey
	Blenheim Violet	Principe Bonnie
Ch. Rock Falls Cavalier		Kanandarque Rackets Boy
	Ch. Blue Bar Limited	Inglehurst Matchless
	Ch. Linda of Blue Bar	Ch. Mallhawk Jeff
	Gretta of Blue Bar	Ch. Lakeland's Peaches
		Spiron Jagersbo
	Rummey Stagboro	Selkirk Snooksie
	Ch. Grayland Rackets Boy	Int. Ch. Racket's Rummey
	Blenheim Violet	Principe Bonnie
Ch. Rock Falls Belle		Ch. Mark of Stagboro
	Ch. Blaze of Fallondale	Ch. Grayland Orange Blossom
	Nocturne of Crowlcroft	Ch. Ladysman of Jagersbo
	Romance of Crowlcroft	Patrician Lady of Jagersbo

Sire of 29 Champions: Out of:

Can. & Am. Ch. Silvermine Jackpot (3)	S-491402	Silvermine Corrine
Aspetuck's Red Letter (1)	S-648297	Aspetuck's Red Sumac
Can. & Am. Ch. Chatterwood's Hot Toddy (2)	S-696509	Ch. Aspetuck's Diana
Betsworth Gold Flake (4)	S-601825	Aspetuck's Red Sumac
Silvermine Roderick 2nd (1)	S-651705	Wamlay Snow White
Chatterwood on the Rocks (2)	S-696508	Ch. Aspetuck's Diana

Silvermine Roulette	S-491401	Silvermine Corinne
Ike of Blue Bar (6)	S-586365	Ch. Rip Tide of Blue Bar
Can. & Am. Ch. Silvermine Custom Maid	S-491405	Silvermine Corinne
Zamitz Exciting Expose	S-660334	Ch. Zamitz Bread and Butter
Chatterwood Lyric	S-824737	Aspetuck's Diana
Aspetuck's Chief Waramoug (1)	S-883218	Ch. Aspetuck's Feather
English Accent of Valley Run (10)	S-893847	Ch. Starbright of Valley Run
Waseeka's Jiminy Cricket	S-778397	Ch. Scyld's The Black Widow
Zamitz Export Edition (2)	S-660332	Ch. Zamitz Bread and Butter
Deepwood Danny (2)	S-669036	Ch. Aspetuck's Feather
Betsworth Blue Print	S-663667	Ch. Scyld's The Black Widow
Aspetuck's Golden Touch	S-696515 ⎫	
Chatterwood Marmalade	S-824735 ⎭	Ch. Aspetuck's Diana
Betsworth It's A Racket	S-635115 ⎫	
Candlewood Destiny (2)	S-668475 ⎭	Duchess of Iversley
Valley Run Starbright's Gina	S-918827	Ch. Starbright of Valley Run
Zamitz Early Edition	S-660329	Ch. Zamitz Bread and Butter
Aspetuck's Shadow (8)	S-957593	Ch. Aspetuck's Diana
Star Rocket of Valley Run	S-976906 ⎫	
Sweet Suzanna (1)	S-858168 ⎭	Ch. Starbright of Valley Run
Aspetuck's Red Satin, C.D.	S-915777	Ch. Aspetuck's Diana
Archibald of Valley Run	S-983561	Ch. Starbright of Valley Run
Cedar Retreat's Rocket (1)	S-853876	Folly of Cedar Retreat

Ch. Chatterwood on the Rocks

CH. ROCK FALLS SKY WAY, S-585551
(Am., Can. & Cuban Ch. Rock Falls Colonel x Rock Falls Peggy)

Sire of 9 Champions: Out of:

Rock Falls King Whit	S-702000	Colonel's Manlove Lady
Moorland Nocturne	S-611765	Ch. Destiny's Small Talk
Rock Falls Tarheel Tillie (2)	S-728820	Ch. Rock Falls Daisy Mae
Moorland Racketeer	S-611772	Ch. Destiny's Small Talk
Ladaredge Angel Face	S-710418	Ch. Haon Peggy
Rock Falls Sky Rocket	S-627367	Colonel's Manlove Lady
Rock Falls Rummey Special	S-685966	Ch. Rock Falls Daisy Mae
Moorland Jubilee	S-611767 }	Ch. Destiny's Small Talk
Moorland Stag	S-611768 }	

AM. & CUBAN CH. ROCK FALLS TROUBADOR, S-370334
(Ch. Rock Falls Cavalier x Ch. Manlove's Goldie of Stagboro)

Sire of 6 Champions: Out of:

Iverlee Fortune Hunter (2)	S-690255	Gorgeous Goldie of Orkney
Rock Falls Happy Hunter	S-435818	Rock Falls Dianna
Memory of Orkney (1)	S-658281	Gorgeous Goldie of Orkney
Orkney the Great (2)	S-770671	Ch. The Blue Princess of Orkney
Laguna Honda Gold Flake	S-701933 }	Gorgeous Goldie of Orkney
Orkney Bob	S-709645 }	

CH. THE ROCK OF STONE GABLES, C.D. - S-770432

	Ch. Jack O' Rackets	Ch. Grayland Rackets Boy
Thelan Sir Rocklyn		Ch. Linda Lou of Blue Bar
	Ch. Rock Falls Lady Marilyn	Ch. Grayland Rackets Boy
Ch. Mike of Meadboro		Nocturne of Crowlcroft
	Ch. Honor's Even Marksman	Can. & Am. Ch. Maro of Maridor
Lady McBeth		Ch. Rodger Dale Dean
	Royal Whirl	Ch. Rummey Sam of Stagboro
		End O'Maine Tangerine
	Ch. Dean of Blue Bar	Ch. Mallhawk's Jeff
Ch. Rip of Blue Bar		Ch. Lakeland's Peaches
	Ina of Blue Bar	Roy of Blue Bar
Ch. Vivacious Sally of Vilmar		Ch. Fly of Stagboro
	Banker of Fallondale	Can. & Am. Ch. Maxie of Stagboro
Vivacious Lass of Vilmar		Ch. Grayland Orange Blossom
	Delta of Larana	Ch. Sturdy Max
		Ch. Lakeland's Dawn

Sire of 12 Champions:

Out of:

Autumaura Carefree Bev (1)	S-985345	⎫
Autumaura Corpsman Joe, C.D.	S-985348	⎬ Ch. Elaine of Elm Knoll
Autumaura Corporal Chet	S-985347	⎭
Skyline of Stone Gables (3)	S-898822	Pleiades Electra of Deer Run
Autumaura Cheery Miss (2)	S-985343	Ch. Elaine of Elm Knoll
Blue Rex of Stone Gables	SA-20547	Blue Bess
Can. Ch. Truebarn's Baroness	476346	Can. Ch. Skidby's Deborah
Prince of Deerfield (8)	SA-55588	Ch. Frosty of Stone Gables
Autumaura Captain Jim (2)	S-985350	Ch. Elaine of Elm Knoll
Thenderin Friar of Chiltern (2)	SA-106711	Ch. Autumaura Carefree Bev
Swagger Boy of Stone Gables	SA-49061	Blue Bess
Thenderin Maid Merian of Kent	SA-144089	Ch. Manlove's Mona

CH. ROCKY NEVADA, S-504146
(Ch. Rock Falls Cavalier x Ch. Miss Tilly of Blue Bar)

Sire of 5 Champions:

Out of:

Can. & Am. Ch. Madame Hi-Tone of Rocky Nevada (7)	S-980585	
Can. & Am. Ch. Desert Sage of Rocky Nevada	SA-1669	Ch. Blue Cinders of Blue Bar
My Fair Blue Lady from Nevada	S-980583	
Truckee Triumph	S-979286	
Rocky Nevada's White Gold	S-980582	

CH. SILVERMINE CHAMBRAY, S-338511

Ch. The Snark of Scyld
  Ch. Sturdy Max
    Rummey Stagboro — Spiron Jagersbo / Selkirk Snooksie
    Rummey Girl of Stagboro — Ch. Pat II / Selkirk Snooksie
  Ch. Samantha of Scyld
    Rummey Stagboro — Spiron Jagersbo / Selkirk Snooksie
    Jane of Maridor — Ch. Sturdy Max / Hi Nellie P.S.

Silvermine Wanita
  Can. & Am. Ch. Silvermine Wagabond
    Ch. Rhett Butler of Silvermine — Rummey Stagboro / Lady Dian of Silvermine
    Keyfield Judy — Fox Flame / Lavender Lady
  Rackets Gene of Silvermine
    Vera's Adonis of Jagersbo — Can. & Am. Ch. Rackets Rummey / Molly Jagersbo
    Ch. Sandy's Racket Gene — Ch. Sandy D / Heather Gale

Dam of 6 Champions:

Sired by:

Can. & Am. Ch. Ben-Dar's Advance Notice (6)	S-568625	
Can. & Am. Ch. Darby of Carylane (1)	S-660482	Can. & Am. Ch. Ludar of Blue Bar
Can. & Am. Ch. Ben-Dar's Carbon Copy (7)	S-655200	
Can. & Am. Ch. Hidden Lane's Michael	S-854561	Can. & Am. Ch. Manlove's Ike
Can. Ch. Ben-Dar's Little Slam	340693	Can. & Am. Ch. Ludar of Blue Bar
Silvermine Citadel	S-474604	Sturdy Max 2nd

CH. SILVERMINE GREAT GUNS, S-549503
(Ch. Silvermine Whipcord x Ch. Silvermine Candy Bar)

Sire of 5 Champions:		Out of:
Cedar Retreat's Pretty Pat	SA-37749	Cedar Retreat Lady Gwendolyn
Cedar Retreat's Aunt Laura	SA-822142	Cedar Retreat's Tostie
Cedar Retreat's Dandie Dan	SA-95532	Cedar Retreat Lady Gwendolyn
Cedar Retreat's Nimrod	SA-140680	Knollwood Dutchess Delight
Butternut of Hubbel Hill	SA-192291	Golden Gal of Hubbell Hill

CH. SILVERMINE SWIFT, S-143413

		Rummey Stagboro	Spiron Jagersbo
	Ch. Sturdy Max		Selkirk Snooksie
		Rummey Girl of Stagboro	Ch. Pat II
Ch. The Snark of Scyld			Selkirk Snooksie
		Rummey Stagboro	Spiron Jagersbo
	Ch. Samantha of Scyld		Selkirk Snooksie
		Jane of Maridor	Ch. Sturdy Max
			Hi Nellie P. S.
		Ch. Sturdy Max	Rummey Stagboro
	Ch. Maro of Maridor		Rummey Girl of Stagboro
		Ch. Lakeland Dawn	Rummey Stagboro
Silvermine Story			Lakeland Nymph
		Ch. Rhett Butler of Silvermine	Rummey Stagboro
	Melanie of Silvermine		Lady Dian of Silvermine
		Nellie Flagg	Ch. Gilroy's Pal
			Rackets Nell

Dam of 5 Champions:

			Sired by:
Silvermine Decal (5)	S-509712	⎫	
Silvermine Delicious	S-509709	⎬	Sturdy Max 2nd
Silvermine Delightful 2nd	S-509711	⎭	
Silvermine Matchless (3)	S-353042	⎫	
Silvermine Messenger	S-353043	⎬	Ch. Silvermine Wagabond

CH. SILVERMINE WHIPCORD, S-338513
(Ch. The Snark of Scyld x Silvermine Wanita)

Sire of 7 Champions: Out of:

Zamitz Bread and Butter (3)	S-566271	Dora's Misty
Silvermine Connie (1)	S-662383	Mary Ann 2nd
Silvermine Havoc (1)	S-483735	Silvermine Nylon
Silvermine Great Guns (5)	S-549503	Ch. Silvermine Candy Bar
Panthorn's Gold-of-Pleasure (1)	S-676963	Ch. Silvermine Decal
Hyrec Whipson (1)	S-976951 ⎫	Ch. Manlove's Beckey
Whipcord's Cherie	S-975267 ⎭	

CAN. & AM. CH. SIR KIP OF MANITOU, SA-240824
(Ch. Skidby's Bosun of Stone Gables x High-Tor's Spicy Lady)

Sire of 11 Champions:

		Out of:
Clariho Bit O'Candy	SA-410611 ⎱	
Clariho Rough Rider	SA-402848 ⎰	
Tom Terrific of Stone Gables	SA-411562	Clariho Piper of
The Hallmark of		Stone Gables
Stone Gables (3)	SA-411561	
Leelyn's Top Brass of		
Clariho (2)	SA-400988	Navy Blue of Stone Gables
Clariho Blue Horizon	SA-513092	Druids Brew of Stone Gables
Clariho Copper Coin	SA-478745 ⎱	
Can. Ch. Clariho Double O'Seven	799239 ⎰	Canberra's Copper of Clariho
Sir Eric of Valley Heights	SA-540294	Druids Brew of Stone Gables
Can. & Am. Ch. Surrey's Charm		
of Stone Gables	SA-563193	Clariho Pell of Stone Gables
Can. Ch. Wragge Run's		
Wine and Roses		Clariho Out of the Blue

CH. SKIDBY'S BOSUN OF STONE GABLES, SA-14977

```
                    Thelan Sir Rocklyn
           Can. and Am. Ch. Mike of Meadboro
                    Lady McBeth
        Can. Ch. Wamlay Mike Chism
                    Ch. Rock Falls Sky Way
           Chism's Queenie
                    Colonel's Manlove Lady

                    Silvermine Hotshot
           Ch. Raskalus Raff of Stone Gables
                    Cinderella of Oak Valley
        Royal Blue of Stone Gables
                    Rock Falls White Cloud
           Tower Hill To And Again
                    April of Blue Bar
```

Sire of 8 Champions: Out of:

Lady's Fairfax of Stone Gables	SA-179978	Ch. Wamlay's Lollypop
Can. & Am. Ch. Yankee's Maid of Stone Gables (3)	SA-225262	Peggotty of Stone Gables
Penmaen Lady Richmond	SA-102565	Penmaen Lady Beaufort
Lemon Delight of Carowa	SA-292824	Campus Belle of Stone Gables
High Havens Queen Bess	SA-198223	Blue Lisa of Stone Gables
Tiffany of Clariho (4)	SA-237547	
Lady Tempest of Long Valley	SA-238792	High-Tor's Spicy Lady
Can. & Am. Ch. Sir Kip of Manitou (11)	SA-225262	

AM. & CAN. CH. SKIDBY'S CAMBRIDGE MISS, SA-94250
(Can. Ch. Wamlay's Mike Chism x Royal Blue of Stone Gables)

Dam of 9 Champions: Sired by:

Top O' Penmaen Lord Willin' (2)	SA-266552	⎫
Penmaen Wandering Home	SA-274296	⎪
Top O' Penmaen Widsith	SA-266553	⎬ Ch. Top O' Tamerlaine
Penmaen Wood Sprite	SA-274298	⎪
Penmaen With Love	SA-274297	⎭
Shawsheen's Penmaen Camber	SA-148073	⎫
Penmaen Suzanne of Forest	SA-143385	⎬ Ch. Shawsheen High Tide
Penmaen's Meg of Gypsy Lane	SA-512960	⎫ Ch. Gilroy's Chancellor
Penmaen Blue Cambric	SA-510511	⎭

CH. SPARK 2nd of CHERRY LANE, SA-159967
(Ch. Windsor of Cherry Lane x Lady of Cherry Lane)

Sire of 10 Champions:

Out of:

Sparkson of Ramar	SA-298010	Mary of Haleridge
Raybar's Orange Blossom	SA-346878	
Raybar's Brandy	SA-344333	
Raybar's Champagne Velvet	SA-345008	Phantom Brooks Forever Yours
Raybar's Boilermaker	SA-345782	
Raybar Wisp of Lonesome Lane	SA-418085	
Raybar's Ain't She Sweet	SA-408421	Ch. Frenessa of Calamity Lane
Anita of Cherry Lane	SA-506730	Belinda of Cherry Lane
Raybar's Mai Tai of Taporcan	SA-410686	
Raybar's Early Times	SA-357836	Phantom Brooks Forever Yours

CH. SQUIRE OF BLUE BAR, S-660757
(Ch. Gus du Hameau x Ch. Mary of Blue Bar)

Sire of 5 Champions:

Out of:

Tarnock's Terry (1)	SA-18885	Ch. Top O' Tarrina
Devoncote's All The Way (1)	S-961065 ⎫	Ch. Cocoa of Calamity Lane
Devoncote's At Last	S-961063 ⎭	
Ranger of Merrie Sherwood	SA-44215	Ch. Manlove's Anna Lee
Devoncote's Betsy Boo (2)	SA-67069	Ch. Manlove's Patsy Girl

CH. STARBRIGHT OF VALLEY RUN, S-545136
(Sturdy Max 2nd x Silvermine Confection)

Dam of 5 Champions:

Sired by:

Valley Run Starbright's Gina	S-918827 ⎫	
Star Rocket of Valley Run	S-976906	
Sweet Suzanna (1)	S-858168 ⎬ Ch. Rock Falls Racket
Archibald of Valley Run	S-983561	
English Accent of Valley Run (10)	S-893847 ⎭	

STURDY MAX 2nd, S-750816

Spiron Jagersbo Rummey Stagboro Selkirk Snooksie **Ch.** Lakeland's Yuba Can. & Am. Ch. Rackets Rummey Lakeland's Nymph Lakeland's Fascination Rummey Stagboro Ch. Sturdy Max Rummey Girl of Stagboro **Ch.** Dora of Maridor Rummey Stagboro Ch. Lakeland's Dawn Lakeland's Nymph	Int. Ch. Spiron Arbu Lala B Can. & Am. Ch. McConnell's Nori Can. & Am. Ch. Selkirk Juliet Ch. Mallwyd Ralph Stylish Pretty Polly Meadowdale Mallwyd Count Myer's Blue Bird Spiron Jagersbo Selkirk Snooksie Ch. Pat II Selkirk Snooksie Spiron Jagersbo Selkirk Snooksie Can. & Am. Ch. Rackets Rummey Lakeland's Fascination

Sire of 14 Champions: Out of:

Aspetuck's Red Robin	S-569092	Aspetuck's Red Sumac
Silvermine Citadel	S-474604	Ch. Silvermine Chambray
Silvermine Delicious	S-509709	Ch. Silvermine Swift
Starbright of Valley Run (5)	S-545136	Silvermine Confection
Silvermine Decal (5)	S-509712 ⎫	
Silvermine Delightful 2nd	S-509711 ⎭	Ch. Silvermine Swift
Aspetuck's Diana (7)	S-622274	Aspetuck's Red Sumac
Silvermine Domino (1)	S-570672	Silvermine Wanita
Sharoc's Monte of Oak Valley	S-279044	Ch. Sharoc Dolly Madison
Aspetuck's Feather (3)	S-584358	Aspetuck's Red Sumac

344

Prune's Own Amber	S-105416	Peggy Jane
Orange Man Machold (1)	S-297568	Rummey Sam's Sally
Mr. Watt	S-235418 ⎫	
Chief of Armsworth (1)	S-213489 ⎭	Maxson's Delight

CH. THELAN MARK OF DISTINCTION, S-507401
(Ch. Mike of Meadboro x Ch. Rock Falls Lady Marilyn)

Sire of 5 Champions: Out of:

Javelin of Button Ball	S-868833 ⎫	Can. & Am. Ch. Crawfie of
Vaulter of Button Ball (3)	S-868839 ⎭	Blue Bar
Al-Kay's Lady Marilyn	S-681570	Idessa of Al-Kay
Discus of Button Ball (1)	S-868838 ⎫	Can. & Am. Ch. Crawfie of
Al-Kay's Sky Watch	S-868836 ⎭	Blue Bar

CH. THENDERIN GOLDEN DREAM, SA-328321
(Ch. Thenderin Friar of Chiltern ex Autumaura Christmas Debut)

Dam of 5 Champions:

Sired by:

Thenderin Merry Belle O'Delta	SA-436794	
Thenderin Jessabelle O'Delta	SA-505716	
Thenderin Revor of Delta	SA-413620	Ch. Merry Rover of Valley Run
Bem's Sir Anthony of Delta	SA-400906	
Thenderin Headliner of Delta	SA-461548	

CH. TOP O'TAMERLAINE, S-820752
(Am. & Can. Ch. Ben-Dar's Advance Notice x Flecka's Hush Puppy)

Sire of 5 Champions:

Out of:

Top O' Penmaen Lord Willin' (2)	SA-266552	
Penmaen Wandering Home	SA-274296	
Top O' Penmaen Widsith	SA-266553	Am. & Can. Ch. Skidby's Cambridge Miss
Penmaen Wood Sprite	SA-274298	
Penmaen With Love	SA-274297	

346

CH. ULYSSES OF BLUE BAR, S-654297

Ch. Rube of Blue Bar
- Ch. Sir Herbert of Kennelworth
  - Ch. Rip of Blue Bar
    - Ch. Dean of Blue Bar
    - Ina of Blue Bar
  - Vivacious Doll of Vilmar
    - Banker of Fallondale
    - Delta of Larana
- Ch. Norma of Blue Bar
  - Ch. Lem of Blue Bar
    - Lone Ace of Kanandarque
    - Lovely Dawn of Kanandarque
  - Zo of Blue Bar
    - Ch. Dean of Blue Bar
    - Ch. Rita of Blue Bar

Ch. Ripple of Blue Bar
- Ch. Lep of Blue Bar
  - Ch. Matt of Blue Bar
    - Ch. Pilot of Crombie of Happy Valley
    - Inglehurst Matchless
  - Dora of Blue Bar
    - Ch. Jesse of Blue Bar
    - Ch. Lola of Blue Bar
- Ch. Penny of Happy Valley
  - Happy Valley Creole Chief
    - Happy Valley Punch
    - Lipstick of Stucile
  - Happy Valley Cobalt Queen
    - Happy Valley Ragged
    - Happy Valley Lady Mellhawk

Sire of 10 Champions:

		Out of:
Zamitz Invader (3)	S-793017	Silvermine Athalee
Zamitz Intended (2)	S-793023	
Mt. Mansfield Independence	S-949182	Mt. Mansfield Sugar Slalom
Mt. Mansfield's Sugar Bush	S-928028	Ch. Mt. Mansfield's Tear Drop
Mt. Mansfield Spring Song	S-928030	
Mt. Mansfield Gregarious	SA-70045	Mt. Mansfield Mata Hari
Mt. Mansfield Moonbeam	SA-60161	Ch. Mt. Mansfield's Tear Drop
Mt. Mansfield's Pumpkin	SA-70240	Ch. Phantom Brook's Pepper Corn
Mt. Mansfield's Tilt (1)	SA-172553	Mt. Mansfield Mata Hari
Can. Ch. Mt. Mansfield's Hillbilly (3)	513636	Ch. Mt. Mansfield's Tear Drop

CH. VIGIL OF VILMAR, S-116734

	Ch. Mallhawk Jeff	Ch. Mallhawk Rackets Boy
Ch. Dean of Blue Bar		Flora Mallhawk
	Ch. Lakeland Peaches	Rummey Stagboro
Ch. Rip of Blue Bar		Lakelands Nymph
	Roy of Blue Bar	Ch. Mallhawk Jeff
Ina of Blue Bar		Kanandarque Loveliness
	Ch. Fly of Stagboro	Inglehurst Rock
		Selkirk Snooksie
	Int. Ch. Moxie of Stagboro	Rummey Stagboro
Banker of Fallondale		Kate of Stagboro
	Ch. Grayland Orange Blossom	Rummey Stagboro
Victory Maid of Vilmar		Mallhawks Lady Dawn
	Ch. Sturdy Max	Rummey Stagboro
Delta of Larana		Rummey Girl of Stagboro
	Ch. Lakeland's Dawn	Rummey Stagboro
		Lakeland's Nymph

Sire of 7 Champions: Out of:

General Lee Jones (2)	S-421813	Roxana's Cynthia
Sir Bedford of Pickard Square	S-423108	Reba of Blue Bar
Kiko-Kiko of Lua-Lua-Lei (1)	S-452629	Mallhawk Snowflake
Waterford My Choice (1)	S-524753	Reba of Blue Bar
Sleeper's Ghost	S-418033	Roxana's Cynthia
Vig-Re's Timothy of Waterford	S-518705 }	
Thenderin Mallhawk Merrily (4)	S-441317 }	Reba of Blue Bar

348

Ch. Elice of Hale Ridge, by Ch. General
Lee Jones ex Ch. Waterford My Choice.

CAN. CH. WAMLAY'S MIKE CHISM, S-812817
(Ch. Mike of Meadboro x Chism's Queenie)

Sire of 8 Champions: Out of:

Can. & Am. Ch. Skidby's		
Cambridge Miss (9)	SA-92450	Royal Blue of Stone Gables
Skidby's Bosun of		
Stone Gables (8)	SA-14977	
Dover's Molly Pitcher	SA-253022	
Can. Ch. Dover's Betsy Ross	639235	Ch. Confetti of Calamity Lane
Can. Ch. Colonel Mike of		
Wellington	635224	
Can. Ch. Wragge Run's		
Cinnamon Cinner	635220	
Can. Ch. Wragge Run's		Can. & Am. Ch. Wragge Run's
Senator Mike (2)	635225	Roulette
Can. Ch. Wragge Run's		
Hello Hattie Lu	635221	

CH. WASEEKA'S ACE HIGH, S-781463
(Can. & Am. Ch. Silvermine Jackpot x Ch. Doting Girl of Blue Bar)

Sire of 5 Champions: Out of:

Sir Featherston of Berriwood	SA-81476	
Popcorn of Berriwood (5)	SA-81478	
Barnaby of Berriwood (1)	SA-;57946	Ch. Beta of Deer Run
Haleridge Poppy of Berriwood (3)	SA-83511	
Sir John Bull of Berriwood	SA-81477	

YORKLEY WISP O'HEATHER, S-506234
(Ch. Sunny Jim x Ch. Southern Lady of Aragon)

Dam of 5 Champions: Sired by:

Ben-Dar's Replica (5)	S-689328	
Yorkley's Statesman	S-689326	
Ben-Dar's Special Edition	S-689329	Can. & Am. Ch.
Ben-Dar's Winning Stride (22)	S-689327	Ludar of Blue Bar
Ben-Dar's Sweet Sue (2)	S-689331	

Other Sires and Dams: In a compilation of this type it is impossible, due to expense, to list every stud and dam worthy of attention. The pictures and pedigrees you have just seen give you the dogs found in the majority of recent pedigrees in the United States and Canada.

However, a few dogs that had not produced five or more champions of record when this compilation was made are deserving of mention. Some of the following may well become the top producers of tomorrow.

Sires with Four Champions:

Can. Ch. Banner of Spruce
Ch. Bantam of Truslers
Ch. Canberra Blue Shadow
Ch. Commodore of Merrie Sherwood
Ch. Hidden Lanes Mark Me
Ch. Kerry of Berriwood
Am. & Can. Ch. Krisquier's Lone Eagle
Ch. La May's Jim Dan Doo
Phantom Brooks Cholmondley
Ch. Phantom Brooks Blue Spruce
Ch. Pirate of Polperro
Ch. Prune's Own Parade
Ch. Rock Falls King Charles
Ch. Silvermine Wagabond
Ch. Sir Guy of Ellendale

Ch. Kerry of Berriwood

Ch. Silvermine Jackpot

Sires with Three Champions:

Ch. Adam of Lonesome Lane
Blue Warrior of Lynncrest
Ch. Candlewood Distinction
Ch. Ernford Highflyer
Ch. Faneal's Blue Danube
Ch. Flecka's Andy
Ch. The Hallmark of Stone Gables
Can. Ch. Helen's Pride
Ch. Kelly's White Lightning
Ludar's Better Still
Ch. Manlove's Marksman
Can. Ch. Mt. Mansfield's Hillbilly
Mt. Manfield's Spruce Peak
Phantom Brooks Briar
Ch. Rascalus Raff of Stone Gables
Robin of Merrie Sherwood
Ch. Sargeant of Kenmore
Ch. Silvermine Jackpot
Ch. Skyline of Stone Gables
Ch. Sundridge Antiphon
Ch. Thenderin O'Revendale
Ch. Tioga King Arthur
Tioga Robin Hood
Ch. Vaulter of Button Ball
Ch. Windsor of Cherry Lane
Ch. Yorkley Ensign Roberts

Dams with Four Champions:

Ch. Betsworth Gold Flake
Ch. Blue Diamond Mist
Bunnydale's Daisy Belle
Clariho Piper of Stone Gables
Ch. Destiny's Small Talk
Dover's Patriot of Berriwood
Flecka's Hush Puppy
Ch. Golden Dawn of Dogstar
Am. & Can. Ch. Hillsdale Susan
Lo Erls Sensation at Dusk
Ch. Manlove's Beckey
Manlove's Bess 2nd
Ch. Manlove's Goldie
Manlove's Judy
Manlove's Nancy Lee
Ch. Mayhew's Game Girl
Notice-Me of Carylane
Ch. Princesa de Rancho Tranquilo
Ch. Robinwood's Dot
Silvermine Wanita
Spruce Blossom
Ch. Thendorin Mallhawk Merrily
Ch. Tiffany of Clariho
Ch. Wallis of Cherry Lane
Am. & Can. Ch. Wragge Run's Roulette

Ch. Betsworth Gold Flake

Dams with Three Champions:

Ch. Aspetuck's Feather
Blue Ecstasy of Stone Gables
Blue Mist of Stone Gables
Cinderella of Oak Valley
Ch. Cynthia Darbella
Ch. Eadie of Elm Knoll
Ch. Flirtation of Meadboro
Gilroy's Dixie
Ch. Guys 'N Dolls Miss Adelaide
Ch. Haleridge Poppy of Berriwood
Hasty Miss of Meadboro
Ch. Hidden Lane's Scheherazade
High-Tor's Spicy Lady
Kennelquest Spring Delight
Ch. Lady Dana of Ellendale
Ch. Lady Jane of Polperro
Ch. Lady Marco
Can. & Am. Ch. Ludar's Ludette
Ch. Lynda's Melynda of Tel-Mo
Ch. Manlove's Lovely Lady
Ch. Manlove's Mona
Margand Jacquelyne
Navy Blue of Stone Gables
Ch. Parpoint Precarious
Ch. Parpoint Pretti-Tri
Ch. Phantom Brooks Pinafore
Ch. Pretty Maid of Cherry Lane
Ch. Prize-Par Sal of Stone Gables
Rebel Roc's Song Leader
Regattadale Countess Susan
Reveille's Pandora
Rock Falls Amber
Ch. Rock Falls Dixie Darling
Rock Falls Eve
Rock Falls Libby
Ch. Shiplake Skyblue
Silvermine Athalee
Silvermine Corrine
Ch. Silvermine Matchless
Ch. Tioga Wild Honey
Ch. Top O'Sagi
Ch. Top O' Yankee Doodle Candace
Ch. Vivacious Sally of Vilmar
Ch. Zamitz Bread and Butter
Zip of Hi-Flight

The pretty miss is Marsha Hall, (now Mrs. Brown) – her companion,
Ch. Vivacious Sally of Vilmar.

Ch. Zamitz Bread and Butter
(Ch. Silvermine Whipcord—Doro's Misty)

14

Leading Winners of the 1950's and 1960's

A NUMBER of the great producers listed in the previous chapter also distinguished themselves in the show ring. Other English Setters of these two eras also deserve mention for their awards achieved in heavy breed, sporting group and Best in Show competition.

Ch. Rock Falls Colonel and Ch. Rock Falls Racket, litter brothers, did their best winning in the early 1950's. Colonel was well into his fabulous BIS record by the turn of the decade, but the period of 1951 and 1952 saw him virtually invincible. While his brother amassed the top awards, Racket managed to win several Specialties, groups and a few BIS.

In the midwest and Canada, Ch. Ludar of Blue Bar came through strong in the early 1950's with an enviable BIS record of his own. Later in that decade, Ludar's son, Ch. Ben-Dar's Advance Notice, took over for his sire in the same territory.

Ch. Guys 'N Dolls Miss Adelaide

Ch. Zamitz Jumping Jack

In the east during the middle 'fifties, Racket's sons, Ch. Ike of Blue Bar and Ch. Silvermine Jackpot, and Ch. Mike of Meadboro made a good record for themselves with Ike and Jackpot acquiring several BIS and Mike winning the breed and groups at major events. This period also brought forth a truly great bitch, Ch. Zamitz Bread and Butter, that won a number of sporting groups, a rare accomplishment for one of her sex.

The year 1957 witnessed the rise of a truly superior star in the English Setter sky, Ch. Chatterwood on the Rocks. Never a BIS winner (though in the writer's opinion he deserved it), this great dog dominated the eastern Specialties in his all-too-short span of four years. Most regrettably, he was rarely used at stud. His line—Rock Falls and Sturdy Max II—has proved to be a strong one through other representatives of it.

In the midwest, another Ludar son, Ch. Ben-Dar's Winning Stride, began his move to fame in the later 1950's with

Specialty, group and BIS wins. Eastward, the dominant winner became Ch. Zamitz Jumpin' Jack, a tri-color and the first of his pigmentation in a long time to win the breed, group firsts and Best in Show.

The opening year of the 'sixties produced a number of promising winners. While Jumpin' Jack topped the breed's BIS record for the year, Ch. Skidby's Sturdy Tyke—the Canadian dog bred by the Polleys' Skidby Kennels—and Ch. English Accent of Valley Run, Ch. Manlove of Ellendale (in California) and Ch. Margand Lord Baltimore (from the midwest) started their runs of Specialty and group wins, and in the case of Tyke and Lord Baltimore, Bests in Show.

In 1961, English Accent, Jumpin' Jack, Lord Baltimore and a new flyer, Ch. Candlewood Distinction, were the leading breed winners. Two other notable bitches, Ch. Dover's Ticker Tape and Ch. Rebel Roc's Queen of Avalon (another California representative), also scored.

For 1962 and 1963, Ch. Candlewood Distinction and a lovely, smooth-going bitch, Ch. Winifred of Cherry Lane, topped the wins for their respective sexes. In the East,

Ch. Candlewood Distinction

Ch. Flecka's Flash of Cabin Hill won Specialties and groups, and two sons of English Accent, Ch. Gentleman Jim of Valley Run and Ch. Prince Charlie of Valley Run, took Specialties. Ch. Oak Lynn Top Brass and Ch. Chandelle's Anchor Man, from Minnesota, made several strikes in the breed and groups around the center of the country and far west. The midwest claimed another breed topping bitch in Ch. Anne of Sherwood who in 1964 won the first BIS for her sex in many a year.

In 1964, too, Candlewood Distinction increased the celerity with which he was winning groups and BIS; Chandelle's Anchor Man continued his meteoric rise; and a newcomer, Ch. Merry Rover of Valley Run, launched his illustrious career.

Anchor Man and Merry Rover dominated the English Setter scene in 1965 and 1966 with substantial group, specialty and BIS wins. I judged both these magnificent specimens a number of times, once together when the decision was the closest and most difficult I have ever adjudicated. In their prime they, and Chatterwood on the Rocks, represented—in my opinion—the finest English Setters of the past twenty years. (In fact, I tried mightily at different times to acquire each!)

For "English Setter of the Year" another flyer, Ch. Sir Kip of Manitou, became a close runner-up to Anchor Man in 1967. And it was in this period that another beautiful bitch made her mark: this was Ch. Valley Run's Dinah-Mite who had taken the measure of male champions at a New England Club specialty in 1965. Dinah-Mite's overall excellence, flawless gait and superb condition won her a BIS from me and several groups from other judges later on. In 1967 Dinah-Mite's son, Ch. Stan the Man of Valley Run, sired by Merry Rover, won two BIS awards and was named the top English Setter of the year under the Phillips' point system.

1967 was also the year that brought a triple tie for the ESAA's Rock Falls Colonel annual award for the breed's leading BIS winners. The three worthy dogs were Chs. Merry Rover of VR, Jaccard Hill Alastaire and Bucket O'Bolts by Law.

The banner year for the breed was 1968 with no less than six BIS winners: Ch. Sir Kip of Manitou, Ch. Stan the Man of

Ch. Anne of Sherwood

Ch. Jaccard Hill Alastaire

VR, Ch. Guys 'N Dolls Miss Adelaide (over a 2,000 all-breed entry), Ch. Bucket O'Bolts by Law, Ch. Jaccard Hill Alastaire, and Ch. Kerry of Berriwood. Sir Kip led these winners by gathering to himself the annual award as English Setter of the Year and the number one rating for the breed in the Phillips System. He also won the ESAA's National Specialty, with over 100 entries, and two regional club specialities.

As the soaring Sixties came to a close, Sir Kip continued his winning ways with BOB at both the ESAA Specialty in New York and its National Specialty in California. A new star in the distaff firmament, Ch. Canberra's Legend, began her career in 1968 with two regional club specialty wins and in 1969—to the best of memory and research—became but the second bitch to win the breed at the Westminster Kennel Club show in Madison Square Garden.

In 1970 Legend became the first English Setter bitch to win **three** Bests in Show in the breed's American history, all accomplished by her amateur-owner, Joyce Rosen. Legend retired with a record of eight group wins and six specialties which, considering her sex, was remarkable. Also in 1970, Ch. Guys 'N Dolls Shalimar Duke made a splendid Best in Show and group record under the breeder-ownership of Neal and Harron Weinstein. Duke doubled up breed wins at the Combined Setter Specialty in New York and Westminster for that year and in 1971 as well.

The final half of the decade produced other noteworthy English Setters. Chs. Margand Wildcatter, Baker's Northern Lancer, Hidden Lane's Busy Imp, Hidden Lane's Merry Max, and Wragge Run's Pride of Replica (Canadian) rose to BIS heights. Also in this era Chs. The Rock of Stone Gables, Spark II of Cherry Lane, Candlewood Quest, Prince of Deerfield, Top o' Penmaen Lord Willin', Galahad of Polperro, Bucket o' Bolts by Law, Blue Diamond's Abner Yokum, Burr Ridge Boomerang and Sis of Lonesome Lane ranked among the group winners.

In the 1950's and 1960's no English Setter came within striking distance of Rock Falls Colonel's record of over 100 BIS, and his even greater number of group and breed wins. Only two dogs have ever surpassed Colonel's BIS achievement,

Ch. Bucket O' Bolts By Law

Ch. Canberra's Legend

a Boxer and a Pekingese. The numbers' game in the 1960's, after Colonel passed to his reward, produced the following top winners and runners-up in the three classifications shown:

Best of Breed: Ch. Candlewood Distinction 179
                        Ch. Chandelle's Anchor Man 152

Group 1:   Ch. Candlewood Distinction 47
                        Ch. Chandelle's Anchor Man 30

Best in Show: Ch. Merry Rover of Valley Run 10
                        Ch. Candlewood Distinction 7

Any such listing must take into consideration the number of times each dog was shown. The ESAA 1968 **Annual,** from which these figures were taken, gives 187 as times shown for Distinction, but no figures for Anchor Man or Rover. It is safe to say that of the three dogs above, Merry Rover was shown the least.

Certain professional handlers seem to enjoy a high affinity and rapport with English Setters. The late Harold Correll campaigned the Blue Bar dogs most successfully, his last being Ch. Ike of Blue Bar. Jane (Kamp) Forsyth has piloted a number of this breed to top awards, including Chs. Rock Falls Racket, Ike of Blue Bar (after Correll), English Accent of Valley Run, and Candlewood Distinction. Ch. Ludar of Blue Bar, and his son, Ch. Ben-Dar's Advance Notice, were in the capable hands of Horace Hollands. Robert Forsyth piloted Chs. Zamitz Jumpin' Jack, Valley Run's Dinah-Mite and Stan the Man of VR in their careers. Robert Walgate showed the sound and typey Ch. Skidby's Sturdy Tyke. The great sire, Ch. Margand Lord Baltimore, did his winning with Richard Cooper.

In 1965-1969, a handler new to the breed steered two top dogs to their show pinnacles. This was William Trainor with Chs. Merry Rover of VR and Sir Kip of Manitou. Dick Webb is another superb professional who piloted the successful campaigner, Ch. Guys 'N Dolls Shalimar Duke.

Ch. Guys 'N Dolls Shalimar Duke

Ch. Valley Run's Dinah-Mite

Several amateur owner-handlers gave the professionals a hard race. Though William T. Holt's record of 101 BIS with his Rock Falls Colonel is unlikely to be equalled, other owners merit high praise for campaigning their dogs—Howard Smith with Ch. Mike of Meadboro; Dr. Raymond Chase with Ch. Chatterwood on the Rocks; Rachael Van Buren, for a time, with Chs. English Accent and Merry Rover of VR; Joseph Kaziny with Ch. Chandelle's Anchor Man; Gladys Nichol, also for a time, with Chs. Valley Run's Dinah-Mite and Stan the Man of VR; Neal Weinstein with Guys 'N Dolls Miss Adelaide; and Joyce Rosen with Chs. Aspetuck's Shadow, Canberra's Blue Shadow and Canberra's Legend—to highlight a few.

As the sixth decade of this century drew to a close, it became clear that no one area of the United States could claim a monopoly for good English Setters. The East, West and Midwest all had their stars, and no one dog was virtually invincible in the breed or the group to which it belongs. All of which is perhaps a better state of affairs for English Setters than obtained some twenty years ago.

Ch. Rock Falls Racket

Ch. Candlewood Quest

Ch. Baker's Northern Lancer

BIBLIOGRAPHY

ALL OWNERS of pure-bred dogs will benefit themselves and their dogs by enriching the knowledge of breeds and of canine care, training, breeding, psychology and other important aspec of dog management. The following list of books covers further reading recommended by judge veterinarians, breeders, trainers and other authorities. Books may be obtained at the finer bo stores and pet shops, or through Howell Book House Inc., publishers, New York, N.Y.

Breed Books

AFGHAN HOUND, Complete	Miller & Gilbert
AIREDALE, Complete	Edwards
ALASKAN MALAMUTE, Complete	Riddle & Seeley
BASSET HOUND, Complete	Braun
BEAGLE, Complete	Noted Authorities
BLOODHOUND, Complete	Brey & Reed
BOXER, Complete	Denlinger
BRITTANY SPANIEL, Complete	Riddle
BULLDOG, New Complete	Hanes
BULL TERRIER, New Complete	Eberhard
CAIRN TERRIER, Complete	Marvin
CHIHUAHUA, Complete	Noted Authorities
COLLIE, Complete	Official Publication of the
Collie Club of America	
DACHSHUND, The New	Meistrell
DOBERMAN PINSCHER, New	Walker
ENGLISH SETTER, New Complete	Tuck & Howell
ENGLISH SPRINGER SPANIEL, New	
Goodall & Gasow	
FOX TERRIER, New Complete	Silvernail
GERMAN SHEPHERD DOG, Complete	Bennett
GERMAN SHORTHAIRED POINTER, New	Maxwell
GOLDEN RETRIEVER, Complete	Fischer
GREAT DANE, New Complete	Noted Authorities
GREAT PYRENEES, Complete	Strang & Giffin
IRISH SETTER, New	Thompson
IRISH WOLFHOUND, Complete	Starbuck
KEESHOND, Complete	Peterson
LABRADOR RETRIEVER, Complete	Warwick
MINIATURE SCHNAUZER, Complete	Eskrigge
NEWFOUNDLAND, New Complete	Chern
NORWEGIAN ELKHOUND, New Complete	Wallo
OLD ENGLISH SHEEPDOG, Complete	Mandeville
PEKINGESE, Quigley Book of	Quigley
POMERANIAN, New Complete	Ricketts
POODLE, New Complete	Hopkins & Irick
POODLE CLIPPING AND GROOMING BOOK,	
Complete	Kalstone
PUG, Complete	Trullinger
PULI, Complete	Owen
ST. BERNARD, New Complete	
Noted Authorities, rev. Raulston	
SAMOYED, Complete	Ward
SCHIPPERKE, Official Book of	Root, Martin, Kent
SCOTTISH TERRIER, Complete	Marvin
SHETLAND SHEEPDOG, New	Riddle
SHIH TZU, The (English)	Dadds
SIBERIAN HUSKY, Complete	Demidoff
TERRIERS, The Book of All	Marvin
TOY DOGS, Kalstone Guide to Grooming All	
Kalstone	
TOY DOGS, All About	Ricketts
WEST HIGHLAND WHITE TERRIER,	
Complete	Marvin
WHIPPET, Complete	Pegram
YORKSHIRE TERRIER, Complete	
Gordon & Bennett	

Care and Training

DOG OBEDIENCE, Complete Book of	Saunde
NOVICE, OPEN AND UTILITY COURSES	Saunde.
DOG CARE AND TRAINING, Howell	
Book of	Howell, Denlinger, Merric
DOG CARE AND TRAINING FOR BOYS	
AND GIRLS	Saunde
DOG TRAINING FOR KIDS	Benjam
DOG TRAINING, Koehler Method of	Koehl
GO FIND! Training Your Dog to Track	Dav
GUARD DOG TRAINING, Koehler Method of	
Koehler	
OPEN OBEDIENCE FOR RING, HOME	
AND FIELD, Koehler Method of	Koehl
SPANIELS FOR SPORT (English)	Radcliff
SUCCESSFUL DOG TRAINING, The	
Pearsall Guide to	Pearsa
TRAIN YOUR OWN GUN DOG,	
How to	Gooda
TRAINING THE RETRIEVER	Kersle
TRAINING YOUR DOG TO WIN	
OBEDIENCE TITLES	Morse
UTILITY DOG TRAINING, Koehler Method of	
Koehler	

Breeding

ART OF BREEDING BETTER DOGS, New	Onsto
HOW TO BREED DOGS	Whitne
HOW PUPPIES ARE BORN	Prin
INHERITANCE OF COAT COLOR	
IN DOGS	Littl

General

COMPLETE DOG BOOK, The	
Official Pub. of American Kennel Clu	
DOG IN ACTION, The	Lyor
DOG BEHAVIOR, New Knowledge of	
Pfaffenberger	
DOG JUDGING, Nicholas Guide to	Nicholas
DOG NUTRITION, Collins Guide to	Collins
DOG PSYCHOLOGY	Whitney
DOG STANDARDS ILLUSTRATED	
DOGSTEPS, Illustrated Gait at a Glance	Elliot
ENCYCLOPEDIA OF DOGS, International	
Dangerfield, Howell & Riddle	
JUNIOR SHOWMANSHIP HANDBOOK	
Brown & Mason	
SUCCESSFUL DOG SHOWING, Forsyth Guide to	
Forsyth	
TRIM, GROOM AND SHOW YOUR DOG,	
How to	Saunders
WHY DOES YOUR DOG DO THAT?	Bergman
WORLD OF SLED DOGS, From Siberia to	
Sport Racing	Coppinger
OUR PUPPY'S BABY BOOK (blue or pink)	